Watson Lake

DEASE R.

LIARD R.

LIARD R.

FORT NELSON R.

SSIAT

ASE R.

ALASKA HIGHWAY

Fort Nelson

TURNAGAIN R.

KECHIKA R. (BIG MUDDY)

GATAGA R.

FORT NELSON R.

MUSKWA R.

PROPHET R.

PITMAN R.

FOX R.

STIKINE R.

Eddontenajon

COLD FISH L.

Hyland Post

Caribou Hide

KWADACHA R.

Fort Ware

SPATSIZI R.

SKEENA R.

NASS R.

KLAPPAN R.

FINLAY R.

ROCKY MOUNTAIN TRENCH

FINLAY R.

INGENIKA R.

MESILINKA R.

OSPIKA R.

HUCKABOO CR.

SUSTUT R.

IRVING R.

OSILINKA R.

PEACE R.

Bear Lake

Finlay Forks

OMINECA R.

TELEGRAPH TRAIL

BABINE R.

TAKLA L.

NATION R.

PARSNIP R.

NATION R.

NASS R.

Hazelton

BULKLEY R.

Smithers

BABINE L.

STUART L.

Fort St. James

STUART R.

SKEENA R.

0   Miles   100

NECHAKO R.

Vanderhoof

BOOKS BY EDWARD HOAGLAND

Cat Man

The Circle Home

The Peacock's Tail

Notes from the Century Before

Notes from the Century Before

Notes from
the Century Before

A JOURNAL FROM

BRITISH COLUMBIA

Edward Hoagland

Random House / *New York*

FIRST PRINTING

Excerpts from this journal have appeared in different form in
The Paris Review. The Hyland Family Diary is quoted by permission
of Steele Hyland.

Library of Congress Catalog Card Number: 69–16423

Manufactured in the United States of America

Typography and binding design by Guy Fleming

For M. M. H.

CONTENTS

Contents

[xi]

LIST OF MAPS

Notes from the Century Before

[I]

Where and Why

MAPMAKERS MUST enjoy marking in *Telegraph Creek*. They've had it on Woolworth-type maps of the world and on desk-size globes, in the same lettering as Nice or Chicago. It's a town of 150 people in northwestern Canada, 800 air miles from Vancouver, but still below the Yukon and near enough to the coast to have tolerable temperatures, rather like northern New England's, and yet a dry climate. The mountains on every side make for drastic climatic changes within a few miles, and until ten years ago there was no through road. Access was mostly limited to the ice-free months, involving a three-day boat trip up the Stikine River. While the town is only 165 miles in from the sea, the river is very robust, proportioned like the Hudson, and the round trip continues to take about as long as an Atlantic crossing. For the seven nonnavigable months of the year there used to be no access except on snowshoes or accompanying the mail. Mail arrived once a month by dogsled until the bush plane era began, in the thirties. Then the service was boosted to once a week, as it remains nowadays, although the Alaska Highway can be reached in a car by driving all day.

Telegraph Creek came into being when the Collins Overland Telegraph Company conceived of running a telegraph line from New York to London the long way around the world, by way of Alaska and Russia. It was a grandiose plan. At the end of two years, in 1867, they had managed to cut a thin trail through the wilderness from the existing transmission lines in southern British Columbia as far north as the Stikine. At the same time, however, a rival group had been racing them, laying a cable under the ocean, which was the short route. When this unlikely idea suddenly succeeded, the line which had been intended to cross the continents was abandoned just as it stood, with hasty loops drooping from the poles and reserve coils of wire in the crew cabins. The village on the river at the terminus did survive, since the area had had a gold rush shortly before. Another minor rush occurred in 1873, to Dease Lake, seventy-odd miles further inland. Also, it was fine fur country, and the Tahltan Indians had their capital village close by at the mouth of the main salmon tributary. Between the whites and Indians, the population of a region of eighty thousand square miles, like two Ohios, was estimated at two thousand people by a board of citizens in Wrangell, which is the settlement lying in the Alaskan panhandle at the mouth of the Stikine. Right now the population might be half that.

The mammoth Klondike strike, way to the north, stirred the Stikine into a froth of activity in 1898. The river was considered to be one of the possible corridors. After reaching Telegraph Creek by boat or on the river ice, a prospector could get to the headwaters of a tributary of the Yukon River by hiking across a couple of hundred miles of tough bush—there, theoretically, to piece together a raft and drift at his ease for the rest of the trip. Scarcely anybody did drift; in fact, rather few reached the Yukon Territory at all by this route, but money and stampeders poured into town. The government even revived the Collins Overland line, pushing it hurriedly north to the gold town of Atlin, on the provincial border, and thence to Whitehorse and Dawson, the hub, which had had no direct communication with the rest of the world before. It became called the Telegraph Trail, especially the stretch of 210 miles from Telegraph Creek to Atlin and the southerly part which passed 400 miles through unremitting mountains from Telegraph Creek down to Hazelton. Men who couldn't afford the boat fares or who wanted to stay on Canadian soil all the way, or those deluded by looking at a map (perhaps by *not* looking), attempted to walk it. The trail was soon strewn with dead pack horses and cast-off equipment, the game scared away, the trees scrawled with messages. The people who limped into Telegraph Creek generally beat a retreat to the coast and out.

The town grew hectically as a transit point, then shrunk, and, dwindling, slumbered along. Four boats instead of seventeen operated on the river, then two, at last only one. The telegraph wire was shut down after thirty-five years, replaced by the radio. A few ready settlers migrated into the country during the Depression, but not like the numbers who had come after the First World War, drawn by the nineteenth-century concept of frontiering adventure. None came after the Second War. The old-style prospecting was finished, and trapping prices dropped off with the invention of fur farming and chemical furs. Of course Telegraph Creek was kept alive just by the immensity of two Ohios standing empty around, but it was simply an Indian town and a supply town, with a Mountie, two rival missionaries, a Hudson's Bay store, and a "free" store. As for the Stikine, a river 325 miles long, not until now is a road being constructed which crosses it, by means of a tenuous cable ferry that is out of commission much of the time, and the only road alongside is a hairpin dirt track which turns to the north after two dozen miles.

[5]

In 1960 my first wife and I happened to live in Hazelton for a while. We were traveling in British Columbia by a system of going to the ends of the furthest roads and renting a cabin from somebody there and seeing how it was. Hazelton is at the very top of the road maps of the province—the top third or so, being virtually roadless, isn't shown. We found ourselves in a lovely, musty, log-house village, surrounded by an Indian reserve, a large green valley, and beyond that, an uneven ring of snow mountains, forested part of the way up. Several of the old homesteads could bring tears for the view they had and the height the hay grew, the rhubarb and phlox and sweet william and tiger lilies still in the kitchen garden, the scarfing of meadow along the river, and the waterfall that fell into the pasture in back of the house. Telegraph Creek was too far away to be talked about much, but we did hear a lot about the Telegraph Trail. As the jumping-off point, Hazelton's fortunes had been tied to it. After the relay men had been withdrawn, the service cabins where they had lived, spaced out every twenty miles, remained as a sort of challenge to the local oldtimers and trappers. Though First Cabin had burned, a jeep road took us to it. Second Cabin had been at the site of a Tsimshian village called Kuldo, meaning "back in the woods," now abandoned, said to be littered with relics which the Indians, according to custom, had left exactly in place on the morning when they moved out. Up to Seventh Cabin, the operators had been supplied by a yearly pack train from Hazelton. From there on, the trains worked down laboriously from Telegraph Creek once a year, and after Ninth Cabin, the distances between them increased to thirty miles and they weren't numbered; they had place names like Bob Quinn Lake, Quinn naturally being the operator himself. The elder Indians in town had packed a good way on the trail, as had the whites, but since everybody had depended at least to some degree on the kindness of the men in the relay cabins, when the line shut down these trips stopped, first the through trips, then all trips. In the time since, there seem to have been only two or three passages clear to Telegraph Creek. A motley party of Tsimshians and teenage girls from Vancouver sent by their parents for a summer's jaunt tried to drive sixty-two horses through in 1946 for an outfitter, who chose to skirt round by water himself after seeing them off. They lost twenty-three animals in mishaps and delays, arriving finally at the other end, completely foodless and quite stupefied.

Hazelton lies at the head of navigation on the Skeena River, just as Telegraph Creek does on the Stikine. Both rivers rise in the same remote knot of mountains a long distance off, have the same turbid color and character, and run in complementary crab-armed courses through a half dozen axe-cut, muscular ranges. During a boom like Telegraph Creek's, six hotels flourished in town, along with a "Bucket of Blood" block of saloons, and, what with the homesteading going on and the Indians' blueberrying fires, more land was cleared in the early years of the century than when we were there. But the last riverboat had long since been retired, logging machinery was moving in, and in spite of the then chronically troubled Canadian economy, a new spreading out had begun, with modernization of many kinds. The lower Skeena, indeed, has had a railroad since 1913 and a road of sorts since the 1940s, which has gradually been improved and paved. The main difference between the two rivers appears to be that the mouth of the Skeena is Canadian, while the mouth of the Stikine is American, so that on the Skeena there hasn't been the difficulty of persuading the ministers of two nations to combine their moneys in order to develop divided land.

However, it was still very silent and wild. The dirt roads seemed to us a hazard to drive. Horses roamed loose, grazing downtown. Most any day you had only to go into the woods a quarter-mile to see bear tracks. People shot them like squirrels and papered the barns with their skins, and when my wife taught a Sunday School class and asked about pets, it turned out that everyone's cat or dog was getting shot after a couple of years too. Their father would find them another, but when the winter was spent by the window shooting at coyotes and such, it was hard not to knock over Spot if he started to dig in the garden. The Skeena flowed past our cabin from sources known only from aerial photographs, some of them where nobody alive had ever been. It flowed with the élan and inscrutable speed of a river as unmapped as that, a churning silt brown—a working river—yet the whole upper portion hadn't even a path. The few people who had been to Telegraph Creek described a generous raw town, unimaginably isolated, where they served caribou in the café and the Indians had round Asian faces and were friendlier than the Tsimshians, and where there was nothing for a white man to do but loaf around and "make little Indians."

We went out to the Kispiox, a fish-filled and fabled side river, and met Tommy Jack, who has a 6900-foot mountain named after him on the Skeena above Kuldo, near where the Slamgeesh comes in. He was haying with his two soft-haired daughters and two fat horses and a rubber-wheeled cart, very prosperous-looking, but very old. When I said I was thinking of trying to go over the Telegraph Trail again, he wanted to drop everything. He got drunk in town that night and kept knocking at the house, his eyes glittering, his face a deep dark, shouting that he was all set to go. He pointed me out to his friends, waving a can of near-beer. I felt a bit guilty for talking so soon. The Tahltans couldn't be any friendlier than this, but the Tsimshians had been acquainted with the white man for a longer time and were ordinarily indifferent to the passerby. They'd been a sizable tribe, strung all along the Skeena, and had warred with the sea-going Haidas, who lived by the mouth, whereas the Tahltans, less numerous and faced with the Tlingits at the mouth of the Stikine, had had to take care to preserve the peace. Tommy Jack's grandfather had participated in that final battle when the Haidas were expelled from the valley. A village called Kitwancool kept the tradition alive, even as regards the whites. Shots had been fired as late as the 1930s, and people like teachers and dentists tiptoed in. When a truck from Kitwancool arrived in Hazelton, the driver dealt me a flat stare of hate.

We got to know Jack and Frances Lee also. We stayed for a week with them on the Kispiox about thirty-five miles above Tommy Jack's house. It's a feline river, all dazzle and slash and then quiet pools where the steelheads spawn. With their son they were building a cabin in a horseshoe curve on a kind of a promontory, upriver from their original farm. The Sweetin entered close by, a sweet little river that you could throw a stone across, and it was at the end of a road which the jeep was able to negotiate by sticking to four miles an hour. Most old-timers who accomplished much in the bush haven't got any sons because they married too late, or, if they have one, like Jack's, he's something of a square peg. But it was a fine week. Frances brought along a pail of turnips, a pail of milk, a pail of peas, a pail of beets, a pail of beans, some slabs of beef, and a pail of cream. These all kept perfectly well, and as soon as the meat ran out we caught a salmon the length of the kitchen table. Frances was a buxom woman, born in the valley, and younger and bigger than Jack, and she could do anything that a man could do without in the least being mannish. She still dissolved into giggles, although she was getting more serious because of the success of their guiding enterprise. Jack, a former bronc rider, was slight and wiry with quick slogging strides, like a woodsman's goose step, for covering the ground. He was ten years younger than Casey Stengel, but looked just like Stengel, aged by his years in the rodeos. His facial expressions were those of someone in his late twenties and his mind was always at work along its own lines, but he had loosened and gotten talkative lately, worried by a deep-seated pain in his chest. He let down his teeth and sucked at them like an old man. For hundreds of miles he was the best guide and sage, popular except with the Indians, who claimed he had disowned a child he had had by an Indian girl once, years before. He had walked into the Skeena country in 1935 from a place called Caribou Hide, 230 miles in the north, by way of the Firesteel

River and the Mosque and Sustut. That winter he lived with a pickup trapping partner, fishing through the ice and boiling up mink. Then he homesteaded on beautiful bottomland ground next to the sidehill where the most deer were, living off them. He got married, and he'd go out and trap in the Groundhog Range, which is eighty miles up the Telegraph Trail. During the winter after that big herd of horses tried to go through, he found three of them and shot them for bait and to eat himself.

His longest trip was in 1941, when he took a government engineer to Telegraph Creek and beyond for a hundred miles more, to the Nahlin. They were measuring snow for a study of routes the Alaska Highway might use. Afterwards, they walked back to Telegraph and caught the first boat of the spring. In 1948 he guided two hunters nearly as far, in a loop. And in the early thirties he had roamed and trapped on the Finlay River. The Finlay starts in the same pathless tangle of mountains as the Stikine and Skeena do, but flows east and south, helping to form the Peace River, which flows north and east into the Mackenzie and into the Arctic Ocean after 2500 miles. Though not unduly long in itself, the Finlay is the wildest river of all. Only two parties of white men have canoed all the way to its source. One was the discoverer's in 1824, and one a surveyor's in 1914. The tiny Hudson's Bay posts which were established on the lower reaches have since given up the ghost and most of the tatterdemalion Indian bands who existed there have moved out. The government, in a flourish of pique and despair, is flooding a lot of the valley. As Jack describes the Finlay, however, it was not an impossible place. He fell in with a tolerable partner each year. The two traders were decent enough, a pegleg at Fort Grahame and young Ware at Fort Ware. Ware had succeeded his father at the post, but he married in with the Indians and grew too free with his credit policies, so the Hudson's Bay Company fired him. Ben Cork became the trader at Fort Ware and Ware went south and fell into a sawmill saw and was killed. If the Indians around were miserable, it was because a priest flew in and flew out with their beaver catch every Easter, and because otherwise they made hay while the sun shone; they feasted and starved. They'd camp below Jack's and come bum a hatful of flour to make gruel, and later he'd watch them pole by, flying a batch of new, colored streamers from their canoe that they'd bought at the Fort. Their first meal from a cow moose would be the fetus, if they found one, but the game warden used to arrest them and send them away for six months for that.

There was a murderer named Shorty on the river, who used to shoot people from ambush, or entice them into his boat and tip them overboard in the rapids. He trudged in to Finlay Forks himself to report finding the body, but by the time the Mountie could accompany him back, "wolves" had invariably got the head off and concealed it, so who could say what the cause of death was? Shorty pulled for the Indians in quarrels along the Finlay, which didn't endear him either. He was eventually imprisoned a couple of years for siphoning gas for his outboard kicker from a cache of emergency airplane fuel, afterwards filling the barrels with river water. He came out of jail a chastened man, a respectable citizen, trained in the tailor's trade.

Jack Lee himself had a good many adventures. He was with Shorty's friend, Hamburger Joe, on the caribou hunt when Joe wet his feet in the overflow on the Finlay ice. All the toes froze and the flesh peeled away until you could hear his bones click on the floor of the cabin when he walked barefoot. Finally he stubbed them one time too often and he sat down and cut them off with his own jackknife. And it was Lee who dug a trapper named Eric Smallstead out of a snowslide that killed him in the narrow neck of the Obo. The bears had already tried, earlier in the spring, but his snowshoes had caught and they'd only managed to tear him in half. Jack Lee likes bears and he says they weren't trying to eat Smallstead, just trying to haul him out of the slide. He's deaf now and these tough-hearted memories give him a sense of all he's survived—he packed a man out of that country who had turned black from scurvy and wasted away to ninety pounds. I saw Jack almost killed by a car which he didn't hear coming up on him on the highway. When he whipped his face around to look after it, he was wearing his same survivor's grin.

One Christmas the temperature dropped down to 72° below. When Jack threw his breakfast wash water out the door it hit the snow as a spatter of marbles, leaving tracks where it rolled. And once, traveling home on the Finlay on the ice, he turned the dogs loose and let the toboggan just blow along, the wind was so strong. He trapped on the Carpet and Wicked and Crooked rivers. He trapped the Prophet. He trapped and traversed the Toodoggone, which leads from close to the head of the Finlay towards the upper Stikine at Caribou Hide. A creek there is named after him, where he had trouble throwing a footlog across. At Caribou Hide, a village now also abandoned, sixty or eighty Indians lived, a collection of Tsimshians, Tahltans, and Finlay River Indians, the Sikanni. It was about as far to Telegraph Creek as it was to go down to Hazelton, but when he was ready to move on again he happened to cast his lot with a Tsimshian, so he walked south with him.

Lee is white-headed today and gives off silver gleams when he walks, which, combined with the fast pace he sets, his diminutive height, and his hollowed, dark face pounded by rodeo falls, makes him a marked man wherever he goes. He too said he would take me over the Telegraph Trail if I got the financing from a magazine. It was plain that like Tommy Jack, though, who had been gleeful, he was speaking from pride: neither of them actually expected to make it. Besides the matter of their age, the trail where it wasn't absolutely erased would be a morass of windfalls. Only one young fellow in town had it in him to complete such a trip. He was a black-bearded hermit who lived in a hillbilly shack with a sign out in front, "Mean Cow," and a cowhide draped over the fence. When he wanted a woman, I was told, he crossed fifteen miles over a mountain spur to Kitwancool, not wanting to mess with the Kispiox squaws. He was cut from the old cloth, all right, but doing the trip with him would probably end in the old way, people said. I would break down with diarrhea and sprained legs by the time we got onto the watershed of the Nass, and he would quite blithely leave me to die, hiking on through the Telegraph Creek.

After we had returned to New York City, I gave up the notion of rewalking the trail as my own bones stiffened a bit. But what I had heard kept a grip, perhaps partly because the Telegraph Trail had been cut to go around the world. Cutting a trail to go around the world is a beguiling idea, an idea that skitters off into space. I got interested in the Stikine also, left as it was in the nineteenth century by a fluke of geography and by the low-keyed Canadian temper. A river in the Arctic wouldn't have interested me as much, but this was a livable river which had had homesteads along it, and whose tributaries still supported one of the great concentrations of game. Although the bush fliers could land practically anywhere now, in Hazelton I had seen the way people were lingering behind their technology. They were awed by the places they were able to reach, where nobody but a Jack Lee had gotten before, and then only after a month's savage walking.

I wrote to the guide whose 3500 square-mile hunting territory adjoined Lee's at the top. It centered on Cold Fish Lake, on the trail from Caribou Hide to Telegraph Creek, and included the head of the Stikine, just as Lee's included the head of the Skeena.

Mr. Tommy Walker was an enthusiastic Englishman, but his pride for his own area seemed monopolizing. Even Telegraph Creek, he indicated, was worth hardly a visit. A photo of the town I got hold of was unpromising enough. It looked wedged in the trough the river had carved, claustrophobically tiny, all too isolated. To me it was a crossroads nevertheless, where I could step back to the Snake River of 1885, hearing stories which hadn't worn threadbare with handling. Except for the draw-and-shoot business, which didn't concern me, it

seemed that the life would be the same. I would be talking to
the doers themselves, the men whom no one pays any attention
to until they are dead, who give the mountains their names and
who pick the passes that become the freeways. I'd meet more
extraordinary old men with the eyes and clear skin and extreme serenity of some of the homesteaders at Hazelton. My
interest was in the continent rather than Canada, and I would
be looking at the Missouri basin not so very long after Park-
man's time. I'm a novelist, not a historian, but at best I'm a
rhapsodist too—that old-fashioned, almost anachronist form.
I've written about the circus—lions and leopards—about the
painterly blizzard of beauty in good welterweight boxing, and
about the Pied Piper. Since childhood I have stuttered severely,
and even in writing rather factual books I'd been depending
entirely upon my eyes to gather the scene. But now I was
going to need to ask many more questions. I decided to do my
writing by means of a journal, since everybody I talked to
would have his own journal. I'd see journals right and left. As
for the tumbling geography, I reveled in that—I'd let the
geography tumble.

It was an exuberant, staccato summer. Luck and events and
kindnesses melded with one another. I rushed along eagerly,
without any special introspection, just putting down what I
found out. I talked to maybe eighty people, and their gaiety,
their consistency growing out of the gaiety and long labor
of opening a new country to settlement, gave the experience
a coherence I hadn't expected. Two years later, in 1968, I
went back again and found the circle of wilderness taking a
terrific pasting. The damming and flooding, the logging and
road-building, the hundred helicopter bases were leaching it
from every angle. Though it was still good ground for a
novelist, an alarming number of the old-timers had been dis-
persed to hospitals, and my memory of this later summer is a
cacophony of get-rich schemes, of white-Indian disparagement
and conflict, and Californians immigrating and buying up the
homesteads, buying whole chunks of valleys, even to the trad-

ing posts and weather stations. There is a frank new air of rapine.

The problem everywhere nowadays turns on how we shall decide to live. Neither the government leaders nor the demographers have been able to supply an answer. Meanwhile, our politics are sulfurous and our streets are a costume ball as we experiment and try out the past. Of course since I didn't wish to emulate the frontiersmen, only to talk with some of them before it was too late, I didn't go to the Stikine as part of this quest. And it hadn't been too late in 1966, but then in 1968 suddenly it was. I got echoes, I got reports and secondhand versions of the old way of life, and plenty of the crosswise, inchoate, prickly stuff dear to a novelist, but the summer of 1968 was never joyful. In the confusion of helicopters and mineral promotions, the question in British Columbia has become the same as everywhere else: How shall we live?

What follows is the diary of 1966.

[II]

New York to Wrangell

THE USUAL EXHAUSTED, NERVOUS departure from New York. A taxi strike, a fight with the landlord about the sublet, general shaky feeling. It's an annual event, this relief at leaving the city, equal only to the relief of coming home. In an airplane I still pray before takeoff; apparently I haven't flown enough. In fact it's the only time I do pray, except for the ritual visit to church at Easter, etc. Occasionally in these moments I've found that I was ashamed of something I hadn't realized I was ashamed of before.

There is a time-capsule element to flying, with the whine of the airstream outside, the bland decor, cellophaned meals, the tap of the hail, the startling announcement of the temperature outside, and the stewardesses, like temple maidens, smiling and giving simple directions. We enter Canada subterra-

[16]

neously, chuted through silent tunnels between planes. The flight to Toronto is very short, the Hudson seeming to join Lake Ontario, but outside, boarding again, the land looks exhilaratingly flat and a farm smell comes through the fuel fumes. The forests, pockmarked with black ponds, soon break up the plowed fields around the Great Lakes until the checkerboard prairie begins at Winnipeg. We fly above a curdled cloud field of fluff with pillars and many spray crests and thin, stationary streamers. At Edmonton the soil shines in the bright sun, the grass is a frenzied, spring green. Pigs are running. The road to town is lined with trailer parks. The men are thin, serious, colorless types and the newspapers puritan. Lots of immigrant faces, but not much life. Since my train was six hours late, I sat in the YMCA awhile, rambled and shopped, savoring an old-fashioned boredom and starting to like the people more. At nine the sun set, round and red. At ten the moon rose, yellow and round.

JUNE 3, FRIDAY:

WOKE UP IN BRILLIANT sunshine in the shaking train, going through the Rocky Mountain Trench, as it is called, a long straight fault valley on the west slopes, with snow ranges on either side, an area where they were building a road in 1960— but still no road. Although the train runs only on alternate days, it stops at each sawmill as if to keep up everyone's hopes. Saw a big moose plunging away, and a buck deer in a marsh. We peer with such instant eagerness at wild animals it must be more than their novelty; it must be the sense that the planet is shared.

Pleasant, mild, modest people, a few with marvelous wildwoods faces, like the man carrying a pack whom the train stopped for in the midst of the bush. There is an Alaskan wearing black boots and a fox clasp for his string tie, a most unfoxlike man with a son named Dana and a son named Wesley. My seatmate is an Ontario nurse going for the summer to work in Prince Rupert. We stand outside on the back platform, grinning in the wind, smelling the spruce. All day a tangle of trees—a single track—and countless creeks with ducks flying up. There are bones alongside from the wolves' winter hunts, and awry, low telephone poles. The train when it brakes smells like gunpowder. Every town is a sawmill, the shavings piled up in mounds to the height of a carnival tent. Indian kids already are swimming from some of the sandbanks, and the boys in the car come out to us to throw rocks at the ducks and to shriek in the tunnels. The girls play old maid, a card game. The nurse has a face which looks lumpy and phlegmatic in profile but, in front, shows big, emotional, blue eyes and an unexpectedly lovely and fluid expression. We argue in order to talk. To feel so tired and yet so fresh! We change engineers at McBride, Endako, Smithers, and Terrace. A smiling bush farmer from Edson gets off at Usk. Joining the Skeena at Hazelton brings a sad spell, because I am now divorced, planning indeed to avoid the town. But the mountains mount in a crowded corridor beside the river, the highest of them all being seven staccato steel tips on a different level altogether. Waterfalls fall like snowstreaks, and there are a half-dozen rough little ranges, which gradually round off and lower at the coast. The Skeena spreads into its estuary.

JUNE 4, SATURDAY:

AFTER COMING AS STRAIGHT as a long fishing line from New York, I'm to make the little hook round by boat to Wrangell, Alaska, and Telegraph Creek.

Prince Rupert is the foggy pretty cannery town where a lot of the Tsimshians work in the summer, living in colonies of shacks that stand on stilts on the waterfront. The rest of the town is on hills among shaggy trees, a town full of foreign accents and ladies of savvy and influence, like the ladies of any pioneer settlement. The gulls mew, the lumberjacks clump up and down. Several acquaintances from yesterday are on the boat—a boy who went to Edmonton to try for a job and didn't get it; a frail old woman from Arkansas who's come all the way on the train to see her sick daughter, not knowing if she's still alive; a raggedy, stooping teen-age boy escorting his brother home. A few young adventurers read *Argosy*. The boat is purposely kept cold for the Alaskans' comfort—not that they take off their checked coats, but they seem to enjoy wearing coats. The dull-boy is in many of them—dim, diligent papas with stolid gray spectacles and faces almost smudged over. One woman lugs her purse like a sack. Everyone offers to take care of everyone else's kids.

King crab for lunch. The waiter is a popeyed appealing fellow from Ketchikan, studying to be an opera singer, and who, by no coincidence, is an old boyfriend of my tablemate. She's snappy and gentle with him, a plain-pretty schoolteacher who is about to marry a fisherman one-quarter Tlingit and one-quarter Haida, these being two salt-water tribes who used to fight with the Tahltans and Tsimshians. The waiter gazes in despair while she relaxes and blooms. She tells me that Prince Rupert students quit school sooner than Alaskan students do, and that her Indian students there are shy, as if jumped on, speaking of themselves only as "from the Nass" and "from the Skeena." She mentions the Unuk River, behind Ketchikan, as being a former Shangri-la of fertile homesteads, now abandoned. Ketchikan, with a population of 7000, is Alaska's fourth largest city, a toylike, polycolored place of homely frame houses and ugly big cement structures a hospital-green which has been hacked out of the base of a small mountain. Since the shoreline is all the space that there is, it's used for the garbage and dumping.

We pass the *Georgia Maru* from Tokyo. A sea lion bobs to the surface—a brother mammalian head—turning like a gentleman looking dignifiedly behind him. In the calm sea, literally every few minutes a porpoise shoots alongside, although too blasé to race the boat, which isn't the kind that can give a porpoise a race anyway. It's a glassy, gliding boat, built for the scenery, which is fine and majestic indeed, a sort of magnified Norway. On both sides, numberless graceful mountains, one tied to the next, move in on the boat and move out. They're speckled with snow and have bars of fog in their folds. We slip through some beautiful platters of fog.

Delicious fried oysters for supper, and a whale in the wake. Wrangell (pop. 1400, pronounced like "wrangle") sits at the low termination of an island, facing west. It's been twelve hours since morning, and I walk hastily and happily around before going to bed.

June 5, Sunday:

Aunt Winnie's Café has steak for breakfast at fifty cents an ounce. The daily newspaper is the Seattle *Post Intelligencer*. Aunt Winnie is reported to be a living legend of profanity. Strong men get up and walk out of a room when she comes in. At the Wrangell *Sentinel* I talk to Lew Williams, the rather limp, mechanical-seeming editor, with a manatee face. He writes well, however, and the antique store front is full of museum-piece machinery and huge wastebaskets for throwing away the stuff anyone else would save. Not only is there no file, the back issues of the weekly, to 1916, are heaped casually in a leaky back room in disorder, rotting. He gets out the one recounting the death of the mayoress's husband years ago, who was killed at Paradise Lake by a grizzly. He was found jammed so tightly between two willow trees where the bear had thrown him that the trees had to be cut to extricate him. The gun had been knocked some yards away. The bear herself, a mother with cubs, was not found, although he had fired once. When his friends heard him fire, they thought that he yelled, "I got him!" but actually what he was yelling was, "She's got me!" An inauspicious beginning.

I talk with Joel Wing, the magistrate. He is forgetful and confused by now too, but is a large, white-haired, idiosyncratic man, a cripple, a bachelor, living in a house too messy to let me in, he says, so we go to his office in the Post Office Building, which is heaped with the paper work of the town, which he seems to do. He's a good, decent, fidgeting, fat man, somewhat effeminate under the beefy Alaskan veneer, exasperated at himself for his slowness at remembering and his difficulties with logic and language. He worries over every word he chooses, as if giving himself the education that he didn't have. His "poor old papa" was a day laborer who dreamed of and saved for the handful of years when he got away from Wrangell and up the Stikine to his mining claim at Trout Creek near the Hudson's Bay Post of McDame. The whole family was up there three winters, so he begs me to take photographs of their cabins when I pass by later this month; he draws me a map. And he talks about Dirty Curly, and two Indian packers named Sambo and Johnny Cigar, and Ah Clem, the last Chinaman of the crews who came into the Cassiar country for the building of the Telegraph Trail. He fans the air, heaves about in his chair, twists his rings, questions some of his recent decisions in court, asking what I would have decided, and digs out historic bits of paper for me from his desk about the founding of Wrangell. Swearing a little, nostalgically, he tells me about the hard blue glacial mud that defeated their tries to reach bedrock on their claim, getting excited again—they wept in the evening sometimes. But they had loyal dogs, and sufficient game, and cabins so warm and thick-walled that they put out the fires at night so as to sleep.

He calls in George Sylvester, whose father once was the big man in town, founding the sawmill, though George is a roofer and fisherman now, with a hollowed, discolored face. Both men are hard of hearing, which makes my stutter especially a problem, and an undefined tumble of mining terms pours out. Sylvester mutters as we pore over my Stikine charts because the names he knew the creeks by, or the names he gave them himself, have not been saved. Jekyll Creek, however, is marked down, for his friend who died in Ketchikan just the other day, as well as Shakes Glacier, named for the Tlingit

Chief Shakes. Sylvester's first trip to Telegraph Creek was in Shakes' long freighting canoe in 1906 at a season when the sternwheelers weren't able to run. It took ten days. A couple of years before, his father had taken $75,000 worth of gold from a placer deposit near the mouth of Snow Creek at McDame, which was reachable from Telegraph Creek by walking seventy-odd miles to Dease Lake and boating the length of the lake and then down the Dease. Among the horde of men who were making that walk twice a year, his father set the record of nineteen hours. Later on, when George was prospecting on his own at Quartz Creek, he tried to equal it, starting late one night in order to keep cool. Plenty of coyotes were howling, but all he was really afraid of was stumbling over a porcupine in the dark. For twenty-five miles where the creeks were dry, he sucked handfuls of cranberries to keep himself going. His time was four hours longer, which was good enough.

Wing locates a letter from Rufus Sylvester to "Friend Metcalf," dated June, 1888, from the Cassiar Range, where he'd gone to trade implements to the Indians and flour to the white trappers. "Lots of Sikanni and lots of Bear Lake Indians and lots of mosquitoes here." As I read, Wing gets on Dirty Curly again, who was a "sniper," a man operating on a shoestring in places other men had looked at and passed by, who could find traces of gold in every creek, effortlessly and where nobody else would have thought to look, but never got rich somehow. Then some greenhorn would come along and take a sixty-two-ounce chunk of gold from under a stone. He says I should look at the Bear-Up-Mountain Totem Pole in town, which records the services of a grizzly bear which during a mythical flood saved the lives of the Tlingits by showing them how to get to high ground. And he gives me this reading of the Frog or Kicksetti Totem at the foot of Episcopal Street, where I stood in delight last midnight, incidentally. It was carved for a widow in memory of her husband to repay a debt owed to the widow; and the face on the top represents a mountain on the Stikine where this legend took place. Below is Ketchikahok, a nephew of the chief who had been guilty of annoying the frogs. One day he fell into a trance and, coming out of it, said he had been to the other world and had been taught by the frogs to treat them better because they were brothers. Below him is the Raven Creator who created the earth, talking to his grandson between his knees who created man because the Raven Creator couldn't find time. Below that is the Beaver, the totem of the man's father's side of the house; and then the Frog, of the man's mother's side. So, the pole reads, *we are a people who once lived on the Stikine River; the Frog is our coat of arms; we are a branch of the Raven people; and the Beaver and Frog are our totems.*

Wing repeats this description by rote, having learned it as a schoolboy, and throws himself around his chair, fluttering his hands in diagrams, closing his eyes to concentrate better, and teaching himself with his index finger. Deep breaths and sighs, a confused, energetic, frustrated precision. "I believe" versus "I hope"—he wrestles with the words to decide which he means. He's an Elk, a public servant, and an endearing man, but it appears as though he is out of practice at talking to people. As a matter of fact, he fell on his hand in the Stikine Bar six months ago and the swelling in one knuckle has yet to go down. While I feel it, he persuades the two bones to creak and grate. The only man he's permitted to shake it lately, he says with the laugh, is the governor once.

The Bear-Up-Mountain Totem Pole is on a nit-sized island in the harbor where the first Russians, led by Dionysius Feodorovich Zarembo, fortified themselves. Instead of their relics, though, a sample Tlingit community house is preserved, rectangular and low, and various poles: the Kadashan Redsnapper Totem; the Sun Totem, very tall, with nine figures atop one another; the Three-Frog Totem, three frogs on a *T;* and the Bear-Up-Mountain, which has a bear on top of a twenty-foot post, looking down at the footprints marking his climb. Chief Shakes is buried on the road outside town with two fish on his grave.

Fisherman go by, wearing a pistol for seals, since there is a bounty of three dollars a nose. A plane bustles in with a movie film, the bank manager, and some boxed funeral flowers. It flitters and flops in and out all day, boiling a plume of spume behind the pontoons. A plane is a taxicab here—all contact flying, without instruments, by daylight, and dodging the fog. The pilot is a natural-mannered Alaskan who looks overworked and pale, like any agreeable young man running a demanding business, and his wife is a tinkly, slow-speaking Texan who disgarbles his radio messages from the static when no one else can.

I like Wrangell. Remnants of the old board sidewalks remain, the streets are a plainspoken gravel, the houses are wound round with vines. The dogs that aren't white are black. They are reticent, sleepy, severe work dogs of a size for pulling a sled. Man or child, everybody presents himself downtown at least eight times a day, and on the upper street are two lovely churches, the St. Rose of Lima, and the First Presbyterian, Alaska's oldest Protestant Church. The U-shaped sourdough beards are tiresome because they look fake, but a good many people are Indians, beardless. It's fun to know every alley in town by the end of a day and know where the principal citizens live. Mostly the Stikine is not an object of interest here now. Its mouth is seven miles off and except for the pleasure-boat owners, nobody much cares. Wrangell faces Seattle and Japan.

In the evening I meet John Ellis, a young fellow who repairs outboard motors. He's a strapping, mature nineteen, raised as an orphan, with a red complexion and a short beard. Though he's a gregarious boy, the river is his constant resort. Every day off, he winds up sixty or eighty miles, poking into the tributaries and through the sloughs, usually alone, because no one else is as involved as he. Just today he has shot a black bear where the Katete empties in. He's been to Telegraph Creek maybe ten times and has traced all the old settlers' cabins that can be found. He says he wishes I'd been in his back pocket these last ten years. In the summer he's patched the holes gored in his boat by the rocks with peanut butter, and in the winter he keeps skates cached away, to go up to his haunts, since the wind blows paths through the snow on the ice. Once, when he wasn't on skates or armed, a wolf followed him for quite a while, first staying about seven hundred yards behind, until he waited for it. Then it came within one hundred yards and circled, checking him thoroughly. He had stopped on a patch of slick ice where his boots would grip better than the wolf's paws, but it didn't attack. He wasn't worried until afterwards, when he found from the tracks that a second wolf had been waiting on shore, perhaps to see whether he retreated there, where the footing would favor the two of them. However, he doesn't believe they really would have ventured an attack unless he had been already wounded or starving and on his last legs. He's seen a total of eighteen now.

Grizzlies are shy on the Stikine but are common on several of the short fjords. The goats on the cliffs can be shot and will fall right into the water beside the boat. A hermit named Ham Island Slim lived on one fjord until last year, a Norwegian whom his brother won over by knitting a pair of red socks for him. He became friendly with the Ellises, baking his private bread in loaves the size of stovewood for them, a wonderfully tasty bread made with five or six different food grains. Ham Island Slim felled trees and every few years floated a raft of logs out to where the sawmill tugboats could come, saving the money from that to go back to Norway in the end. Another hermit, Dirty Bart Gillard, lives on an island fifty miles out in the ocean and comes into town about three times a year. He's quite amiable then, not as though starved for company, but agreeable, and seems rather a child in his chuckling and in his thought processes. Since he has a small radio for music and news, he isn't exactly a Rip Van Winkle and has retained the ability to speak. These wilderness souls are always noticeably nutty, Ellis says, but the only mystifying, possibly dangerous one lives on Wrangell Island itself, on the opposite side, going so far as to put out his fire so the smoke won't show on the rare occasions when a boat putts past. He rows into town just once a year, buying great hundred-pound bags of dried provisions, and has never been given a name, since virtually nobody knows about him. From a sort of perversity Ellis visits him, though the man dislikes the visits and stays silent except to answer the most direct questions. He'll definitely shoot if you don't announce yourself from shore, and once he disappeared for two years but then turned up again. Ellis, to be helpful, had hidden certain belongings of his under the cabin's floorboards, but was afraid to tell him so.

He gives me the dates of spring break-up recently from an album he keeps of the river—pictures of bears and bare girls with beer cans. May 16, '64, April 26, '65, May 1, '66—it's a cold river. He and his brother own one of the five old homesteads on Farm Island nearby. The cows needed to be boated out before winter and the vegetables from Washington State were cheaper to buy, so the property's just for parties now.

June 6, Monday:

Grilled halibut cheeks for breakfast. The counterman says his cat will eat nothing except jumbo shrimp, and talks about the perils of driving in Seattle. "You just need to hire you a nigger chauffeur, that's all." The game warden, a retired police officer from Yakima, Washington, says that relations are better between natives and whites here than there. The Tlingits are of a higher class and, not being on a reservation, marry and compete with the whites. He's a heavy forceful competent man, so his game estimates, which otherwise might seem high, sound accurate. He claims five thousand bald eagles gather on the lower Stikine for the smelt run, and that in his patrol territory of a hundred by two hundred miles there are two to three thousand bears, a third of whom are grizzlies, and maybe as many as one thousand wolves—too many, driving the deer population down, swimming from island to island to hunt them. The logging moves them around but doesn't abruptly reduce them. He says they are parti-colored, sandy and buckskin, silver and brown; and two of Ellis's eighteen were black. Of the Canadian game on the Stikine, the Alaskans don't see caribou, sheep or cougar. Fisher and lynx and coyotes are rare, but a rabbit famine upriver has pushed a few down. The wolf bounty is $50, coyotes $30, wolverines $15, though only a couple of trappers are left to practice the trade. From air counts, he guesses at two or three hundred goats, mostly on the mainland, and three hundred moose, new immigrants who have eaten their way to America down the floodplain of the Stikine, feeding on willow and alder.

It's overcast, with 8000 miles of ocean out there and the prevailing winds westerly. The midriff of the day I spend with Tom Ukas, who is a totem-pole carver and story teller and nephew of the last Chief Shakes (they gave each chief the name). He's about seventy-five, he says, and all the rest of his generation have been burned or drowned off. He learned English at nineteen aboard the U.S. *Skedney*, a coastal trading and survey ship, working later for years in the engine rooms of various boats. The mill will still call on him when they have boiler trouble because he can patch it without needing to wait until everything cools. He's a short, froggy, dignified, expressive-faced man who wears glasses like most older Indians. One wonders what they did for their eyesight before the whites came.

After quitting school, he trapped and hunted with his father —in the winter for marten and mink, in the spring for beaver, along with a long bear hunt while the bears were hungry and roaming around and encounters were easy to come by. Grizzlies hibernate high up, emerging in March or April to nibble fastidiously the new shoots at the edge of the snow or to root at the bottom of the snowslides for possible victims. As they gradually pick up the threads of their lives again, and the wish to roister and eat and drink, they descend to the river bottoms, where the black bears are, and dig up the edible plants, watch

[27]

for fish, dig out muskrats, and look for intrigue. Then they climb to groundhog, grass country on the high slopes, each to an established territory, and mellow and settle a bit while the black bears stay low the whole year. By knowing where to look, the Ukases would bring back ten hides or more, worth fifty dollars apiece. Sometimes they used deadfalls too, built like a tiny house, until a white man crawled into one and the government outlawed the system. This sort of hunting went on until the First War, by which time the bears had become very scarce, much scarcer than now.

Ukas speaks casually, saying he was never attacked except once when he shot a yearling for food, out beaver trapping. Instead of one bear, suddenly there were three. The mother and another yearling tore out of the woods. He clambered onto a hummock. Whereas a black bear bites and worries a man at knee-level like a dog, a grizzly will raise up to get a good view. In any case, he was on the hummock, and when the mother reared up, he shot her twice in the chest and finally once in the head. When she fell, the second yearling took her place, stood up, and he shot right into its mouth. So that was a jackpot, fifty years ago, when he was young.

He talks faster than a good raconteur, but in the same spirit, running his stories together, playing with his glasses and resting his hands on the pile of magazines on his desk. The room is full of comfortable old chairs.

Scutdoo, a Wrangell Tlingit, was hanged for killing a soldier in the 1880s, although an inspecting officer later complained that this was the second Indian the post commander had hanged without adequate evidence. The chiefs insisted that he was innocent at the time. They refused to deliver him up and then said he had run away and couldn't be found. An ultimatum was given. When it expired, the garrison shelled the Indian town, which was next to the fort. The people fled, the shelling went on for hours, a woman and baby were killed. At last, with most of the houses in splinters, Scutdoo was led forward by the chiefs. He asked for his dancing hat so that he could dance before he died. In Tlingit he whispered to the messenger that his mother should put a knife in the hat, but when it was brought and he felt inside, no knife was there. Scutdoo despaired. He danced, and he lifted his hand to his mouth and bit off a great hunk of flesh and spat it into the soldier's face who was doing the hangman's job. The mourning Indians of the town had been forced to take hold of the rope that would pull the trap door, but before the soldiers could make them do this, Scutdoo went into his final dance, with his hands tied and the noose round his neck, he sprang high into the air and off the platform, breaking his neck and saving his friends the task.

Ukas won't stop. When I ask to see his totem pole in the shed in back, I feel rude because he's afraid I won't come back afterwards to the living room to hear about the Raven's grandson . . . Man wouldn't be mortal if the Raven's grandson had kept his stove properly hot, and wouldn't have to work so relentlessly. Out of man, bears and seals were created during an earthquake, because the men who jumped into the water for safety turned into seals, while the men who ran into the woods became bears. The Raven led those who remained up onto Cascade Mountain, on the Stikine, in the flood which ensued, and took hold of a cloud with his beak and hung there until the water subsided, so that his people, the Tlingits, who clung to his feet, were saved.

Near Shakes Glacier is the hole through which the Raven dived another time, when he went down to visit the Underworld. Ukas and a friend found the hole while they were hunting one spring, a hole as large as a car, with no breeze or sound coming from it. They crouched at the edge and listened. Although the hole is far up the mountainside, according to the legend the Raven emerged in the river eventually. Each of them dropped a bottle cork through to see whether the corks would repeat his journey, and then forgot about them the rest of the day as they hunted, until sunset, when they were rowing home to their camp on the riverbank and there were the two corks floating.

The totem is made of a fresh, beautiful, pale yellow wood.

I'm amazed by it. Completely filling the shed, lying on several supports, it thrusts like a rocket, many times taller than me. Carving from the bottom upwards, he has finished all but the hat at the top, even the long Raven beaks which attach separately. The little tools rest on a bench. He walks back and forth, touching the segments with a certain humility, this probably being the last totem pole he will have enough energy for and the last anybody in Wrangell will carve. He is delaying finishing—an hour's chipping at the hat would take care of it. The wood is red cedar, and it will stand in front of the post office, a marvelous huge piece with six succinct figures. At the top sits the hatted, ruling Raven. At his feet is the Power Box (like a box), holding the Tide Control and the Daylight Control for the moon and the sun. Under the box is the Raven again, though only his head, with a bright halo disk around it —this representing the Raven in his special capacity as Creator. Below the Creator Raven, scrunched up, is a kewpie-doll Man, and underneath Man is the Raven Mother, whose beak is carved to lie on her chest, not stick out grandly like the Raven Creator's. At the bottom, under the Raven Mother, sits the Tide Control, who escaped from his box and triggered the flood and is personified by a big beaver. It's all magnificently bright and incisive, as I try to tell him mainly by my excitement.

John Ellis gets through work, gobbles a meal, and from six to nine o'clock we head off to pick up the bear which he shot yesterday. After bringing it out of Canadian territory, he draped the skin in a tree until he could find out whether the bear season had opened yet in Alaska. The skiff whirls and scuds over the water at 30 mph, with its bow high. We pass Dead Man's Island, where the early Chinese cannery workers were buried; also Dairy Island, and Farm Island, five miles by fifteen, which splits the mouth of the Stikine. A boy of eight named Timmer is along, so John shows him the remains of the homestead on a point of the mainland where his mother grew

[30]

up. We stop to look at a gold-rush message cut on a rock at the edge of the water. Only the simple numerals of the date are still legible. And an old bridge crosses a slough—two logs fitted onto a rock-packed frame, wide enough for a wagon. We whip and zoom into and out of the principal channel, which builds into slanting slopes of water against the sandbars. It's as wide as the Hudson but is a rich brown-gray, littered with floating trees and boiling and pimpled with miniature whirlpools, with circles of surface water spinning and intersecting. Stunting for Timmer and me, Ellis shoots into the narrowest sloughs, curving with them and out at the end, after a mile between the close-set walls of the rain forest. Mink, moose, beaver tracks. Cottonwood Island, Government Island. Government Island lies off the cove where the customs man had his cabin in the old days, in a thicket of tall hemlock trees and windfalls and brush. The roof has fallen in from the weight of the winters of snow. Nearby is the bearskin, about five feet long, representing an animal of two hundred pounds. John was watching a cow and calf moose in a slough, trying to photograph them, when the bear showed up on the opposite side and started across. He left the head intact when he skinned, and the mouth is still biting a mouthful of grass; the tongue is out, the lips are red-flecked. The ears are floppy, personable ears and the muzzle is well proportioned, the eyes not too small—a likable face. Fine, unblemished fur, prime-of-life claws. Gracing the prow, stretched out, the skin makes the skiff look very big, but to me it's a sad memento, and as he says it's the sixth bear he's killed, he begins to sound as if it were sad to him too.

Again we skylark between the drift piles and swampy islands and crocodile logs, making the seething brown river a raceway, an obstacle course. The sun is low. The thick shoreline is that of a jungle river. Hundreds of great trees are stranded about in the shallows, so that parts of the estuary look like a naval graveyard. We swing near a beaver house, and swing near an eagle plunked in a tree. From time to time a seal surfaces and dives—whole herds go upriver during the salmon run. Besides the continual gulls, we start up a flock of ducks every couple of minutes, thirty or forty ducks, and since the boat zips along as fast as they do, we wheel them towards shore like a troop of horses, until they gradually outdistance us. These are the speedy Merganser ducks, but there are so many species about that the "thundering herd," as John calls them, who come out on Sunday in their motor boats, classify them as fishing ducks or as eating ducks. When they catch a bear in the water, they all herd and tire him thoroughly, then let him get out on the beach and chase him on foot for the illusion of running him down.

We visit the Farm Island farm, swerving up a creek, planing along. John points out where a goat came down to the house, and where a wolf sat last August listening to the Beatles on the Victrola. Inside are eight bunks and a guest book where everybody signs and which Ellis has filled with pronouncements from "Captain Crunch." Nailed to the front of the house are the outboard propellers he's "crunched." It has a glass porch and a white exterior, and he is determinedly at home and cheerful here. His brother and he are just pulling themselves clear of the bitter childhood they spent.

On the way out, we spot an otter and chase its ripples around. On the bank its whole dachshund body gets in operation when it runs; its legs do the work of a centipede's. Then the river's mouth again, with seals surfacing, and eagles and fleeing ducks, the snowy horizon—a profusion, a gushing of life. I goggle and grin quite helplessly, for this was the way the world was made.

The crewmen of the *Kogaku Maru* are fishing from a raft of logs attached to the ship. At the dock, two boys Timmer's size have brought in a pair of salmon to be weighed. The biggest is forty-eight pounds. A man laughs, seeing the bear, because yesterday his kids crossed paths with a bear behind town. The kids screamed and ran, and the bear turned tail in absolute terror. "His hair practically turned white, he was so scared. He must be the only polar bear in southeastern Alaska now."

[III]

The Boat, the Stikine

I'M WRITING THROUGH MEALS at the restaurant as well as at night to keep up. Today I'm leaving for Telegraph Creek. Dashed around in the morning to locate George Engelmann, an old wolfer, seventy-four, who is noteworthy because he got seven wolves on Etolin Island last year. In modern Wrangell he is unknown. He lives on a cramped, grimy boat moored at the commercial wharf. He's a thin man in gray drooping pants that would fall if he sneezed. He has watery blue eyes, a patient drawl, and a small face gone gently to seed. Like Judge Wing, when I say I'll be back in August to talk some more, he says, "If I'm alive." He's painting somebody's boat; it's a sunny day that will hold the paint, and a lot of these good days he does no work at all; he'll sleep right alongside the work. I've taken a liking to him and I plead for a little time, but in banged, weary stamina, he is adamant. We argue like friends. He tells me to see a fellow who has "forgot more than I know," a shrimper now, but used to "go all up into that country, the Queen's land." The Canadians almost caught him, but he'd throw his gear into a cache and get all his furs on his back and carry them out, walking faster than they. Not long ago he had a stroke, alone in his boat, and drifted two days before he could get the kicker going and come in. As for Engelmann, his best trapping year he wound up with forty-nine wolves, which looks like a lot of wolves when you have them stacked up. He had a partner last winter, because he is getting old, but the partner only smelled up the trapline with the diesel oil on his boots that he wouldn't wash off, and scared the wolves.

Before sailing time I drop in on the previous riverboat captain, who shows me some photographs of moosehide canoes, and a paddle he cut with an axe in an hour and a half, and a baleful, lone trapper rafting downriver with a slew of sled dogs just before he was drowned. He piloted on the Yukon and Taku too, and trapped on the Iskut and Unuk, and prospected and mined, but he seems brisk and flat and we don't hit it off.

At 4:30 P.M. the boat leaves, timed with the tide. A scow loaded with groceries for Telegraph Creek is tied to the bow. Captain Callbreath, a young man my age who was born there, checks the coverings with a high-hipped Indian stride. The boat is the *Judith Ann*, sixty-four feet, drawing 2½. It's an expert shoebox of a boat, narrow, blunt, and the engine pounds like a foundry. He grips and tugs at the wheel when he is spoken to, bashfully searching the water, but he's a presentable steersman. He's a gentle man with a perky, affectionate mouse of a wife back cooking in Aunt Winnie's restaurant kitchen.

A brown stain of silt spreads out in front of the mouth of the river, curds of foam everywhere, which are "squaw soap." Like yesterday, there's the wild Eden sense—troops of birds dashing. In its spring flood, the river slides like a river of mud.

Map of the Stikine River and its Watershed

We angle from island to island to catch the short stretches of slack water and pound like a busy smithy in order to make 5 mph. Snags stick out of the river like the heads of seals, and the islands taper like arrows and look hot, but ashore a forest of cool Sitka spruce rises two thousand or three thousand feet, with patches of snow going on up from there. A few spooky cabins appear. Side valleys split away into *Y*s, blocked by mountains. Horsetail falls hang from the cliffs. Every curve reveals bigger mountains. We pass Shakes Glacier, in a scoop valley with a huge landform at the back like a buffalo's head. The occasional eagle sits quietly at the top of a cottonwood tree. Like seeing one's first lion in a zoo, he's already a neighborly sight, except one is surprised when he just sits and doesn't perform. His head is a startlingly lineny white.

The wind as a rule blows downriver during the day and up the river at night. At 11 o'clock the snow all around is still gathering light; the water acquires a glittering mercury sheen. We tie to a log on a sand bank and sleep for six hours.

JUNE 8, WEDNESDAY:

NOBODY KNEW WHERE ALASKA was when it was sold, which may be a reason it was so cheap. Much later, the Canadians and Americans compromised on the boundary in the panhandle area by giving the fjords in their entirety to Alaska and giving the rivers to Canada, except for their mouths. To the traveler on the Stikine, the boundary is peaks and peaks, in a wheel, because the river swerves and view closes in. Ringed round like a lake, all we can see is peaks. The rest of the passengers are a likable lot: a randy, lively retired photographer and his wife; a gaunt, white-haired electrician "from Walla Walla" and his wife; the assistant comptroller of the University of Alaska. My favorite is a banker from California who served a chain bank in five different towns and in each had to take his turn as president of the Kiwanis, a chore he should only have been given once. He's a solid, laconic fellow. My roommate is a

compulsive clown with an overfast laugh, something of a luna-
tic. He looked like Billy Graham at first, but he looks like Red
Skelton now, a bay-colored, lonely, baying man dressed in
ash-brown.

The rumor is that the river will be too high in one canyon
ahead for us to make it to Telegraph Creek, though the captain
is eager to try, as I'm probably the only passenger he will have
this year whose aim is really to *get* there, not the round trip.
He's desperately shy when anybody enters the wheelhouse, so
we've worked out a system whereby he tells me through the
window what we are passing, and the boat doesn't get pulled
off its course from his gripping the wheel.

Incredible spoked sundials are set up along shore where the
big cottonwoods have been undermined and have fallen over
with their bleached roots exposed. The Katete debouches
through a thick screen of swamp. A wide valley funnels back
to mountains and saddles which encircle the end. The Iskut,
the largest tributary on the Stikine, is next, even more barri-
caded behind islands and sloughs. It's a classic straight corridor through a vast steep valley of virgin trees, each as straight
as if it had been plumbed. The Stikine weaves, like the highway it is. As we approach the mountains before us, they slowly
open a gap, which closes again after we pass. We feel our way
over the snags, often nuzzling so closely against an island that
we can hear the songbirds over the noise. Crossing again, we
slip backwards eerily for what seems a long time, only just
succeeding in holding our slant. The scow up in front is fun to
ride because it slides vibrationlessly, but so is the galley of the
Judith Ann, where the floor jangles in frenzy and the glasses
and plates deafen the floor. The river is often a mile across, an
eddying gale of gray water. A half-skinned cedar floats by with
flesh-colored protrusions where the limbs were. Great Glacier,
in its majestic slash of a valley, takes two hours to pass; Mud
Glacier, two hours more. This is the spine of the Coast Range.
The mountains go 6,000 to 10,000 feet, to gunsight peaks and
to sailing, razory needle peaks. They're blue, cut with shadows

and loaded with snow, and they carry small glaciers slung on their hips. A sudden slide wipes out a waterfall before our eyes, and the black and white patterns of snow that are left are like a dramatic couturier's dress.

I glass the high pasture pockets for a file of sheep or a grazing bear, or maybe some good yeti tracks. As far as our rate of speed goes, this is rather like walking to Telegraph Creek. And a walk in a million it is. Three Canada geese, a beaver, a moose. The Porcupine River, like the Iskut, comes in from the southeast past massive mountains. Having bogged up its proper exit, it sneaks out at right angles to its own valley. We spend several hours fighting our way in a circuit around. Cowboy music from the wheelhouse. We tie onto the downside point of an island where the current from either side will keep the boat straight during the night.

JUNE 9, THURSDAY:

IT'S TOUCH AND GO whether we will reach Telegraph Creek. Rain last night didn't help; the river is flailing and high, eating the banks. Every once in a while a tree falls with a splash. I had hoped to have come in a week or so from the largest city in the world to the littlest, and in Wrangell I heard about Telegraph Creek's home-brew beer and the famous Indian-girl complaisance, which went with the era before. Finally we tie up to wait at the mouth of the Anuk, a tiny river about midway, where the captain trapped when he was a boy and where Hudson's Bay established its first trading post on the Stikine. There are some crowing pictographs drawn by a Tsimshian war party who captured a family of Tlingits as slaves. The water tanks of the *Judith Ann* need to be filled in any case, and Captain Callbreath likes the taste of his trapline creek, but he's mortified for my sake. The cook, Florence, is his go-between with the passengers. She's a chubby, cream-colored woman who summers on this riverboat and bats around the rest of the year to places like Samoa. Last winter she worked in the Royal Hotel in Honolulu as pastry cook, but "didn't last six weeks." She tells me about a character on the river, recently dead, who walked in from Hazelton, taking four months to do it, living off the country and enjoying himself. When he arrived he was carrying just his blanket, out of all the belongings he'd started with. After that, he would disappear each summer, looking for gold, though by then everyone else was after molybdenum or mercury. He lived below town and couldn't get in for supplies for two months one time because of the trickiness of the thaw, so he lived on beaver meat. His dog fattened right up, but he said he dropped down to skin and bones.

Groundhog Jackson lived not too far beyond here, by Dokdaon Creek. It was Groundhog who discovered the great Groundhog Coalfield near the Telegraph Trail that somebody will reach with a road some day. He sold his claim to a German firm for $3,000,000 just prior to World War I, taking the downpayment, a fraction of that, to San Francisco to celebrate. He blew it and brought back a wife in the spring, and when the government seized the German firm's claim, he got no more. Whatever his wife had married him for, they lived out their lives on the Stikine. She grew into an even better trapper than he.

In the drizzle, I'm reading the disputation between Reverend Kingsley and Cardinal Newman, two solemn walruses at war. There's a copper find nineteen miles to the east, so that a helicopter is lifting tanks of fuel from the mouth of the Anuk, where they were dropped off by barge last week, to the drilling test site. It hovers with a rigid slide-rule precision while the hooks are hooked, but swings off swiftly and grandly. The pilot tells me the rate is $177 an hour, if I want to hire the thing. While we watch, the banker catches a whitefish. Suddenly luck lands on the river in the shape of a Kennecott boss in an airplane. Callbreath charters it for his oranges and eggs (planes are much cheaper), and I get aboard as well, to handshakes and waves. It's a wee two-seat Cessna. The pilot is a dark, speechless, underfed boy about twenty-one who has never flown to Telegraph Creek before, and so is a little bit nervous. Climbing on the wing, he pours in ten gallons of fuel, just the color of strawberry pop, and, tucking his copy of the same map that I have over one knee, he takes off along the washboarding current, a headlong bumping. It's too gay to pray—too great to pray. We circle back down to the Porcupine, gaining height, then up the Stikine, which immediately looks more imposing. The sweep of it didn't appear below, the innumerable braided channels half drowning the lush valley forest. Another major glacier feeds in: blue ice and a black moraine like coffee grounds. Far from diminishing the mountains, as I thought that it might, flying gives them their due. We're a third of the way up, at most, and so they crescendo and culminate above the plane in all of the shades of forest-green, meadow-green, with their moose ponds and long, long, pendant streams, and their snow cirques, and muscular shoulders, and sheer rock escarpments.

The Scud River, next up the line, is so turgid and big it looks like the Stikine, except that it climbs right into a cloud-bank where we couldn't go. Willy-nilly, we continue along the main fork. The mountains bulk into sawtooth massifs too superb to be true. We curve carefully with the river gorge to keep out of their way. Air pockets rock and adjust us, and I'm so exhilarated I'm throbbing. The Chutine, opposite to and beyond the Scud, is a clear-water, green-water river with a wooded valley, not the glacial effluvium. Now the trees have begun to change. The mountains dry out and draw back, leaving a wide plateau on both sides of the Stikine. We fly over an old clearing, with its sole horse and its laborious log houses close enough to the bank for a fishing line to be run out the window. Telegraph Creek is a scatter of buildings, fantastic after coming so far. Both relieved, we land on the lake behind and unload the groceries. Nobody meets us except a curlew that does a curlew. I take it to be a good omen. The sky is clearing. The boy roars into the air, and I walk the two miles to town. The brush is full of birds cheeping and whistling. There's an elaborate system of flumes and trestles which carries spring water, and I follow them down. The town is wonderfully sprinkled out on a half-dozen terraces, high levels and low. People wave and smile. I can scarcely remember ever being any happier.

[IV]

The Old Men of
Telegraph Creek:
The McPhees and
the Others

JUNE 10, FRIDAY:

I AM STAYING AT the Diamond C Café, "Pioneer Outfitters,
Est. 1874." It's the only lodging in town, and is run by
Edwin Callbreath's parents. The Anglican bishop is here for
his annual visit, a stooping listener of a man; also a Kennecott
survey crew, so we're jammed. In the morning I climbed up
the hill a couple of levels to the two McPhee brothers. Alec has
the best vegetable garden in town. Dan, who lives up the last
flight of stairs, is something of a landlord, owning a shack and

two houses left him by friends who have died, in lieu of money that he had loaned. Both McPhees arrived in the West about 1904 and worked on the railway that runs to Prince Rupert and on a network of government trails to the north, building a wagon bridge across the Bell-Irving River, which hasn't been bridged since. While they were doing this, they'd walk back and forth across on a cable, daredevil-style, balancing themselves with their loggers' peevies. In 1912, when they were cutting a trail in the valley of the Nass, which is only now seeing its first roads, the local Tsimshians rode out to intimidate them, circling on horseback and firing their rifles. That winter was Alec's last visit south to a city.

Dan was the first to move to Telegraph Creek, although not until 1930, when he was put in charge of the maintenance crew on the village roads. He arrived on the riverboat, looked around at the size of the town and said to the Hudson's Bay man, "If I'm here next Saturday night, I'll kiss your blessed ass." ("Been here thirty-six years," he laughs.) He's a lean, wry, humorous man, haggy and coltish by turns. He looks like a canny grandpa from Tobacco Road—long nose, floppy hat, black shirt and pants—and when he tells a joke, he seems to swallow it, like a shot of whiskey, and feel it go down and simmer nicely. Dan always kept the security of the government job, but for the winter he picked up a trapline on the Scud River and Yehinko Creek from a moonshiner whom the Mounties kicked out. He used to average thirty marten a year. Martens are so dumb, he says, that if you see a marten's tracks that marten is yours. On the wall is a picture of him behind his dog team, in a high-collared native sweater, holding the hand grips and looking abrupt and rough and ready to shout. He had a half-breed wife who died three years ago and left him lonesome and rather itchy and at loose ends. One of his several sons still lives with him, bringing the money in, while Dan cooks. As the family absorbed his attention, he traded the trapline to another Scotchman for twenty-six cleared acres on the Chutine, intending to farm. The Chutine was better for farming than the Scud was, just as the Scud, with its twisting sloughs, was better for trapping. Nothing came of the trade, however, since Dan remained the road foreman and his wife ran a small hotel in town: not for the Scotchman, either, who drowned the next year in his new territory while cranking his motor. That was the way it usually happened. The outboard would stall, and the man couldn't keep hold of the oars at the same time as he cranked. The boat swung into a riffle and swamped and the river swept him under a driftpile, where it didn't make any difference if he could swim or not.

It's hard to elicit descriptions of the other people on the Chutine. Some were wanderers, always out after gold or hunting somewhere, living from hand to mouth on what they could get at the moment. Others organized their lives as a farmer does, raising a regular schedule of vegetables, which they canned for the winter, filling the potato house with potatoes and onions and salting away a winter's supply of fish. Since there wasn't a market, of course, it couldn't expand beyond subsistence farming. If the man didn't leave, he cleared more and more land and built more and more barns, with the time on his hands, until by and by he died.

Alec McPhee is a shorter, more ebullient man. He has blue eyes, yellow-silver hair, and a red toothless mouth, and he scrunches over his crossed knees like a boy, sniffs a breath in through his nose, and stares boldly out of the window to see who's going to be coming past next. When he speaks he shakes his head and his whole body shivers delightedly, because everything that he finds to say amazes and amuses him. He was the town's gravedigger; he was the carpenter and electrician; he was the powder man on the public-works crew whose job was clearing the river of snags. So he's a fortunate man, he says, never to have blown himself up, or to have caught a fever from a corpse. When he was stringing wiring to the school from the government generator near the Mountie's house, he slipped on the icy steep slope, tangled the top of his hand in the spool, and although he was wearing mittens, lost only a single finger. Explain that good luck if you can. Never having married, he has an uncared-for, jumpy air that brings him cookies and stews from the widow next door and the nurse down the hill. He's an irresistibly blithe man, an urchinlike man. Apparently he did approach marrying an Indian girl once, but in some way or other she banged her head on the gunwale of the boat when they were down by the Iskut, and fell overboard in a rapids and drowned.

In the winter of 1932, with a responsible job in the Prince Rupert area, Alec was out prospecting along the Nass together with a friend. It wasn't the right season for prospecting, but it was their only chance. They had a dog team and were having a lark, crossing into land new to them, Damdochax Lake, Muckaboo Creek. They kept postponing returning, and since Alec's brother already had gone to live in Telegraph Creek, all of a sudden, when they noticed that they were on the Telegraph Trail, they decided to forget the ties which they had and hike to the Stikine. This they did, potting game as they went and bumming tobacco from the relay men on the line. They had so much fun and poked up so many side creeks, dawdling along, that they were at it 105 days, all told. Not until 40 miles out of Telegraph Creek did they run out of snow. They simply packed the stuff that was left on the backs of the dogs. They couldn't stop, they'd grown so attuned to moving. After seeing how Dan was, they went right on to the Jennings River country, which is 160 or 170 miles farther north, and back again. On Level Mountain (the historic hunting ground of the Tahltans) one spring night, sitting in front of their tent, they watched every imaginable sort of game cross before them: caribou, moose, deer, black and brown bear, mountain sheep, mountain goats, like a splendid parade, as if on display.

He was in his forties by then. This lilting, long, weightless trip was just the latest of many for him, and as handy and busy as he was about town, he kept going out. He prospected to the Big Muddy River and the Turnagain River, 150 miles to the east, a rugged country of big boulders and scrub spruce where he saw not a soul for weeks, not even a Siwash—maybe a rusted old stove in a lean-to or a rotted deadfall. He wound back by way of Cold Fish Lake and the valley of the Klappan and the high source plateau of the Iskut. Another year, in the winter, he traveled northeast a couple of hundred miles to the Rancheria River in the Yukon where there was a strike—this the teeming caribou country, so that every night he was able to shoot one and camp right beside it, gorging himself and his dogs. When he went out in the fall, in some places he hadn't been able to find a drink of water for miles, but next April, on the return, he could hardly struggle through the very same streams which had been dry, and in every half-promising creek a man would be gophering with a shovel and sluice, throwing up sand. It amounted to working for wages, like other work, since each creek settled into providing a set rate of pay, which then diminished gradually over the years until it wasn't enough to live on, although the gold dust on the bottom continued to sparkle.

Alec's registered trapline was in another direction entirely, down by the Boundary on the Stikine, and included the Katete to its head as well as the first seven miles of the Iskut River. For years he averaged as many as one hundred beavers a season, each worth about $30, and perhaps fifty marten ($15), and thirty-five mink ($20), and two or three otter ($10), and one or two fisher ($75). He'd fish through the ice for rainbows and cutthroats and Dolly Varden, besides shooting a couple of moose. Down where he was, ten feet of snow lay on the ground by February and the moose endured by huddling in the spring-fed sloughs alongside the river, which didn't freeze over, or else under the thickest cover of spruce. Whenever they were forced to cross between sanctuaries they were helpless, wallowing like an overstrained snowplow, leaving a mournful, deep trench exactly the shape of their bodies, whereas he ran lightly on top on his snowshoes. The wolves traveled the open ice where the wind scoured it bare. He used to see twelve or fifteen at once playing on the sandbar across from him, big ones with little ones. Eight wolves, loping tightly in a pack like a gang of sleigh dogs, came up the river from the direction of Wrangell one day. He thought a friend of his was arriving to visit. Dirty and shaggy, they whirled into the yard and sniffed his two bear dogs, a unique and spindly little breed about the size of a terrier, developed by the Tahltans. The wolves didn't kill them, and when he clapped his hands, they turned and ran for the opposite bank of the river and got up in the woods and howled. Another time, in the spring, a grizzly got caught in a beaver trap and so tangled up in the willows it didn't have leverage enough to break free. The willows were waving as though in a wind. John Creyke, who was staying overnight, went down and shot the bear with nothing more redoubtable than Alec's trapline .22.

Grizzlies are the gorillas of the continent, the man-of-the-mountains, of interest to everybody, but Alec speaks of all these animals and people with equal affection and gaiety, poofing his words out, laughing, nodding, shaking his head, recrossing his legs and swinging the top one, blinking, and looking boldly out of the window. He says he's seen an eagle dive on a salmon and get taken under when the salmon sounded. He says the Siwash kids will be into his yard after his radishes as soon as they're up and he just wonders whether he's planted enough for both them and him. When he was on the lower Stikine, he might not see man, woman, or child for seven months in the year, unless maybe he snuck into Wrangell. It got a bit stiff toward the end, but it was the richest territory anybody had, and when you're alone you keep busier. It's surprising the company a bunch of sleigh dogs is. He had a jovial four-dog team that could pull a quarter of a ton. In difficult snow he'd break trail ahead of them, as when they went to his overnight cabin up the Katete. Once out of the coastal belt, though, running for home on the ice, he went seventy exuberant miles with them in a day —jogging behind the sled, jumping on, jogging again, and jumping on. When he trapped, he had his summers off except for being powder man, and when he was prospecting, if he made any money he took the winter off, except for wiring and carpentering the town. He sold his furs to the local man, but his friend Gus Adamson preferred to ship to Montreal in hopes of a better price. One particular year the bottom fell out of the market when Gus did this, so that the catch he was offered $1500 for in town had fallen in value to $900 by the time it got East.

Dan McPhee even prospected for sturgeon in some of the lakes. Since these can go over a thousand pounds, it wouldn't need many to set you up. The Bear Lake Indians caught one very occasionally and kept it alive as long as they could, tied in the shallows, cutting steaks off its sides. Both McPhees have a smile they reserve for such antics. Dan's is ironic and civilized and Alec's is curious and buoyant. Tired from my visit now, they both look like small hooligans, Dan rather trembly and drawn. His word for most people I ask about is "born locally," with a pursed smile, meaning illegitimately, but his smile means mostly that he wishes that he'd had a hand.

I love the town, with its up parts and down, its steep roofs, usually tin, so that they shine. The Anglican church is bread-brown, with a leaning steeple, high, miniature windows, and a needlework-chiselwork interior. The river clips by in front in a channel of three hundred yards, and graceful, swaying catwalks go out for disposing of trash. The old telegraph cabins are across from the Diamond C Café, and the Catholic church, a hefty log house painted yellow, is on the highest terrace. The school is out of sight on the bluff. The Tahltan Reserve, which is called Casca after a related tribe, is behind that, higher still, and is reached least strenuously by walking a mile up the draw which Telegraph Creek cuts through the bluff. On Front Street, by the river, besides the Anglican church, the Mounties' office, and a row of weathered board houses where several Indian families live who have chosen to leave the legal shelter of the reserve, are the two stores. The lofty, immaculately red-and-white one is the Hudson's Bay store, and the other belongs to the traditional private trader in competition, who right now is a young Alaskan. Each has considerable traffic, and in each the nurse has posted a list of the children who are late for their second Salk shot. The children are rounder- and flatter-faced than the Tlingits, and a redder brown. They are louder, wilder, more hammery, from being so much farther off. They treat me to the Bronx cheer as I go by, they mock my stutter and range the town, climb the rock chimneys, which go giddily hundreds of feet up the bluff, run down the paths to the thickets along the Stikine, and throw stones at the birds harder than children in Wrangell would. At the same time they're shyer and more intrigued, studying me, asking my name. They flop into soft puppy-piles on the grass, listening to an older child talk. As this is a thoroughly Indian town, they're at home everywhere, like the men, who are not defensive or grudging. And the girls have a yielding daintiness, a real doe-deer quality, along with the prettiness of the Tlingits.

JUNE 11, SATURDAY:

NEXT TO DAN McPHEE's is Ah Clem's old house, with a long green dog sled in the yard. Snowshoes hang under the eaves, as well as a packboard, a saddle, saddlebags, salmon nets. There's an easy chair with a hide over it, and a dog on the porch who stands up very tall, his coat like a luxury fur. Ah Clem had many jobs—cook in the hotel, rock man constructing the orderly terraces. Also, he fed the dogs in the summer, when upwards of two hundred of them were staked on the bank of the river, howling and yapping; he cooked up a gruel of salmon and grease and potatoes twice a week. He is survived by his half-breed son, a fat, sleek-haired man more Chinese than Indian in appearance, and by his grandchildren, who look more Indian.

Gus Adamson lives next and last, beyond Ah Clem's son. Since Alec McPhee went on pension, Gus has been the river snagger. It may be an office joke somewhere in Victoria that a person still exists who keeps the deserted Stikine navigable. Gus, however, thinks about scarcely anything else, between the paperwork and his troubles with crew. They complain because in an effort to save the government money he feeds them on rice and tapioca instead of on fresh beef and fruit, like McPhee used to do. He has two men to help him, and they make three two-week trips to the Boundary during the season, blowing away obstructions. The boat is an old-fashioned longboat, infinitesimal alongside the bank as we look down on it. He's a sturdy, feisty, bald bantamweight, so remarkably small that he seems to be blown up like a balloon, the way small men by a process of inversion sometimes do. He's deaf now, has dental difficulties and a bright red complexion, and is missing the central part of his nose. He speaks slowly, choosing his words, and he lives in a pocket-sized, shipshape house, with a large middle-aged Indian woman.

Perhaps so I won't meet her, we sit outside in an ancient car. He feels he hasn't been authorized to talk to me about the river and doesn't want to stay with me longer than politeness demands, but he's such appealing company, with his close-to-the-vest manner, that he's hard to let go. He looks in my eyes. Deciding there's something kindred in me, he says we could talk for a month about the river if he were authorized to. He arrived in Telegraph from the Peace River in 1935. After scouting around, he affixed himself on the Dease and Stikine as a river freightman, and trapped in the winter between Great and Mud Glaciers and the Porcupine—or, in other words, between Alec McPhee's strip of the river and the Callbreath family's. The man there before Gus had just drowned—Jack Fowler, who had prospected to Nome and to Dawson City and had carried the mail and done other glamorous things, and was living with his second wife by this time, a strong-winded squaw named Annie, although he had waited too long getting started to leave any kids behind. Gus's prize year was in the late forties, when in a quick twenty-five days he caught sixty-two beaver. Recently he built a new hut on the spot to sleep in when he snags down that way. He rubs his back; he's been having an old man's ominous pains. Small ear, big hearing aid, facing me. And that's all that he'll say.

In the afternoon John Creyke's son is married. Creyke is the best hunting guide anywhere around and would be the leading citizen if he weren't Indian; as a result, there is no leading citizen. Since I'm too timid to invite myself, I take a walk along a sandy scratch trail above the river, with flowers and pretty ground pine. A rolling game country stretches fifty miles south to about the Scud, where the mountains fist up nine thousand feet. Coming back across a grassy range, I meet a loose troop of horses, who slide out of reach like so many fish, wheeling in a flat, careful curve as if they were tied head to haunch: insouciant, bonehead horses, sinister in the face. No wild animal looks any tougher. They have the corrupt, gangster faces of mercenaries and that tight herding instinct. A roan and a white do a little kicking, and when the roan yawns, all the rest catch the yawn. Incidentally, I understand that the fat horse I saw from the plane flicking his tail, was completely alone and had wintered alone from last September, so he's lucky to have survived the wolves and the snows.

Can't get over the river. The gorge emphasizes its cutting power without hiding it, but it wiggles offstage right away. This is the one place it's looked at, but after a few working curves, it's gone.

I stopped at the Wriglesworths'. They live above Alec McPhee and next to Dan, on the other side of his house from Ah Clem's son. Theirs is a nonmorganatic marriage and an unambiguous one, so it's a pleasant glimpse after the pictures I've had of the wife going home to her relatives every afternoon after cooking lunch. Mr. Wriglesworth has a rather strange biblical face, quite like Lincoln's on top, with a forehead like a furled flag under a shock of upright hair. He looks like the prophet who walks in front of a migrating people carrying a staff, and as though his face were younger underneath the skin than outside, as if the deep lines had been cut from grinning more than from anything else, grinning at the bright sun more than at friends. Mrs. Wriglesworth isn't as prepossessing. At first she seems like any well-meaning, shrunken-down woman from a farming community who has done her best all her life, and done well, yet has always worried a lot and never felt that her best was worth much. She ducks in and out apologetically, serving a marvelous home-brew beer which is as sweet as cider—I can't get enough. Her hair is a frumpy dab, her mouth bends like a bobby pin. "Don't tell him that," she interrupts. "He's not interested in that." She says that she never is favored by such an outgush of words from her husband, so why am I? But she grows on one, what with the sweet-tasting beer and the smells of supper. The nagging turns out not to be nagging, but only her end of a constant byplay. He's a witty man and he's on her whenever she sheds a tear chopping the onions. He boasts to me about a world-record "broad jump" she made years ago, after she'd brushed up against a hornet's nest. "That's quite a surprise, when you turn around and you see your wife in midair, doing fine, when you never knew before that she could jump at all, even a little ways. There she is, taking off."

She has the knack of turning a bottle cap over by pressing on it with one finger, a delicate motion, using the pad. I practice as though we had a winter of long nights ahead. She's about ten years younger than Mr. Wriglesworth, and they married in 1934, after he had already been on the river for ten years. They met in fact at Groundhog Jackson's place, near the Grand Rapids, as it is called, and they settled on the homestead which Wriglesworth had established at the mouth of the Chutine. For a while a tentative placer-mining operation was going on some distance up a tributary of the Chutine, where he earned wages on the "grizzly," which sorts the big nuisance rocks out of the sluice. Generally, though, they lived on what they raised and what he was paid for his furs. Beans, cabbage, turnips, potatoes, carrots, peas, squash, lettuce, tomatoes: everything grew. The thriving grouse were their chickens; they let the woods raise the chickens, and they ate snowshoe rabbits and a yearly moose or two. Each moose furnished six hundred pounds of meat or more. It would get a crust on the surface but would keep through the winter in the cold. In the spring they often ate beaver, which they enjoyed. The year-round utility food was salmon belly, or salmon prepared in some other way. It could be dried and smoked, each fish being split into four parts and finally folded up again into its original form. This was what they fed their dogs and was the form that the Indians used, smearing grease on the fish to soften them up before eating them and sticking them up around the campfire like so many boards. The Wriglesworths also canned salmon, or slimed them with brine strong enough to blacken a potato, or else kippered them, which was delicious, the fish being soaked in a liquid mix of brown sugar and smoked salt and taken out, smoked, and then rested and given a second smoking. They could net such great batches of salmon from June to September that really the only limit was how many hundred pounds they wanted to do the work on. They ate the young mountain goats too, though with an old billy you might as well boil up a stone—and the yearling black bears, tasting of berry fields, whereas a grizzly's meat was fishy and scavengerish.

Since the Chutine ramifies into a full river system in its own right, Mr. Wriglesworth had more of a trapping territory than he could use. Because the number of men who were still active declined to a tiny group, he got Shakes Creek and Yehiniko Creek as well, both tributaries of the Stikine, both about twenty-five miles long. Yehiniko has a lake at its head with mineral licks and the sheep coming down, and on Shakes Creek, where Chief Shakes made his last trading trips to meet the Tahltans, he counted eighty goat in a streaming, stretched-out band. Maybe three times a year he went to Telegraph Creek, on the ice with his dogs, or in his skiff. Otherwise, the purser on the riverboat, whose name was Dar Smith, would do errands for him and pick up the mail. During these brief stops, the various cooks on the boat gave Mrs. Wriglesworth some tea and some chat, and she went down to Wrangell to have her first baby. The second was due in the winter when the boat didn't run, so they went to Vancouver for that. They had several neighbors—the Dan McPhees, of course, at one time, and the Groundhog Jacksons, and the Clearwater Jacksons, no relation, whom she liked better. There was a Monkey Jackson living in Telegraph Creek, but this Clearwater was the unfortunate Jackson who brought a boatload of domestic goats into Wrangell one time and tied them under the pier and went into a bar for a drink. When he came out the water had risen and they all were drowned. The closest neighbor was old Kirk, two miles up the delta of the Chutine. He was a gentleman of the old school, a bachelor with an antiquated horse and a snow-white beard, and was a remnant of the Ninety-Eight Rush and of old Jack Fowler's generation. He couldn't hunt any more, but he had about twenty acres that he had painstakingly cleared, which has vanished in jackpine now, and he lived pretty well from his land. Twice in the beaver season when Wriglesworth was away, Edith packed her children through three feet of floodwater to him.

They were all conscientious neighbors. There were no bushwhackers, no screwballs, no suicides. I walk around and around the experience with my questions, but I can't dislodge it from its naturalness. They made berry beer from the soapberries and wine from the saskatoons. The children did correspondence courses in a regular regimen, so that the son has gone whole hog lately and become a computer programmer. Even the bears were good neighbors. Once when Mr. Wriglesworth had fastened his canoe to a tree, which happened to be on a bear's trail, the bear yanked it out of the water by hitting the rope with his paw, and then reassumed ownership by sitting down with his back to the tree and rubbing a swatch of bark off. And once when Mr. Wriglesworth had paddled forty-five miles from his cabin to the source of the river near Chutine Lake, which has V-walls and icebergs tumbling in and a truly stupendous relief, he was leaning over, punching holes in the thin coating of ice which had formed along the bank. He couldn't locate several traps; although it was only a modest little stream here, it had risen two feet overnight. But he heard the ice breaking across from him. Feeling for a trap chain, he paid no attention until he noticed a grizzly wading directly his way. When he let go of the bank to drift downstream, the bear swam towards him convergingly. After he shot it, the body floated grimly ahead of his canoe for a long while. But these were two incidents in a life's residence on the river, a continual association with game. Except for shooting stew meat and beaver with a light gun, he'd go through the year using two cartridges, one for his first moose and one for his second.

The tumbling market in furs, as well as their children's needs, ended the Wriglesworths' tenure at last. He hasn't the stories of rambles like Alec McPhee's, but he used to see thirty moose at a time up on the Chutine where a fire had burned out the evergreens and let the willow and alder grow chest-high. As the different old-timers died or retired, the huge labyrinth of the Stikine itself belonged to him. He went down ninety miles to Great Glacier, where one side of the valley is a wall of green ice and the other side is a hot springs, dammed by the beaver and surrounded by vegetation as in a botanical garden. It was a kind of exotic swimming hole, the water lukewarm. The steep slippery clay banks made a slide. You'd slide in and splash and look up at the ice.

JUNE 12, SUNDAY:

A COLD SUNNY MORNING like November in New York. The town still delights me, its brown bluffs and tumultuously climbing green hillside across the way and hand hewn, eloquent cabins spotted around. Saw Mr. Wriglesworth go by, with his patriarch's head, and a springy, dignified step, a pack on his back, for a prospecting trip of three days.

I spoke with Mike Williams this morning. He's a husky old

Indian on Front Street. He says that John Bull takes care of him now; his knees have gone bad. He has a booming hoarse voice, a short nose, bushy eyebrows and a wrinkling smile under his eyes. He trapped the rich Iskut and Porcupine country with Fowler before Fowler died. He and Dora, his wife, would hike down in March with their boat on the sled and live alongside Fowler's house. One year they cleared $7000 between them, with Mike's two brothers. Mike remembers him from back in 1908, when Fowler was already old, and yet when he died he was starting a mink ranch, spending the day fishing and cutting up fish. He didn't drown, as Gus Adamson said, because Mike found first his snowshoes stuck in the snow, then his hat, and finally Fowler himself, "croaked," face down in a bank of snow. Apparently, after falling through the ice, he'd crawled out of the river and was trying to get back to camp before he froze. One winter when he was younger his prostate gland burst, but he toughed that out and survived. And he spent an entire year alone on the Taku watershed, a large river system to the north, where he thought he was onto some gold. When he returned, he was batty and babbling; he was handing out gifts on the trail. He gave his shirt and snowshoes and shoes away to the Indians he met, and gave them his samplings of ore and his fisher skins.

Mike remembers being told by his father how during the months of the gold rush, people slept all over town, in the streets, on the woodpiles. His grandfather owned a farm on the Scud which might be worth $$$$ today because of the copper find, except that he let it go for back taxes one time when he was poor and sick. Mike grew up a trapper and hunter, and says he likes sheep meat better than goat, and groundhog better than beaver. Moose is tastier and tenderer than caribou, except in the spring, because caribou pick up their summer flesh quicker. He says the supply of furs partly depended upon how plentiful the rabbits were, although the coyotes came in with the rabbits and sometimes raised cain with the furbearers. In a pretty fair winter he might catch ten wolverine, twenty or thirty marten, fifty or sixty beaver, ten to fifteen mink, maybe thirty fox, two or three otter, and all the squirrels he wanted, although he didn't eat squirrels like some people did. He knows that long ago the Indians used snares for everything, before they had guns, but he's never snared. He does speak the Tahltan language, however, because his parents spoke nothing else. When the rabbits are numerous the salmon are not, and vice versa, so this is a salmon summer coming. His nets are coiled in a washtub in the living room while he works on them. The run of kings will begin very soon. Then the sockeyes begin to arrive in July, and the cohos the first of September. He says you can see them break water where a creek empties in, jumping the obstruction of the current. You set your net in an eddy alongside the main flow. In the Sheslay River, which is north on the Telegraph Trail, you get salmon so big you can't use a knife to cut their throat, you need a hatchet.

A neighbor drops by, a brawny sensible man with a large face who, like Mike, is a great deal friendlier to me than I remember the Skeena Tsimshians being. The cabin is comfortably high-ceilinged. The walls are pink. There's a low sofa, a vase of wax flowers, a horseshoe over the door, a few Christmas bells tacked up from last Christmas, several mirrors around, a sack of Five Roses flour in the corner, and a stove made out of a metal barrel. Three decorative paper balls hanging from the center of the ceiling seem to be lights for a moment, but of course they aren't. The talk turns to beer—the types of home brew, the commercial Old Style which we are drinking, and the Over Proof that you get in the Yukon. There's a motto on the wall from the Alaska Highway:

> Winding in and winding out
> Leaves my mind in serious doubt
> If the dude that built this road
> Was going to hell or coming out . . .

Dry Town is upriver from Front Street and considerably higher. It's a row of shacks on a giddy shelf over the river where not many families live any more. The roofs have acquired a right- or a left-handed lean. Gap-runged ladders rest against them which used to be employed in getting the snow off. The shingles have warped in the shape of fish scales and are patched with pieces of rusty metal. The windows are boarded up, and when one peeps through, the interiors are heaped with chests and trunks, as if a traveling troupe had lived in them. The dozens of holes under the porches, dug by the sled dogs, add to the same atmosphere. This was where a number of Indians moved when their ancient capital town at the junction of the Tahltan River was abandoned; it was the first of a series of anxious, aimless shifts and switches for them. Some of the houses are locked and in better condition, but the only person I ran across was a bloated and addled fellow, evidently feeble-minded. The one dog there played with me as Indian dogs always do, quite as any pet might, except that he never actually ventured within reach. He acts out the fooling and fun, like a charade, not undoing it by trusting himself in anyone's mitts.

Dry Town was dry by law, of course. Across the river is another cluster of houses, newer-looking because the roofs are painted bright colors and the willow tops wave animatedly in front of the windows, where the Caribou Hide Indians lived from 1949 until three years ago. A village is being founded for them at an old campsite of theirs called Eddontenajon, at the head of the Iskut River. Before 1949 they had lived in total isolation at the head of the Stikine and Finlay, ten days on horseback from Telegraph Creek. The Caribou Hiders were mostly Sikanni, a tribe of the Athapascan family, and when they were moved close to town they didn't mix with the Tahltans, as the government had expected they would. The Tahltans thought them backward and slightly dumb and silly. Their missionaries were Catholic, not Anglican, and before the age of the missionaries, the Tahltans ruthlessly lorded it over them. Under threat of death, they were not allowed near the Stikine, either to fish or to trade with the Tlingits and Russians. Appropriating their furs, the Tahltans doled out traps and gunpowder to them in dribbles just sufficient to keep them from starving, so they had been eager indeed to make the long move to the legendary river of salmon, with its white-man's facilities. The trouble was that the moose close around had been hunted out, though they did find plenty of salmon, and the Tahltans were not enthusiastic to have them, and their missionaries were unenthusiastic about the Anglican Tahltans. So now they have started again from scratch.

From a distance, overgrown as it is, it looks rather gay on the other side, not transient and dusty and scuffed like Dry Town. The trail down to the landing and the trail over the mountain to Eddontenajon and Caribou Hide and the forts on the Finlay River still show. According to Alec McPhee, the Tahltans said that the Caribou Hiders spoke "broken Tahltan." They ran up debts at the store, they were the bad guys, though nobody thought them so very seriously. In Hazelton too, I remember a small band of interior Indians lived across a river canyon from the settlement of the Tsimshians. The name of their village, Hagwilget, meant "quiet people," and so little contact was maintained between the two groups that they only knew who had the best baseball team by comparing their scores against the whites' team.

Alec McPhee has unearthed a map of Fort Wrangell from the nineties for me, including routes to the Klondike. It's full of bold speculations, distortions and bluff. Printed notes say "smooth trail here," "very rough country." The back is over-spread with an excited penciled diary about porpoises and bluefish killed on the lower Stikine, and moose sighted and prospectors seen. Miner and cartographer are equally thrilled, but unfortunately most of the diary is illegible; a magnifying glass would be needed. It's not his own, and one hears about so many diaries in a place like this where time has stopped still that I guiltily let drop the matter of finding a way to preserve it.

McPhee is bolt upright in his chair, holding his crossed knees and sniffing breaths in, twitching his head. When I ask for more stories of trips, he says that they were just wonderful trips, that's all; no disasters on them. He even brought a horse to carry the grub, so all that he had to do was to saunter along and enjoy himself. He says once he found a five-dollar nugget which had just the shape of the long-handled shovel that he'd dug for it with. A guy from Seattle in the next tent to his cleared out one night and cleared out with the nugget as well.

Have been lying down with a sore throat part of the afternoon, but talked to the Anglican reverend a little. He's a tiny, struggling man with a hard-pressed, accentuated air. Being a veteran of six years in town, he has a strong glare-squint, and rather a frontier stomp to his walk. He has a grating voice and a brave, lonesome smile. He carries a Kleenex in one hand and seems to be always dandling some phlegm on his tongue, as if to prove to himself that his cough doesn't frighten him. Having got past the bishop's visit and the Creyke family's wedding, he's greatly relieved at the moment. Last night he played piccolo until very late at the wedding dance; it was one of his successes. He eats supper in the café for company, standing in the middle of the floor to be close to everybody and darting over to his plate at the counter from time to time for a brief mouthful. Usually he speaks of himself as "we," repeating the sentence once or twice in a lower and lower murmur, like a man who forgets that he isn't alone. He's a person of pugnacious judgments which revolve around each other. He respects the Indians and resents the outer establishment of cozy bishops and clever young men from the University, such as the two schoolteachers up on the hill. He lives in a wretched flimsy mess of a house and tells me sternly that I probably pad my books and am a hypochondriac. We retire from front-line work like this and discover we haven't even a roof over our heads, he says, so he spends every leave driving back to his parents' old house in Saskatchewan, repairing the chimney and paying the taxes, though he isn't particularly fond of the place. He takes a couple of local kids along to show them a bit of the world, but it sounds like a desperado drive, like the nurse's month in Las Vegas every fall or the riverboat cook's voyages to Samoa.

The nurse is another lorn figure, a jittery, bombastic lady who stalks the streets with the martial haste of someone with nothing to do and the eyes of the village on her, as she supposes. This is her tenth year, and she's so abusive to patients that nobody goes to see her unless in extreme situations, when she turns about and becomes first-rate. If a baby in Casca goes into convulsions, she'll order in a government plane.

I haven't neglected my landlord, who's full of lore locked away, but he's elusive. He's recuperating from an ulcer operation, so he sleeps in the afternoon and the rest of the day is underneath one of his 1930s trucks. He also has a vintage tractor and three vintage cars which he's picked up over the years from people who were leaving town. If we do exchange a word, he's under the chassis transferring parts and I'm squatting next to the running board. Although he's not as gentle a fellow as the captain, his son, he's a milder Callbreath than the grandfather was, the forceful Callbreath of 1874. He's a lean-knit half-breed with high cheeks, walnut skin and a delicate nose—he looks like a honed Indian. His lips are so swollen from the sun that he can't adjust them into an expression. They're baked into testimonial form, or a sort of art form, like the curve of a fish backbone on a beach. His wife is the kindest woman in town. People call her Aunt Eva, which embarrasses her when it's a drunk stumbling in the café. She is always at work, and she reminds me of photographs from the thirties, with her sagging dresses and her wayward, meek nose. She cooks maternally, is indulgent in her gossip, and strangers pretty well put themselves in her hands. Since there have been times when her husband hasn't been expected to live, they argue whether they should stay on. He wants to be here with his motors and she wants to move to one of the cities where her children are.

The two patron families of Telegraph Creek were the Call-breaths and Hylands. The Hylands were businessmen. They kept a store and married white women and managed their ranches tidily rather than hurling themselves at the occupation. But old Callbreath married a native and plunged into ranching hard. He lived downriver fourteen miles, on the far side. He tried to raise chickens and cows, in spite of the rugged climate, and kept a huge, milling string of horses which Roy spent his boyhood in the midst of. It was all work and no money, cutting hay, putting up shelters, provisioning the Telegraph Trail, and he got out of it as soon as his father died. The estate was a crosshatch of debts anyway. He liked trucks, not horses, tinkering, not business.

He doesn't know what to tell me. In so much wild country there has only been one outlaw, and his era coincided with the First War. He was from Hazelton, named Gunanoot. When we were first here, my wife taught his great-grandsons in Sunday school. Callbreath describes Gunanoot as a pleasant-looking, short, popular guy who would turn up every once in a while to outfit himself at the Hylands' store. The alarm wasn't raised until he left town. He had a space the size of Minnesota to dodge about in, and did trapping in order to pay back the friends who were keeping his family fed. It was emotionally punishing, however, going on for thirteen years as it did, because the Mounties weren't able to catch him. He killed a white man who had assaulted his wife and was taunting him about it. A few hours later he shot a second man, a friend of the other white man who was trailing him, but by accident, thinking this was the same enemy and that he had missed. He didn't kill anybody after that, though the Mounties sent out harassing expeditions. He would often drop in on a big-game party for an evening's talk and to borrow some salt, and he appeared at the various trading posts on the Dease and Finlay —he would ask the factor what he would do if Gunanoot ever showed up. Some of the hardy prospectors helped him out, as did the Nass Tsimshians. At last, after such a display of long-suffering woodsmanship and civility, his side of the story was told. The Mounties agreed through his relatives that if he would only please turn himself in, they were sure he would be acquitted. Late in life he was bitter about these years, but he was the guru young men came to see before setting out on the Telegraph Trail. A mountain was named after him (7250 feet, with a glacier on it) in his stronghold, right at the mythical head of the Skeena.

JUNE 13, MONDAY:

A DAZZLY MORNING. IT'S like having a second language to be at home here. I'm a different personality. In the city I over-plan, I'm a worrywart, too punctual, but I came all the way to Wrangell after having been told that the boat was booked full and with no idea if I would find anywhere to live if I did get upriver.

You can recognize the old residents like Callbreath and John Creyke by the cluster of vehicles which have accrued to them, a sign of their having survived. Creyke lives in an empty church, a high fiefdom at the end of Dry Town. A sleepy call answered my knock. I went in. The bed compartment in the corner was surrounded by a curtain of cheesecloth, and a woman's annoyed voice told me to "Pull it back. Pull the curtain!" When I did, there they were.

Mrs. Creyke is a bulky woman who looks as wise as a gypsy medium, as Indian women who have borne fourteen children frequently do. She rolled over to go to sleep again, but her husband rose. He's a vigorous sixty, quiet-spoken and tall, with thriving white hair, deep-set eyes and massive ears. He's the son of an itinerant, rich Scotchman who had many liaisons during a period of residence of several years. Some Britishers came to be Indian Agents and trek through the bush, some to be officerly missionaries, but this one came purely for fun. Whenever his family sent money for a ticket home, he spent it all, until they had to enlist the assistance of the Hudson's Bay.

Being polite, Creyke rubbed his face awake. He said it was lucky he lived in a church or he wouldn't have room for these wedding parties. He put on a pair of pinstripe pants and moosehide moccasins decorated with beads, and we sat at the edge of the bluff on two logs. Being used to fancy hunting clients from the States, he was doing the favor, simple and unbuttered-up with me. But he liked the sunshine—it was as though he were washing his hair in it with his hands—and the shimmying, wriggling river below. Occasionally he has snagged for Gus Adamson, but he doesn't like this high water; he'd just as soon stay off the river entirely. Hunting has nowhere nearly that danger; hunting and game are everyday life. Laughing, he said he was old enough to start prospecting now. You fiddle around wherever you happen to have set up your camp and see if you stumble on anything—that's what they call prospecting. In the old days he packed for the Callbreaths and Hylands, as well as the outfit that Hudson's Bay had. He took supplies to Hyland Post, which is a fourteen-day trip with a string of seventy or eighty horses, nine days coming back unloaded. His trapping territory was more or less the same as where he hunts now: that is, to the east along the Klastine River for the fifty miles between here and the head of the Iskut River, and including Ice Mountain, a broad dominant volcanic cone of nine thousand feet; then on another twenty miles over an intervening range to the Klappan River, and all the way up the Klappan to its source at Tumeka Lake; and up the fork of the Little Klappan as well, to its source at Gunanoot Mountain, which is two hundred miles from where we are. He's been south to the Nass, which is further than that, and north to the headwaters of the Yukon, and west to the International Boundary, and east into the Liard River system —one of the iron men, one of the princes.

As I have before with other people, I try to get Creyke to name a favorite valley in this gigantic ocean of heaped-up land almost too enormous to comprehend—some splendid retreat. But he doesn't respond. His conception seems to be very different. His own assigned territory is twice as large as Delaware, limited though he feels it to be. He didn't huddle somewhere in a lovely valley; he traveled through; he went everywhere. There was a range of mountains for hunting caribou and another for hunting sheep—maybe still another for goat. There was a river for salmon and a river for trout. There were rivers after these rivers and ranges after these ranges, uncountable vivid valleys that were a heaving, pelagic green. Once the knack was acquired, it was nothing to go for a month or the summer, lazing along as calmly as a long-distance swimmer, and never encounter an end.

Nowadays everybody has shot their dog team, so if a boy wants to go out in the winter for moose, he borrows Ah Clem's son's dog and Dan McPhee's dog, Mike William's dog and John Creyke's dog, and combines them. Sheep are the glamor game because they live high and because they're high-strung. For some reason, goats don't look up, so that unless you kick a stone down on them, you can stalk them successfully by getting above. But moose are the beef of the north because you can eat the meat day in, day out. Sheep, even caribou, after four or five meals you lose the taste for. Since nobody is trapping wolves any more, they kill lots of moose calves in the spring. The cow will swim to an island in the middle of a lake where the wolves aren't as likely to go, but then a bear may swim over and find the calf hidden. Creyke has about forty head of horses, who winter well, he says. The temperature on the range drops to thirty below but the snowfall isn't excessive. They paw down to the grass, and their bells and their habit of herding tightly spook the wolves off.

Since I rousted him out of bed and since he has given me enough of his time, he goes indoors to wake his wife and get the breakfast fire going. He stands erect as a captain of industry, and although he can't read or write, he's the cosmopolite of the town.

The Hudson's Bay clerk is a frail functionary. For most of his life he has switched about among isolated posts such as

Telegraph Creek, and has grown as pallid as a cave creature. Moveless, friendless, he does without either sun or company. And the one schoolmaster I've met appears to have been completely bleached out by the long winter. He played some chess with the Catholic priest but read very little. He's a zestless young man, but does like the kids. He says they have good imaginations, if little or no curiosity to learn; he hammers the stuff into them. Says the parents get drunk constantly, as though they only existed for that, and the kids sometimes are neglected for days. It's interesting that the only antlers in town belong to him. It's so virginal here that game is still meat to everyone else, not a trophy.

They're a grim bunch, some of these institutional whites— the trudging pastor, the scolding nurse with her bobbed black hair, like a neurotic nanny, and the ashen clerk. The permanent people like the McPhees are wood sprites by contrast, or else witty, mischievous oracles, like Mr. Wriglesworth. They *are* wood sprites. Nothing goes on, and yet the village is carbonated; it tingles. Blithe old codgers walk down the steps from the terraces, like Rumpelstiltskin. For an old trapper to have any neighbors at all is a luxury. The resilience, the self-sufficiency, overflows.

A. J. Marion isn't particularly like that. He was a versatile hobo, a cabinetmaker and carpenter, and he left Ontario for Detroit, then Rochester, then Jamestown, Virginia, where he helped build an exposition that Teddy Roosevelt opened. A pal and he flipped to see whether they'd go to New York or St. Louis. St. Louis won. Later they proceeded to Seattle, where they were sitting around the union hall one time when the business agent came in and said jobs were going begging in Juneau. "Where's Juneau?" Of course they went, though, and sitting around the bunkhouse in Juneau, they heard about the Stikine. They bought eight dogs, two sleds and a ton of grub, and came up on the ice in 1913 (already he was past thirty). From Telegraph Creek they went on for 150 miles into the

Cassiar Mountains. The creek which they staked was barren, but they worked so hard that World War I had been on for almost a year before they heard about it.

Marion has a horrendous reputation in town; he bites people's heads off. His house is a level below Dan McPhee's, and although his door is wide open the whole summer, he's left to his own devices by the others. I was told that the early afternoon was the time to chance him, when he would have warmed to the day but not yet heated up. I found a hard-boiled, amusing, quick-memoried man who reminds me of a circus straw boss I once knew. He opens up to a silent listener. We got out the photograph albums of mustached friends and plump, self-effacing half-breed women. Because he was a money-man too, he talks about the rich scions who arrived on the riverboat to get drunk and hunt, the Mellons, the Schlitzes. A Smithsonian collector who was a crack shot with a .22 searched for bushrats. One squeak of his lips in the right location and out popped a horde. The Museum of Natural History in New York sent a man who gathered up buck brush and leaves, to go with a family of caribou, along with an artist to draw the backdrop. The artist was so talented that at a dance that was held he could sketch a couple circling the floor and present the picture to them before they passed him again. I told him the same museum has a Tsimshian war canoe fifty feet long.

Marion is the "hard" variety of bush professional, like my Hazelton friend Jack Lee was. There is a hard variety and a mild one, such as Alec McPhee or George Engelmann in Wrangell. It's a matter of style, not of prowess. You can visualize two men gutting a deer. One of them goes at it like a soldier who is stripping a foe, and the other rather resembles a woman poking through her purse, examining what it contains, although she knows what everything is. Marion operated a fleet of canoes and scows on the Dease River to Lower Post, as well as a bunch of wagons and trucks on the tote road between Telegraph Creek and Dease Lake. The Stikine then was a conduit to a vast interior area, before the Alaska Highway. Indians poled and paddled for him, and he managed a Hudson's Bay Post on the lake, buying $18,000 to $20,000 worth of furs every year. Altogether, counting the take of the independents and the other Bay posts, $175,000 in furs used to leave Telegraph Creek in the spring. A village grew up around his cabin, and the small strike on Gold Pan Creek in 1924 provided a lucrative flurry for the traders like him, the pack-train men and the river men. For the miners, however, rushing into the country and paying through the nose, it was a dead loss. They found just another stream with a glittering name and too much gravel and too little gold. The village Marion started is a blank now, except for a single old Indian lady, a Mrs. Asp, who has chosen to stay by her husband's grave. Somehow or other she kills a moose every year and scratches up a potato patch. She can only be reached by boat, and she is said to be past talking to, if indeed she is still alive. Nobody really seems to know.

His own wife is dead. His children's vacations are marked on the calendar, and he is waiting impatiently. As busy as they are with their families, maybe none of them will be able to come. It's a lonely wait, obviously—no telephone service—and he talks about quitting the Stikine. Except for the Anglican reverend, he's the loneliest man in town, and the only person for whom becoming elderly is an ordeal. He has a sarcastic mouth, used to getting things done, and piercing blue eyes, bushy white eyebrows, a purple nose, which he rubs, and an energetic voice, and he sits here reading an old *MacLean's* magazine for the seventeenth time. He says he bought a ranch on Shakes Creek for his kids; built an oil house for fuel and a mouse-proofed grub house, both on the river, with the ranch house set back, which the bears have ripped through several times now. But nobody took the idea up; it's all gone to scrub and jackpine. He wears clean engineer's clothes, a railroad man's cap, and little springs wrapped around his arms to hold up his sleeves. His stove and floor are polished to shine. He tells me about the spring cleaning he held—had a native girl in and supervised.

JUNE 14, TUESDAY:

ANOTHER SWEET DAY. THE Kennecott prospectors fly off in their helicopter each morning to unspecified destinations, returning about five o'clock totally fagged. Physically, the boys turn into men before one's eyes. Their faces flatten and redden and harden. I walked to Casca to meet Benny Frank, who is the chief's older brother. The chief has been flown by the government to a convocation of chiefs at Whitehorse, along with the counselor from Eddontenajon. While most of the whites are amused by such comings and goings, as if at children play-acting, the Indians appear not to realize this or not to resent it yet, to be still trying to win and to please. The reverend, who taxis them about in his jeep, is sincere. Visitors from the south, like the mining geologists and pilots who come in and the schoolteachers and the Indian agent himself, are reasonably interested in them, and the old residents among the whites are subdued and mellowed in what they say, so that the spread of attitudes may be a blur; white men have been here for such a short time, anyway.

Casca is high enough so that even in brilliant sunshine the cloud action against the surrounding mountainsides goes on. To see the hurricane heave of the land is very exciting after being down in the gorge for several days. Casca proper consists of two scraggly rows of flimsy frame houses, tarpapered over and painted brightly. Across a ravine full of brush and children's skittery trails is White Casca, which isn't a reserve and is therefore deserted except for a couple of ladies on old-age pensions who don't need the payments Reserve Indians receive. White Casca looks much older, with sod-roofed log cabins that lean and groan, that seem to speak like an elephant graveyard. Thick-walled, hunchy and wrinkled, they look as though their strength long ago had given out, but as if they had boxed in dozens of sad secret histories of humble lives led. They look as if they go back to buffalo days. Casca has the wash lines and kids. Although the shacks are sharecropper shacks, the people seem cheery and confident. They come up to me with an extraordinary sort of trust. Values are face values; I simply tell them what I am after. It's an odd sensation to talk to somebody who is my senior by fifty years and to feel in everything that he says that he has never encountered a crook. The conversation takes on a radiance, like talking to a no-hit pitcher at the end of the game, or talking to someone inspired, whose rules are his own. The very first thievery is now beginning to appear among the Tahltans, but at Eddontenajon the Caribou Hide group are not said to know about dishonesty yet.

Benny Frank lives with his deceased wife's mother, which isn't a bad idea since she is the most beautiful woman who ever graced Telegraph Creek, according to Dan McPhee, who should know. There is still a magnificent resonance to her looks. She's a pale-colored, big clever woman with an air of clairvoyant depth. She's eighty-four, looks fifty-five, and, speaking Tahltan with Benny, looks as if she hadn't troubled herself to learn English but is willing to use her other powers to understand what I have to say. They're having coffee and bread for breakfast in their night clothes, which are simply demoted day clothes. They live in a green steep-roofed cabin of one room, with ladder stairs to a half-loft, although they sleep in a narrow bed downstairs. There's a curtain to change behind and some Christmas cards up and magazine pictures that show a colonial ball, especially the gowns. They have two stoves joined to a shiny blue pipe, and they have a colossal white husky, bear-sized, who is silent and docile, except for his wolflike presence when a stranger appears. He's the rescuer type, like those that children in the Alps ride around on, but besides him they have a valuable yapping little black bear dog to hunt with. It's hard to see why her legs don't fall off, she's so skinny and tiny. The two of them slap her about, and she jumps around our ankles assertively, as if she had heard she is almost the last of the Tahltan Bear Dogs and that when she dies the race will be extinct.

Emma Brown, Benny Frank's friend, really does have the wide mouth and notable cheeks of a beauty. She's got a marvelously second-sight look—her eyes a cat's cradle within a cat's cradle. Nobody's been up here asking questions for umpteen years, and when she and Benny decide to enter into the spirit of what I am after, they go all out. Instead of this dinky reserve, what a stretch of land their tribe controlled before the white man, when they were eight hundred strong. Stikine means "Great River" and they had, in addition to what I have seen and can see implied in front of me, annual summer salmon encampments on the Sheslay and Nahlin, two tributaries of the Taku a week's travel northerly. They camped in numbers on the plateaus of Level Mountain for hunting, their big capital town was on the Tahltan, and they traveled to salt water to trade with the Tlingits, who were more warlike and powerful, but couldn't boast such a tub-thumping spread of territory.

Level Mountain remained a garden of game after the Stikine itself was appropriated by the gold hunters and settlers. They used to construct a corral in a canyon, and when the weather changed and a storm began banging and flustering the caribou, they would drive a knot in and kill them. They snared moose, caribou, even wolves with noose devices, as well as rabbits and ptarmigan. By surrounding a thicket and preparing dozens of snares, they captured baskets of ptarmigan at the exits. The women and children beat through the bushes and the men shot arrows at any that flew. They caught marten in "stick traps"—light deadfalls. Gophers and groundhogs they caught with nooses over the holes: Benny demonstrates the placement of the crosspiece and springpole. The meat they would bone and slit thin, and smoke it, and fill a caribou's stomach with fifty pounds of gopher meat, like a Santa Claus sack, as much as a man could carry over his shoulder. The ground squirrel, groundhog and gopher skins made sleeping robes when sewn together, ninety inches by ninety inches, as soft as a modern eiderdown. They slept under those, or blankets of lynx and marten and mink. The bear and moose and caribou hides they kept for clothing, moose being the warmest. Moose was still good at 50° below, and moose was the best meat also, and everyone's favorite game because a moose doesn't change his quarters and fool you, like the other big game; he will stay just about where he was born. Early in April when a crust had formed on the snow, they would run the moose down with bear dogs—the moose breaking through and floundering—and pull back their heads by the long muffle lips and cut their throats. They didn't ordinarily eat bear, but they sold the hides and melted the fat into tallow for soap and for greasing themselves and cooking—whole barrels of oil.

On the Sheslay and Tahltan, everybody collected to construct a fish trap which for four days or so would catch all the salmon. Then they'd take the trap out and let the rest of the run past to spawn. They cut the bellies off the sockeye and filled up barrels with these in brine. The backs they smoked and dried, along with the other varieties of salmon, the kings and the cohos and humpies. Or sometimes they chose a pond and blocked the outlet with a net made by bending a spruce root into a circle and weaving strips of bark across, and harvested rainbow trout as thoroughly as if they were picking a tree—up to a hundred maybe. Being the same color as the water and smelling natural, the net was very effective. The kids groped under the banks for every last fish, and they dried the delicate bodies on a frame over the campfire. Even beaver they netted, using a mesh of willow withes, before the steel traps became common. A couple of moose hooves were attached as a rattle so that the beaver could be pulled out immediately, before he chewed through. Because he was one of the few who knew how to trap underneath the ice, Benny got an earlier start and lived on beaver all spring. A cousin of his had married a Tlingit girl in Atlin and moved there, and when he died he willed his trapline to Benny, so that Benny was working some two hundred miles north of the regular Tahltan country, trapping between Teslin Lake and Nakina Summit. He'd catch about thirty marten and fifty to sixty beaver a season, but prices declined until in 1948, when he had amassed sixty-seven, he was only paid $400 for them. The previous year he had made so much money guiding that he chartered a plane to fly him to the Swan River with fourteen hundred pounds of supplies, staying out alone for eight months, but he earned only $1900. That's when he quit. Nobody traps any more. The beaver have multiplied on the creeks until a boy can go out and catch more skins in two weeks than he can pack on his back. Then they have to be shipped to Vancouver and the check doesn't come before mid-summer. It's discouraging.

No, the religion died before they can remember, they say when I ask. Benny is another hefty old man with white hair and a large jovial face. In the summers he packed to the south on the Telegraph Trail, through Raspberry Pass, past Ice Mountain, and onto the Iskut; then south to cross by the Ningunsaw River and Snowbank Creek to the Bell-Irving River, and across by Muckaboo Creek to the head of the Nass. They ate rice on the trail once they were working for the white man, but before that the Tahltans had eaten little vegetable food, unlike the Tsimshians. Of course they ate multitudes of berries, and wild rhubarb, either boiled or as a salad spread with bear oil, and nettles and nuts, dandelions, wild onions; also the roots of the horse lettuce, as they call it (the licorice plant?), which grows on wet sandy ground near a spring and needs to be scraped and pounded. The kids liked the sap of the cottonwoods in the budding stage as a foaming candy.

These were the medicines used. For flu, rhubarb roots boiled; to relieve a cough, pitch from a balsam tree boiled; the same solution could serve as an eyewash or, when drunk instead of gargled, to clear up kidney and bladder trouble. The bark of the red alder peeled thin and boiled helped children suffering from diarrhea, whereas soapberry bark peeled and boiled was the treatment for constipation. Another sore throat remedy was a mixture of peppermint leaves and devil's club which had been cooked together. For a fever or indigestion, the scrapings just under the bark of a jackpine was good, or just under the bark of a willow, for fever. Jackpine and balsam pitch mixed would draw the pus out of a boil, and to plaster a wound they stewed jackpine pitch together with cottonwood bark and what they call caribou leaves. About the turn of the century a woman who was snaring groundhogs on Level Mountain was mauled by a grizzly, Emma remembers, and only saved by the village women keeping poultices on her night and day of these same caribou leaves. Her first husband's father was saved similarly, after losing an arm to a bear on Ice Mountain. The root called the poison root (water hemlock?) when applied like a mustard plaster will help ease a sore joint or congested chest. It's also used to train dogs not to snatch from the table.

Benny goes out to chain up the husky, not for misbehavior but just on the principle that he doesn't want to see him too happy. The dog shambles off like a huge bottled genie with a bland, soapstone face. Emma takes me to see her work shed. She has two hides scraped white hanging from the rafters, ready to be cut into vests and moccasins. The first process was to cook the raw skin in a pot together with the moose's own brains, she says. This soaking and cooking was repeated four or five times, drying the skin in the sun in between. The meat side was scraped with a sharp rock on the end of a pole and the hair side with a piece of leg bone, split and sharpened, which she shows me, and the hide was stretched on a stretcher and kneaded and tanned. She shows me a tanned beaverskin and a hard, glutinated dangle of moosemeat that she says is dog food, though it would scarcely fill the husky's mouth once. The dogs fast like anchorites at this time of year because it's too late for moose offal and too early for salmon. She shows me an old clump of sinews from a moose's back, which she laughs and calls Indian thread. It's for sewing leather or making a snare or a net. One of her neighbors has two hides stretched on frames in the sun, tied with the mooses' own sinews through holes round the edge.

Perhaps there are twenty-five houses up here. One is surprisingly suburban, but that belongs to a woman whose husband walked into the blade of a helicopter while he was on a mining payroll. I angle down past the schoolyard—big woodpile, hopscotch and soccer—the kids dressed in vermilion shirts and pink pants. The graves in the cemetery, each with a picket fence, seem to have even more children in them. One cross supports a wooden wolf's head which overlooks the village. Everybody I meet is exceedingly curious about me. They call me Father, assuming I must be a new missionary. News of the doctor's annual visit is posted downtown, and it mentions that "Members of the Indian Band" have automatic appointments, though the fellow is said to run through these shamelessly in order to get done so that he can fish. Apparently the curiosity of the individual Indian about us lasts longer than our curiosity as individuals about him. But the wave of whites on their way, the whole hurrying host of campmobiles, ensures that our curiosity about the Tahltans will only grow greater and greater, long after theirs is at an end. Indeed, with our peculiar matter-of-factness and force and the devouring momentum of the age, their single protection will be our curiosity regarding them.

[V]

Eddontenajon: The Hylands and Frank Pete

JUNE 15, WEDNESDAY:

IF YOU ASK WHO the best dog-team driver was, or the best packer, the best trapper, best guide and hunter, the answer always is Willie Campbell. He's of the generation that worked for the founding Callbreaths and Hylands, raised Benny Frank and John Creyke, and got systematically rooked. His family had title to the land on Dease Lake where A. J. Marion set up his trading post for Hudson's Bay, so the Hudson's Bay Company got the title "canceled," as Marion says with a laugh. Campbell owns a cabin in Dry Town but during the summer lives upriver at Ninemile, close to the old Tahltan capital, on a farm. Yesterday afternoon I paid Callbreath to drive me out through the dry choppy plateau that surrounds Telegraph Creek. Symmetrical saddles lead off through the mountains. A turkey track went from the road to the Campbells'. It wasn't a successful visit except visually—the blue screen door, the red tin chimney and the homemade ladder resting against it, the over-all, weathered, crazy, idiosyncratic slump of the house. On the limping porch hung a dinner gong and a series of traps and saws, and, inside, rifles and hats on the wall, and curtain partitions and cooking pans. Campbell's present wife, who is his third and is in her eighties too, sat back in a corner like a squat peasant crone in a Japanese movie, especially since she seemed to be speaking Japanese. In the yard he'd built several log huts for his dogs, as well as two barns, a corral, an outhouse, a woodshed, a potato house, a root house.

The old woman, huddling forward with her quizzical sing-song face, was convinced that Callbreath and I spoke Japanese. "There's his track," Callbreath said, touching a hazy footprint with the toe of his shoe. He and Mrs. Campbell remained while I followed it to the edge of the river canyon, abrupt and high there, and climbed down about eight hundred feet on a long slant, until a large black sleigh dog sprang into the path, all his hair up. As I hadn't a chance of passing him, I shouted. The canyon was a spectacular black basalt, the yellow river loudly scoured by, and I was grinning, although we were at an impasse. At last Willie turned up, a stooped twisted man on a cane with a young tenor voice and another of those immense Tahltan faces, except that his was pulled out as long as a pickaxe and then bent at the chin. A chin like a goiter, a distorted cone of a forehead. He looked like a movie monster; he was stupendous. He was wearing hide mittens and shoes, and he pointed across the Stikine to where he had seen a grizzly the day before. We went to look at the salmon net he had been tending. The dog quickly became friendly, bounding about with a lilting gait and shining direct yellow eyes.

[77]

Campbell, being almost the oldest person in Telegraph, was past trying to make out my stutter over the river's roar. He was a doer; he had no managerial interest in enlightening me or explaining the operation of anything. But the rocks formed a cove where the salmon would naturally stop for a rest, and a log boom extended out to the middle with a net strung along it and ropes to the shore. He tested one of them to see whether a salmon was pulling. He had an impressive great rotating apparatus fifteen feet high as well, for drying the net, apparatus which he had put together in his full vigor and which was all but beyond his capacities now. It was incongruous, in fact—so masterfully arranged, when he could hardly tug on the ropes any more and the net had a hole through which he said he had just watched a good fish get away. We climbed the path cautiously, stopping for rests. He leaned on his knee and his cane, struggling with asthma, bowed over the grandeur. He knew Tommy Jack down in Hazelton and Tom Ukas in Wrangell. He'd been everywhere within three or four hundred miles, roaming alone. He'd seen all the lost, hidden lakes, crossing through notches, and killed every shade of grizzly, from silver to brown. He said the most meat was on Level Mountain, where the caribou still come in the thousands, and that his own trapline had followed the soggy, rolling headwaters plateau to the east of Dease Lake. For many years he ran the mail to Atlin, two hundred and ten miles up and two hundred and ten miles back again, once a month. The pay was a hundred dollars a shot and a lot of people tried their hand at doing it, usually collapsing after a few trips, but Willie made the job his own.

I call him Willie, although he showed no inclination to talk. The others were waiting for us, and I seemed too young and inept. He was a doer, he was the best in the country, grotesquely slowed down though he has become, and since his manner still carries the certainties of this, I call him Willie as people call Joe Dimaggio Joe, for instance, from meeting him once.

Eddontenajon: The Hylands and Frank Pete

Mr. Wriglesworth has just returned from his prospecting trip, with his rifle and pack, unrecognizable, he looks so young —his stride and height, his shaggy coat. He's mesmerizing, like a reconstituted Daniel Boone. I'm flying to Eddontenajon at noon, so the reverend bustles around in his capacity as the ticket man. He's kind of fun, he grows on one. He's so spunky that one forgets what he's spunky about. The plane, a DeHaviland Beaver this time, makes a very pretty landing, appearing from nowhere over the trees and dropping right on the reeds at the edge of the lake. From the midst of the bags of mail, off gets the Catholic priest, of all people, another disconcertingly graceless man of the cloth, who has bad teeth and a lengthy jaw that he grits frequently. He's been to Whitehorse for a two weeks' leave. My Anglican is wearing a black windbreaker and a black lumberjack's shirt. They grin in gingerly recognition, like a badger meeting a fox. The priest is a younger fellow, with a gaunt frame, pulled, thinning hair, a considerable accent and spectacles nearly as long as his jaw. He isn't belligerent, but as he lifts his baggage out of the plane, including a year's sacramental wine, "Ah!" says the Anglican. He pauses for the precise wisecrack to come to him, then decides he won't make a joke about that after all. "If you'd stayed much longer I would have got your whole flock."

The priest swings around. He's surprised; he's not used to crossing swords. Loudly, shaking for added force, he responds, "I didn't know you were a thief!" He leans to see if the reverend has an answer for *that*. It's a draw, like the badger and fox. They grin wary grins.

We taxi away from the swimming dock. It's another fabulous flight. We follow Mess Creek, which is a series of scrabbling cascades. The pilot flies very close through the passes— we see little stage sets of trees in talky positions, vis-à-vis. It's rainy and bumpy. The parcel post grunts in the sacks in back. Sheep Mountain fronts for Ice Mountain, and Ice Mountain is built with the symmetry of the great volcanoes. The shoulders consist of forests and bare lava surfaces, occasionally cupping

[79]

a pond. They bend in a shield-shaped, bronze-colored curve below and above us—we're crossing the middle level of the mountain. The bottom is lost in mist and the top is hidden in clouds. The pilot today is a youngster of twenty-three, as far as I'm any judge, though he tells me he's twenty-eight. He's wearing a crumpled Hawaiian sport shirt, wash pants, urban-style glasses. He has several days' beard and he earns about a thousand a month. He looks like a college junior riding to class on the bus. The incredible landscape enhances his earnestness, of course—the green gorge of the Klastine and the bending lava slopes of the mountain going up bronze into the fog. We can just see snowline. He's an excellent pilot. He banks steeply and slows, circling the clearing where the storekeeper lives in order to notify him, and lands on Eddontenajon, in the reeds again, at the very earliest moment. Since there isn't even a swimming dock here, he backs onto a gravel beach and carries the mail off along the pontoons. When that's finished, he pushes off, lifting quickly away in a spray, turning towards the mountain, and climbs.

My new host of the moment is a man named Black who, like many Canadians, reminds me of an Irish-American. It's another arrival where I like everybody. We all ride with the mail in his pickup—his very plump wife, their three little daughters in short-sleeved blouses (I have on a skiing coat and sweater), and two Indians. The one named Peter looks just like a Peter. He has a mild-looking mustache, he's solicitous and gentle, not like the earthy Tahltans or the shantytown Tlingits in Wrangell, but like a woods creature, with the nap of innocence still standing all over him.

The clearing is as new as you can get. There's no bomb crater, but everything is knocked flat. Though it isn't esthetic, right away you're rooting for it: the two cabins that have been started, the small fiberboard store, a closetlike post office, a tent for Peter and his son. The girls vanish when they climb out of the truck because the underbrush, or whatever you call what grows up when a clearing is slashed from such a forest, hides them. Like minnows, they're out of sight within a few feet. Darting around, they're as at home as three tropical birds might be. With their apple coloring, they run and scream. Like charmers, they babble at me while their father sorts the Indians' mail, some of it smelling of whiskey because a bottle, flown down from Atlin, has broken. Black says sometimes the kids from the village, which is a mile away, will deliberately drop the packages that haven't already broken during the walk home so that their parents won't be able to get drunk.

Black seems to be a resourceful type—gay and blunt. He has the ability of people who are in their thirties to become either forty-five or twenty-five, according to what is opportune. After putting in a couple of years as Hudson's Bay manager in Telegraph Creek, he has turned himself into a pioneer among pioneers. Though there may be a newer suburban subdivision in North America, there can't be a newer community. The sawmill down the road where he produces roof timbers for Eddontenajon has yet to cut breathing space for its own work. The trees are simply dragged to the saw from the edge of the gash. He sells the timber to the Indian agent and hauls house logs on a contract basis. Being postmaster brings in an additional $60 a month (two flights come in), and he sells the villagers staples and clothing. His wife teaches primary school. His concession to her is to let her get fat, but she's a thoroughly fast-paced fat; she hurdles her chores. Marriages up here are either good or else there isn't a marriage at all. The cabin they're in smells of sap and is nicely set up with a new sink, if not any plumbing, an upholstered rocking chair, and a bookcase of Shakespeare, *The Reader's Digest*, and Burns. She tells me the ferry across the Stikine is starting to operate again after a hiatus from last November, but that from February till early April the rare truck could cross on the actual ice, it was so hard. They have a cable with buckets also, which a pedestrian can ride in an emergency, pulling himself across by hand, as was the system on the Telegraph Trail. The road has been extended ninety miles south of the river so far, and four white couples spent the winter on it.

Just as in Telegraph Creek, there aren't any demonic people around, apparently—no tormented souls of the kind that one would expect from reading about the frontier in fiction or history. Quite likely, they go somewhere else today. This is that same frontier, however, the core that the exploratory energies which got the rest of the continent settled didn't quite reach. As big as the Iskut is, not even the Indians lived in this valley. The ground is so spongy that it's a hike to cross the front yard; I sink in at every step and feel as if I'm about to disappear, like the girls do. Soil—at least soil as we know it—has never had a chance to form because the trees have never been chopped down before. The ground is a litter of centuries of needles, leaves, and dropped bark and disintegrated limbs and storm casualties. The trees don't grow very high because they don't live long enough in this climate to allow a fertile earth to form underneath, but the lush nap of virginity is spread everywhere like on a new sweater.

JUNE 16, THURSDAY:

IN NEW YORK TO dream of a woman is an unremarkable event. Here it invests the whole night with sexual urgency. Instead of the ones I'm supposed to be dreaming about, the women seem to be those whom nothing worked out too well with, however; and so it remains in the dream. I think there is something bogus about it, besides. In the firsthand accounts of gold-rush treks down the Stikine on the ice and the like, the fellow often ends up *gaining* weight. He's a greenhorn, he's scared to death, especially of starving to death, so he mooches from every campfire, gorges, hoards food in his pockets and belly, cadges and begs. Two weeks out of New York, I'm not eating, I'm dreaming.

Bob Henderson fetched me nine more miles down Lake

Eddontenajon: The Hylands and Frank Pete

Eddontenajon late yesterday. He's an open-browed, sunny twenty-one, the assistant to the Mr. Walker I wrote to from New York who guides on the headwaters of the Stikine. He has a store too (two stores and no customers!), but mainly his serves as a supply point for Walker's hunting business, which begins at the Little Klappan, fifty miles in from this new road, and which they can only fly to. Where we are now, the head of the Iskut, is assigned to John Creyke. We cooked supper together, getting acquainted, talking about the geography and game. They have perhaps a couple of thousand caribou, and the Stone sheep that sportsmen come after from everywhere under the sun. Stone sheep are an offshoot species of the bighorns, with lighter, more gracefully flaring horns in scimitar curves. These differentiations occurred in the Ice Age, when tongues of ice split off virtual nations of sheep and let them mutate. In rather a parody of this process, the road is pushing the canny rogue moose back onto the Little Klappan and the sources of the Stikine, so that all of a sudden great stalking giants are appearing in unusual numbers in spots where there were scarcely any before, where the Indian dialect hadn't even a word for moose.

At dusk I went for a walk. We're at three thousand feet. The relief goes up three thousand or four thousand feet more, although not theatrically. It's fine wet headwaters country. Shallow short valleys lead back from the lake on both sides at regular rhythmic intervals. Two eagles flew by. I saw the tracks of a cow and calf moose and one concise print of a wolf. There's a den somewhere close. Walking through the forest, I struggled like a bug in a rug. It's country where if you could walk five miles you could walk twenty-five, but you can't walk five. At the corners of the property the homestead stakes are still standing, curious objects like chunks of kindling. Around the top of each is wrapped a printed form with blanks for red-tape specifications, the answers all typed in properly and signed at the bottom.

I do tiptoe about this matter of roughing it. I curl in my

sleeping bag daintily and I'm awfully fastidious as I wash at the creek, and never quite do my share of the jobs. Today we're driving to the Alaska Highway, if the ferry is in. While Bob gets ready I poke about the store—nail clippers, bug killer, snuff, sacks of sugar and bleach and Robin Hood flour, axes and bullets.

Off we go. The long lake again, as still as green glass this time, filling its valley, with a siding of uniform mountains. The name means Lake-Where-The-Little-Girl-Drowned. We stop at Black's sawmill and meet a bear-backed bullcook who is looking for work. Black isn't hiring. His three little blondes are stowed for the morning in the cab of his truck as if in a playpen. They're so very small against the backdrop that they wouldn't show up if it weren't for the gleam of their yellow hair. At Eddontenajon Bob asks whether a boy who had hurt his wrist is okay, since we're driving to where there's a doctor. The missionary is a wordless thin German with bent teeth in a dragging gown. We cause a hullabaloo, because these are the Sikannis from the wild Finlay. Some of the women are downright grotesque and deformed. The men have wispy beards. The kids have star eyes and crowd forward to touch us. "Where you guys from?" When I say New York, it's as if in New York I had said Eddontenajon. Meat was so hard to come by on the Finlay that the Sikannis lost themselves in the welter of terrain except at the height of the summer, when they'd meet in luminous weather to see who had survived. After the white priests and traders abandoned Fort Grahame, they moved to a chill tapering lake called Bear Lake, mixing with drifters from the other tribes. When that was abandoned too by the Church and by Hudson's Bay, they moved to Caribou Hide. When they were starving in Caribou Hide, the government transferred them to Telegraph Creek; and now the government has helped them move here. The village has an atmosphere of anarchy and uproar—not of violence but of unaccustomedness. Some people are in tents, some in the hut structures that remain from when this was a way station on the network of trails, and some in shiny new cabins of peeled logs. It's very different from what I have seen before.

Bob says that the Sikannis are not protected by any treaty. Of course this is nonsense, but he says that the Indian agent has been experimenting beyond the legal guidelines of his powers and when they've protested has told them this. He's decidedly cheerful about their not being protected and about several families being summarily cut off the rolls, though on the other hand he complains that during the winter some destitute men came to his store and ran up credit which has not been repaid. He thinks the agent coddles as well as bullies the Indians, squandering the taxpayers' money, and that they're spoiled by the missionaries too, who stand up for them on certain occasions. The Walker enterprise has been in conflict with both the agent and priest lately, so that a sourness prevails. Mr. Black seems to be of two minds. He talks of the Indians with insight and sympathy sometimes, and then when he's with Bob, with dislike and sniggers.

Bob is a boy overworked at the moment. His views are a medley of what he has heard and his own frustrations as the advance arranger. When he laughs at the jealousy which he says exists between two of the senior citizens of Eddontenajon, he sounds as if he's been teasing them both until neither one wants to work for him now. And he's been by himself for six weeks, so that practically every other sentence is about the women—whom they spread their legs for, creeping from cabin to cabin like cats, how bad they smell. He says the men are so superstitious about spirits in the bush that they won't sleep out alone, and that their hunting acumen is overrated. As we're driving along, he whinnies imitations of a ragged woman who just now asked him for money, holding her baby. "My baby has no milk! I have no milk for my baby!" Earlier in the spring a girl appeared at the store, sent by her parents, and took up the broom and began to sweep, after the historical fashion of a squaw proposing to a white man. He turned her down but is gentler in speaking of her. Walker and he *do* employ Indians, whereas most white guides don't, and at the end of the season they fly out a load of meat for the villagers in an unusual gesture, the hunting grounds having been theirs before. But he complains that the people accept it too greedily; in half an hour it's gone.

Dreary talk. The newspapers editorialize about the patience due a race from "the Stone Age," and around here they're said to be lazy, erratic trappers and laughably terrified of the grizzlies, as if to deprive them of even the virtues a Stone-Age people might be expected to have. Another generation will try for a fairer estimate, by which time the bears will be gone, the Indians scattered or besotted, and the tales regarding spirits out in the bush will be past recording. These frictions are not to be understood in terms of Negro-white difficulties, however. From the earliest time there was a sovereignty granted the Indian as well as a complaisance on his part. He was conceded to have been the original man-on-the-spot and also, despite the carping, to be at least reasonably stoic and brave, to have endurance and sharp eyesight, the various manly qualities which were exactly what Negroes were denied. The caricature which reached city folk didn't include his curiously soft and amenable edges, though they are the aspects of him the white people living nearby have such a field day making fun of.

Like John Ellis in Wrangell, Bob will be trying to stave off the thundering herd, not fighting the bush as the old fellows did. As caretaker, he's appropriately smoother, more pleasant-tempered. Compared with Ellis, he's a prep-school man—he's from Victoria and isn't self-made or especially flamboyant, but he has that 3500 square miles. Except when accompanying his customers, he doesn't hunt; his interest is only in knowing the game; he'll be perfectly content when hunting as such becomes obsolete, a matter of drawing lots and cropping the range. He drives the truck unflaggingly, if not very well, and works the same way, disorganized but effectually energetic. His legs are short, his torso is blunt like a lifeguard's, and his brown lamb's-wool hair adds so much to his young look that one doesn't immediately see how strong he is.

We go by Mosquito Mountain, a bonnet-shaped, self-contained jungle of alder and violets and spruce, which has a deer population. Elfin, loved animals as they are, they don't make much headway in land as ferocious as this. They need jungle to duck the wolves in, but jungle with only a little snowfall. The streams reduce to trickles, until we cross the Iskut-Stikine divide. Below is a moosey, mysterious valley where the snow doesn't gather too deeply and the Indians hunt in the winter. There's a cache in a tree, hides hanging off it. A friend of Bob's has hacked out a homestead across the road in a platter-like basin next to a lake, fervently green, but he has become a milkman in Edmonton recently. The river, having risen again, is rapidly washing the ferry's approaches away. A caterpillar is working on our side, the question being whether it will be able to finish soon enough to be transported over to the north side before too much damage has been done for it to disembark there. In crossing, the scow employs the action of the current itself, which is crazily fast. We just fit on.

The next divide, between Cake Hill and the Hotailuh Range, is up in the jackpine scrub at treeline and winds down to Gnat Creek. This is Willie Campbell's country. The creeks and the muskeg glitter coldly. Gold-rush ghost shacks, Dease Lake. A raindrop flows to the Arctic here, not the Pacific. You call the bridges Bailey bridges. They clinch into place like an erector-set bridge, just narrowly accomodating a vehicle. It's all airy plateau, but clawed by an ugly burn. The trees stand as black spears speckled with yellow where they have peeled. We wave at all comers: several corporate geologists, another ranch truck with the name of its river painted on it—his is the Kechika, Bob's the Spatsizi. Then we get into the Cassiar Mountains, steep and grand, a wonderful up-and-down, fine-smelling country with lovely tree patterns. We follow the Eagle River, which is a brushy green clear-water river with a stiff mountain ridge on one side. This is the gold country I was hearing about in Wrangell. It's got glistening kidney-shaped lakes, old cabins, and meadows of redtop, vetch and pea vine. For firewood the miners merely girdled a tree they were going to want the next year and let it die and dry out where it stood until they could push it down. We eat lunch while we drive, but stop on a crest to fill the tank from a can of gas. Troutline Creek, Quartz Creek, Snow Creek—the valleys are slung right on the midriff of the peaks, so that the tops are close and accessible to the eye, the streams crisp and fast. Suddenly I recognize the two cabins where Joel Wing lived when he was a boy, like the diagram that he drew. We brake and jump out. Another few weeks' summer growth would have hidden them. Although they're crumbling, they convey how sound and workmanlike they were, wedged into the warm ground, with long-roofed snow porches, and jammed with family debris inside—boots, feathers from quilts, a bedspring, a foundering stove, a bear hide thirty or more years old. There's a heavy box cache on stilts and a screened-in cooler. The mudbank where the Wings dug doggedly and which defeated them remains just as he described.

Set alone, an hour further along, the Horseranch Range rises sheer from a steeplechase valley, announcing itself, big and presumptuous. Several raw Indian cabins have been plumped alongside a Nile-green lake. But the country diminishes again to muskeg and jumbled brush, much of it burned; a dusty washboarded road. The truck limps. We meet the traffic from an asbestos mine, and at last reach the Alaska Highway at Mile 649. We cross the Liard at Mile 642, a breezy, sweep-swinging river, and pull into Watson Lake at Mile 635. Watson Lake, with three stores, four beer parlors, one cocktail lounge and six hundred people in some trailers and prettied-up shacks, is the Yukon's third-largest city. News has been radioed that the ferry back at the Stikine is out, so we may have to ride the buckets across on our return. Our eyes have a squint as if we had driven across the United States.

Eddontenajon: The Hylands and Frank Pete

JUNE 17, FRIDAY:

THE DELIGHTS OF THE Alaska Highway are for somebody else
to explain. They involve the mathematics of distance and something about the gray gravel against the jackpine. The tourists
stream by with their headlights on because of the dust, fearfully tired. Whenever one passes another, the other is blinded
and has to slow down. If this is a frontier, as they seem to
believe, it's because, unlike the Wriglesworths' Chutine, for
instance, nobody has had the desire to settle down here. It's
like standing at the World's Fair and watching a squadron of
people file by, registering exactly the same expression. They
get out of their cars every minute or so and think, *The Yukon!*
Then, for some reason, many of them have brought along a
road sign stolen from home or along the way, and they nail it
up on one of the goal-post frames which have been provided by
the Board of Trade. They're the same citizens who used to
drive back and forth between Seattle and Miami, so they write
on their cars, "Tenn./Alaska!" Of course I'm a snob. I remind
myself that I once felt a considerable enthusiasm for Highway
66, but there was some folklore and poignance there. Here you
have vacationers climbing out of the car in a desolate muskeg
flat, unfailingly registering *frontier* on their face, and finding
after a minute that the motels are filled.

Without exception the Yukonese are heavyset, conscious of
how heavy a punch they can throw. Goodness knows when
they throw it, though; they seem so tame. At first sight the
place has an activity that I've missed since leaving Wrangell,
except it's bully-boy stuff, like mules going around a mill
wheel, proud of the chest they've got for pushing the pole.
Loneliness blows through the town like a gale. One sees lots of
ground-monkey faces among the women. A tree-monkey face
with its roundness and prominent eyes and frontal braincase
can be quite attractive, but the ground monkeys, best represented by the baboon, have close-set eyes and a broomstick
nose. Some of the married women wouldn't be married any-

[89]

where else, although they do run a taut ship for their husbands, keeping the business afloat. The handful of queenly girls smile at the knowledge of how much pleasure they give as you step into the restaurant.

I've had a day hearing stories of streams getting "gassed" of their fish, and Indian women being mounted and screwed. That's the solution to the shiftlessness of the race—breed it out of existence. The Indian women won't suckle their babies for three or four years any more, but want to buy milk. They want to buy bread instead of baking from flour. The bucks are sharp as a needle in trade—as cute as a trick—and if they think they've got you, that's when they'll bear down. Two scruffy bush pilots were in getting soused. Once they have flown an adequate number of hours, the good ones usually go south to work for United Airlines. These are the late sleepers, and one guy indeed had had to fold up a partnership the other day because he almost strangled his partner during a drinking bout; a doctor was called to tend to his throat. I divided my attention between the talk and Georges Simenon.

JUNE 18, SATURDAY:

STOVE OIL, CAR GAS and boat and plane fuel were loaded on the truck, each in barrels of forty-four gallons: also groceries, and bale-sized bundles of other supplies. Saddle tanks, as they're called—auxiliary tanks—were attached to the chassis. We did another cross-continental drive through rain and hail and beautiful breaks in the weather, through the luscious gold country again, sinfully green. A hundred and fifty miles or so from the highway we stopped at the Adrians: "The Adrians, pop. 4." They live at the turnoff to Telegraph Creek and manage the government weather station. The nearest neighbor is the Indian lady who lives by the grave of her husband, a thirty-mile trip by boat. We saw a cow and calf moose in a poplar meadow, and Bob pointed out a growth of wild parsley that the bears love, with paths tramped in it. We went up through the Hotailuh Divide again, the stands of jackpine, which is the rough workaday knave type of pine, just as "every manjack" is a commonplace man and the skipjack is a poor relative of the tuna. Bob drove with grinding stamina. We no longer have much to say to each other.

At nine P.M. we arrived at the Stikine, its great valley leading east in a trough to the mountains some one hundred miles away. It looked like an avenue and the mountains looked small, set sideways. The rain clouds had been battered apart. The low sun lighted a variety of greens. It was a roiling, seething scene. On the bank men in red helmets scrambled over the beached ferry. The footing was all mud to wade through. A cat skinner was working, but whatever he did the river undid before he turned around. Some barefoot Indian children were sitting at ringside watching, while smoke for their supper went up from the hut behind. We got across with the groceries in a skiff, skidding precariously over the flint-brown currents. The fellow who owned the boat had ferried the Caribou Hide group to market and school when they lived across from Dry Town, and when Caribou Hide was rediscovered in a starving state by the authorities after the distractions of World War II, this was the man whose family was functioning, camped by a caribou that he had killed.

"Where are all these big guys?" he said on the other side, because the crowd of kids whom Black had brought from the village weren't helping unload. Mostly they were staring at me. Several of the barrels of gasoline had to be wrestled up the bank too. Irritated at being so dependent on him, Bob told him to quit looking at the girls—"Remember the last time I fired you?" But Black, at his fluid, manipulative best, stepped in. The Indian skipper told me with a smile that he was married to a white woman for a while, and that not long ago they'd split up and split the kids. He took the boys and she the girls. Perhaps because of the supply of fresh fruit and vegetables we had brought, Black was as ebullient as a tenor. The Indians told jokes, trying to please him. We drove the rest of the way chattering, leaning towards each other, and peering outside for a moose, with a rifle in ready position and three cartridges in the ashtray.

Eddontenajon village was another wild spectacle. It was eleven o'clock now, the daylight muted, suggestive. Kids were climbing in and out of the schoolhouse windows and trying to find where I lived on the maps on the wall. The tents billowed; the laundry lines flapped like gypsy pennants. The women in their pants stalked back and forth, bulky and occult. The ground, clogged with stumps, heaped with cuttings, smelled of balsam. The village was encircled by its packs of chained dogs, and all at once these got up, baying and yapping in staccato explosions, as if we were besieged. The children, no matter what age, crowded around me like around a moon man, with a scale of faces like being on the Bosphorus. It was not as though there was one race here; it was all the continents. A drunk stooped into a zigzag silhouette and yelled. Everybody talked about going to Black's house tomorrow for groceries—"downtown," they said.

June 19, Sunday:

A quiet, recouping day. Listened to the news short-wave from Japan and read some Thucydides.

June 20, Monday:

Bright and early we drove south to Kinaskan Lake on the unfinished road. Parking by a strange message box, Bob commenced to honk. The opposite shore was too far for us to see anything. He sat with a bemused expression, he had so much work: a second load of fuels to bring in, a dock to construct for the freight plane, more provisions in Watson Lake, all of which was contingent on the ferry being put back.

A speck appeared, growing slowly. "Two rifle shots is the signal. I don't usually come for a horn, you know," Steele

Hyland said. He was laughing, but not really fooling. "There's going to be a lot of horns on this road in another few years." He glanced me over and decided he'd relieve Bob of me and take me across. As we got out on the water, he said that when he staked his land fifteen years ago, the road had not been laid out to follow the Iskut up to its head, but instead to cross the mountains by Raspberry Pass, which is a day's walk below Kinaskan. Anyway, a snooper would need field glasses to pick out his place and the river bars him to somebody trying to go round the lake on foot through the bush. Kinaskan, as a matter of fact, means Boy-Crossing-on-a-Raft.

Hyland is the surviving Hyland, as Roy Callbreath is the surviving Callbreath on the upper Stikine. He's a jocose, big-faced, meat-faced man in his ageless fifties, a fire warden's button pinned on his chest, with blue eyes and a boisterous boy's mouth. Besides running a store and restaurant-hotel in Telegraph Creek, his family, in the early years of the century, operated trading posts on the Spatsizi River, on Dease Lake, in the Cassiar country, and on the Liard River at Lower Post. The Hyland River empties into the Liard nearby. Steele's grandfather, having shipped around Cape Horn from Ontario in the 1890s, was prospecting with seven other men on Scurvy Creek, as it was named afterwards, which feeds into the Hyland. They'd been eating salt pork for months (even fresh meat will help combat scurvy), and they were all down and dying of the disease when some Indians happened by and brewed up a pot of juniper tea. Five of the party refused to drink, saying it was Indian medicine, but Grandfather Hyland and two of his friends drank it and lived. On their stumbling, hallucinatory trip out, he picked up a chunk of gold ore which prospectors have been searching the river to match ever since. He himself never went back. He became a trader, buying the pressed bales of fur that just fit a canoe, opening up one or two areas before Hudson's Bay. He had two sons who expanded the business. Besides packing regularly on the various trails, they used to run fantastic, meandering, sixty-day hunts for rich men at a hundred dollars per person per day, providing a gaudy assortment of horses and a crew of wranglers and guides. The riverboat would return to Wrangell, piled with skins. They had two ranches for wintering their horses, one on the Spatsizi at Hyland Post, and the other up at Hyland Lake, which is close to the boundary of the Yukon.

Like Callbreath, Steele Hyland abandoned horse-keeping right away when his father died, though he kept the store until four years ago and remained the presiding intelligence of Telegraph Creek. As an historian he's encyclopedic, and he isn't chary of sharing out what he knows. He says the boys grew up to be either hunters or mechanics, usually mechanics, as he did. Then their children, moderate, modern youngsters, have left altogether. He's childless, but of John Creyke's fourteen children, only one boy has turned into a woodsman like his father, and of Callbreath's eight, only Edwin, the captain of the *Judith Ann*, stayed in the north at all. So the people changed faster than the country did.

Obviously one trouble was that nobody else came in. Whatever was being done well finally was overdone. The farmer, with no newcomers to sell his produce to, went on clearing more land and building additional barns and sheds, raising the roofs in inexplicable queer peaks and quirky hexagonals that got almost heroically high. Except for scattered shallow-snow valleys, it wasn't a proper ranching area. The few wild horses that are left on the deserted old sites could be easily caught in the winter if anyone cared. Creyke, Willie Campbell and Roy Callbreath's father were the knowledgeable handlers of horses, and nowadays the one outstanding horseman is an eighty-seven-year-old fellow called Skook Davidson, who still lives alone in the Kechika Valley, which is north of the Finlay and way east of here, and one hundred miles off the Alaska Highway. He arrived with the first surveyors, who traversed through from Fort Ware to Lower Post in 1941. He was their packer, and when they gave him the horses at the end of the trip, he went back up the newly explored valley to its wide spot and wintered underneath Terminus Mountain, he and the wolves and horses, where he's stayed ever since. Now he's got too many horses to count, unbroken, unfenced, no one to sell them to. He has horses he hasn't seen for five years. He can't ride any more, not even sidesaddle and using a box to help himself mount. He's a cranky old man, crippled up with arthritis, cussing into his radio, who gives a report on his wolves instead of his weather, and throws the cork into the creek when he opens a bottle of whiskey so there won't be a way of stopping the fun. In his time, he's raised several waifs to be first-rate wranglers, but the waifs have stabbed him in the back in some cases, and they don't make boys any more who can walk in there, Hyland says.*

Hyland too is an extremist of the old school. If he hasn't heptagonal barns or too many horses to count, he does his hauling by means of a quaint midget caterpillar manufactured in 1922. He's built a large work shed equipped with sanders and drills and saws—a wall floor-to-ceiling with tools; there must be a thousand tools. One side of the shed is for working in metal and one is for working in wood. At the moment he's constructing a fourteen-foot motorized scow for freighting, although he already has a scow bigger than that and seven boats. He has a 5000-watt power plant, when 400 watts would do for lighting the house. He has his own sawmill, with a planer and shingle-maker, and two transmitting radios and all kinds of extra, unexplained huts. Four of them are living cabins, piped for propane and stove oil, each with a tin roof that slides the snow off. Yet this is a lake where you can catch sixty fish in an hour on a barbless hook and the horizon of

---

* Skook is a sort of Jim Bridger, the last of a kind, and a famous man for a thousand miles south. This brief mention does not do him justice. I have heard about other epochs of his life in central B. C., and would have liked to add an appendix on him. In 1968, when I was traveling in Canada again, I went up to Watson Lake and waited three days in the Yukon dust for permission from him to fly to his game reserve on the Kechika for a talk, but each morning his vigorous voice, penetrating the radio static, refused. You don't force your company on a man now eighty-nine, it seemed to me.

mountains around are all still unnamed. Stone sheep browse in plain view on the north flank and goats in plain view on the south.

Hyland's wife's name is Lou. He calls her Girl. They have a constant flirtation going on, like the Wriglesworths', except with more to-and-fro fooling than teasing. She's a tall, playful, skinny person who's always pretending to be serious. They met on the riverboat when she was coming to Telegraph Creek to clerk in the Hudson's Bay store during the manpower shortage in World War II. Six months later the government agent married them and the whole town was at the reception. The miners gave them a deerskin poke with two hundred dollars in it. Like Mrs. Adrian of "The Adrians, pop. 4," she's another extraordinarily soft-natured, feminine, even winsome woman, moving about pleasurably. The boat that's reserved for her seems one of a different color and style which the rest of the boats center around. She has a wonderfully light-filled, uncluttered house with just a handful of pieces of furniture that belong: a table for two to eat at by the window, and a counter in front of the stove with stools for a crowd. None of it is new, just the house. She has a bird-feeder where she puts the leftover pancakes, and a greenhouse for starting the vegetables in the spring. Telegraph Creek, being two thousand feet lower, is a month ahead of Kinaskan Lake and is freakishly snowless anyway, so that she remembers when the boys in town went out to trap they would need to be trucked to the top of the schoolhouse hill before there was snow for the sleds to run on. She has a Victrola and records and mobiles outside that chink in the wind. The lake pours reflected light into the living room, and she boils cookie balls of rolled oats, margarine, marmalade, vanilla, brown sugar and peanut butter, and dashes off letter after letter, like someone else phoning their friends. Sometimes she gets tired of using snowshoes, but in the warm months when she's in the greenhouse, hummingbirds heedlessly hover next to her face, intoxicated by the profusion of smells. In April just as the ice goes out, a couple of hundred swans will splash down for a three-week stay, whistlers the height of a man. They give a musical *wow-wow* call and clamor and whoosh overhead in a waving *V* at twice the speed of a car.

Her husband and she take enough pains to tell me their life isn't lonely to prove that occasionally it must be. Naturally it must be, and, more still, to have every visitor assume that it is must be boring. They draw their income during the bright weeks of summer when fishermen fly in and survey geographers rent tenting space. Another business is refueling bush planes, which have to make at least one stop in crossing these enormous distances. "Steele fills the plane and I fill the pilot." Also they measure the level of the lake at its outlet for the Water Resources Board, which brings in twenty dollars a month, and radio daily weather accounts to the bush airlines. In the winter planes land on skis for fuel or a party, a half-dozen friends surprising them with saki and corned caribou and pastries and fresh greens and fruit. On New Year's Eve, everybody on their frequency tunes in, including cussing Skook, and exchanges good wishes and drinks together. Once a wolverine got in the house, and once a grizzly, which bashed everything frightfully. They were away and the house was on his spring migratory route, but unlike the sort of vandalism that is done by humans, the terror, the phantasmagoric element, was strictly the bear's. He found himself in a Hall of Mirrors, surrounded by storming bears that ripped his paws worse with every window he socked. Lou's reaction when she came back was to fix cardboard cutouts of his red tracks before she began bleaching the floor.

JUNE 21, TUESDAY:

IT'S VERY BUSY AND civilized. She's up at six-thirty. Boyish the way Steele is, he's likely to sleep as late as she lets him, but then is all over the property, repairing equipment, projecting his plans. She keeps to their radio-report schedule with an alarm clock—"Roger, roger. Negative, negative." They drink tea a couple of times in leisurely fashion, and wine before supper. They have a great deal to do if they want to do it, but nothing that must be done. A life like this is either blithely continuous, regulating itself by its satisfactions, or else is insufferable from the start. And it's all *words*. There isn't a sound to interrupt, only each other's conversing. Like the Wriglesworths, they pun and heckle, listen for trip-ups and hold each other to everything said. The names "Wrig" and Steele are names you'd expect to hear a wife say on a tennis-club terrace. Though the Hylands' marriage is frozen at a stage of romance where it mightn't be if they had had children, there is no tinny ring to the fondness, no wistful clinging, and they're the people I've felt the most comfortable staying with.

They're like seafarers in the exclusive interest they have in their setting. The reading material, both magazines and books, concerns nothing else. The decorations are heads of game, pictures of scenery, or mineral specimens. It's amusing to tell Steele about Samos, the Greek island I was on last year, which is two-and-a-half times as long as this lake. The population is something like forty thousand, down from sixty thousand before the war, and the island has been occupied for three thousand years. Yet the end facing Athens is regarded as scarcely explored. A shipshaped mountain rises spiritedly, with a lift at its bow and stern, and nobody knows its entire extent, nobody's been from end to end. Bandits have lived out their lives in its pockets and spurs. It's full of lost meadows, secret wells, honeybee hives and brigands' caves with men's bones mouldering on the floor—incontrovertibly a *wild* place.

He can't believe his ears. "Why didn't they go in and clean them out?"

We sat up late last night in the watery illumination. The sun merely feinted at going down, although in the morning the air was near frost. He says he has five feet of snow on the ground in January. Often a Chinook wind will blow and melt most of it late in February, before the storms renew again, continuing into April. The March stuff packs down and the wolves emerge from the timber and travel the lakes, two or three families together. Last winter a plane crashed on Dease Lake while chasing some. He says the most skillful trappers were the Indians, but that many of the whites carried in larger totals of fur because they were single-minded about it and were trying to raise a stake to get out of the country. The dog teams were small single-file teams because of the timber, not fan-shaped as they were in the Barren Grounds, but a man like Creyke, who had a phenomenally long trapline, or Willie Campbell, running the mail, kept a crack group of dogs. At Christmas the Hudson's Bay man would tap the bottom of the barrel of rum he kept for liquoring the Indians at trading time and get a punchy, thick holiday syrup, and deep in the bush, on the Taku, the boys who had stayed out to trap would visit a relic Russian fort and dress in the uniforms and swords they found and party around a cast-brass cannon so big that although the fort has since been rediscovered, nobody has taken the cannon out yet. The Mad Trapper of Rat River raced through the Stikine country one year, pursued by the Mounties, on to the Liard, to Old Crow in the Yukon, and into the Northwest Territories. Other than him and Gunanoot, the closest they came to having an outlaw was the Boston Burglar, who wasn't a burglar at all, only a retired gunsmith, a nice fellow, a prospector, found dead on the trail from the Turnagain River at last.

Hyland's favorite epithet is "fairy," and he calls the Indian who sometimes works for him "Lover Boy." He's a free-wheeler. The problem is not getting answers, but thinking up questions for him. Who was the last backpacking prospector? The last backpacking prospector was an American who stepped off the riverboat quite recently, set off right away into the bush, walked for two weeks and climbed the mountain that he had picked out during the winter from studying his maps. There in a basin under the peak was a helicopter camp, with the candy wrappers and frozen food cartons and ginger ale

[9 9]

cans lying around. Having left Telegraph Creek, Hyland has cut himself off from the inevitable melancholy of such incidents and the steady drip-drip of the deaths in town. He's here where it's new, listening for planes for his bread and butter. But the promptness of his answers as to what Ah Clem or Callbreath, Senior, was like, and the fact that for some modest reason he's eschewed diaries as well as horses, is sad.

We had tea, celery, potatoes and roast moose for lunch. The moose I assumed to be leg of lamb. Steaks for supper, a tender, coarse-grained meat, beefy except for a subtle sweetness to it, rather like home-brew beer. Hyland shoots moose on his lawn, he doesn't go hunting for them. He points to a bluff where the Indians camped when they passed Kinaskan. They'd sit chipping arrowheads out of obsidian, get a view of the game and let the breeze shoo the mosquitoes away.

Mr. Walker, who is childless too, has Bob Henderson as his probable heir. The Hylands have Cliff Adams, a deliberate young man with two kids and a black-haired mouse of a wife—mouse meaning dodgy and shy. They're living just now in a one-room cabin crammed to the rafters with groceries and gear, their trunks, their clothing, his saddles. He's building a four-room house of yellow peeled logs chinked with oakum, which he twists in ropes and covers with stripping. The floor is of planking covered with plywood. The roof is shingles, tarpaper and planks. To keep the logs looking light inside the house, he will brush on a little white paint, wiping it off immediately with the other hand. The cost he thinks will add up to $150, for the materials. He's to open the new hunting territory allotted to Hyland, which has never before been professionally hunted and hardly explored at all. It's a sea of snowfields and rain-forest jungle, absolutely trailless except for the meager remains of the Telegraph Trail. It extends east from here to the head of the Nass and south to the Unuk, like Delaware and Rhode Island combined, and it's a thicket of peaks, like a class holding up their hands. So we laugh.

Cliff is the first individual my own age whom I've paid

much attention to. There was one in Telegraph Creek with an expanse of territory stretching north from the Stikine clear to the Inklin River, but he was so lackadaisical I haven't referred to him. The refrain of the older people is that they don't make 'em like they used to, when of course it's more that the energies of the age are directed elsewhere. But it is puzzling to find this superbly rigorous country so empty, so unattempted, and yet not be able to pick up a newspaper without reading about a man who has just sailed a seven-foot sailboat across the Atlantic, or rowed across with a friend. I remember once in Wyoming meeting a boy like John Ellis, the one who took me to fetch the bearskin. He was also in his late teens, born on the spot, not an Easterner who had wanted to pioneer, and an orphan, supporting himself very well now—in his case as a plumber—after some earlier privations. He worked mainly in order to stake himself to solo trips into the mountains which lasted for weeks on end, and though he seemed to be the only person left in Wyoming who still did that kind of thing, there was a hunger and passion to it, as in Ellis's trips, which you don't hear of from the McPhees or the rest in Telegraph Creek, all of whom first arrived on the Stikine like young space engineers, in gaiety and glee. You wonder what the result will be when the hungerers are settled snugly and married and no longer feel such a sting. On Samos last year I knew a man who was building a sailboat by hand and planned to sail it around the world. He wasn't like either Ellis or the McPhees. He was an ornery, touchy South African, not as attractive as his ambitions, who had already traveled in Indonesia and Indo-China a considerable while, and whose wife had just died after suffering from leukemia for many years.*

Cliff is in his early thirties, compactly built, and even more

---

* In 1968 I met two young men on the Osalinka River, as skinny as icicles, who were engaged in riding fourteen hundred miles to placer-mine for gold. They had five pack horses with them and a commando collie. There was another fellow my age in that area who still occasionally drove a dog sled a hundred-sixty miles to Fort St. James, though it was a feat to him now, not a matter of course.

compact in speech. He has a focused, pinched, closemouthed face, a likable hook to his nose and a likable nod, a low choked voice with the beguiling mid-B.C. accent, and usually he looks to one side if he does open his mouth. He croaks the words out. He's a cowboy who stopped being a cowboy and moved up here to be in on what's underway—for no odder reason than that. He's like the cheerful, bush-bearded throwback in Hazelton who offered to walk me to Telegraph Creek and whose hobby was taking honeymoon couples into the woods on a hunting trip, and after shooting a bear for them, hanging it up along-side their bunk so they could hear the blood hit the floor, except that he's gentle, not crude. He's in the old style. My technique with most of these people, if I've had one, has been to keep still. Not being as used to company and not being as used to silence as I, they talk in a hastening rush, in nervous, then pleased soliloquys. Cliff rejoices in stillness, though. He needs to be nudged into an embellishment, one question quick on the heels of another one.

We talk about game, since he's among the best guides. He watched the sheep soldier through the winter on a wind-blown ridge above the lake, nit-sized figures in file. It can be sixty below, but the one essential is that they have grass. The goats, though they climb higher in the summer, often go lower in the winter, trying to locate a cave. The next July you'll stumble on it, mattressed with molted hair and sprinkled with bones of the kids that died, like a wolf's cave except for the rumpy antelope smell. Sheep have a special zest and therefore a majesty. They don't occur commonly, and when they take flight it's for that day and maybe the next. Goats seem to feel more secure. They don't bolt when they first see a hunter, but stand and look back before slowly climbing. Caribou too are inquisitive. They will join a pack train, or will continue to mill around even after one in the herd has been shot. Sociable, scatter-brained, where they haven't already been decimated, they're simpler to hunt than the moody moose. In fact, caribou are so ingenuous that if they're starting to run away and you hold up your hand, often they'll stop to investigate why. In snowstorms they come down to an evergreen forest for shelter and eat the lichens hanging from the trees and paw underfoot for the moss. Cliff says he thinks the moose followed the white man into this Stikine country on the tramped trails. Since moose eat willows instead of lichen, they thrive in a burnt-over forest which grows up deciduous afterwards or on land partly cleared and abandoned. Coyotes were another immigrant, coming in with the pack trains. Now they're as frequent as wolves, but apparently it was too tough a wilderness for them in the beginning. In the heavy snow, they huddle under the deepest tree cover and look awfully thin when you see them.

He says he and a friend woke up a black bear in the middle of winter one time and ate him. Grizzlies may do the same thing during a warm spell, since they don't hibernate as uninterruptedly, and then spend the last piece of the winter in the victim's own den. Bear meat is likely to be worm-ridden, however, particularly grizzlies, who eat so much carrion. The bear population is splotched about according to where the marmots are and the various cycles of salmon and berries. When a grizzly kills an animal of some size, he may bury it under a mound of debris and lie on the mound until his next meal; this is a bad moment to walk up on him. The rutting season in the early summer can also be bad, and the sows, as they are called, attack on occasion when accompanied by cubs, at least in the first year. After that, although the cubs keep on their mamma's trail, she gets bored with them and will almost invariably run from a human, whether or not she has ever been hunted. Generally, a bear who is shot runs downhill. In an area like this, not knowing of the existence of man, he doesn't start looking for one, but runs for his life as if he'd been hit by a bolt of lightning. If the hunter has shown himself, naturally sometimes that's different.

Grizzlies are not clanking fiendish machines, they are living creatures. They may flee from a man on a given day and not flee the next; they may challenge him at the top of the hill and

[103]

not at the bottom, or chase him and then unaccountably break off the chase. People who have been attacked on a treeless mountainside have escaped by jumping down a short cliff or by lighting a fire in the grass at their feet or by yelling and fighting bravely with a stick in their hands, as against a Cyclops, or by taking a badgering blow or two and playing dead. Like the French, grizzlies have the merit of being just as hard on their own race as on foreigners. They are solitaries, they are property owners, and they are virtuosos. In the ordinary wheel of events, the more bellicose strains have been eliminated—great bears, such as Lewis and Clark describe, who attacked on sight. Nevertheless, they rear up to see who they are dealing with and to show themselves, a habit easily misread. In their abhorrence of man they are uniquely consistent. They withdraw from a mountain slope when he moves into the valley below, even if no shots are fired. From miles off, the racket and smoke that he makes are enough. They are the first animals to leave and they leave with less fear than any of the others. As they've been doing this now for such a long while, the distaste must have become very strong.

When I ask how his children will get their schooling, Cliff says by correspondence, a bit defensively, as if he'd been arguing with somebody. It's what he's chosen for them, however, it's not anything he regrets. His boy looks about five, the girl younger. Both bounce like beach balls through the forest, assured and grinning, beside a trumpet-colored dog.

Cliff isn't the most popular white man on the road among the villagers at Eddontenajon because he has no powers that relate to them, but since he strikes me as the most observant and as the only one who really likes Indians, I sound him out about how they're doing. He says that no, he doesn't think they resent the whites as encroachers, although he wouldn't have heard if they did. The parents can remember starving when they lived at Caribou Hide. They have an immense trapping range, comprising Creyke's, Walker's and Hyland's hunting areas combined, of which they exploit just the thin strip by the road. This spring many of them didn't go out at all because the Indian agent had delayed in paying them for their catch from the fall. The picture is one of confusion and gradual social disintegration without bitterness.

A fellow named Frank Pete still is an early riser, purposely vanishing on trapping trips before the big drinking set-to's. He'll go twelve miles and shoot a moose, when the rest of the village is crying for meat, and have packed two hundred pounds home on his back before anybody has noticed he left. Or he wraps twice that amount in the skin and skids it home on the snow. He prefers going without dogs, a little more carefully, using his eyes and enjoying himself. He even walks to the store, rather than sled. The dogs are employed a lot, though, and gorge on the hunts while the meat is hacked up. The Indians don't use captured wolves because wolves will sulk and stop responding when they are beaten, as the teams constantly are. Wolves are pacers with long sloping chests and feet that spread on the crust for speed. Dogs have big frontal shoulders for tugging the sled and feet that punch through the crust of the snow.

Cliff says the only danger in the winter is a snowslide, not the temperature or the wildlife. He has wintered at Hyland Post several times, which is one hundred and ten miles or so from here. Land furs, like lynx, wolverine, fox, have been recovering lately in price, and fish are never easier to catch than in the winter. They hang about near the open water at the outlet of a lake where their oxygen supply is refreshed, and yet behind the edge of the ice where they feel safe. So you don't try to fish the open water; you dig a hole several feet back and catch the whole school.

JUNE 22, WEDNESDAY:

A RADIANT POWDER OF snow on the mountains today. Some rain on the lake, burly cloudbanks. I spent the morning on the living-room sofa, listening to Lou Hyland hum and reading accounts of the Telegraph Trail during the rush. It was a long sink of mud teeming with dizzy souls armed with Bowies and Colts and dragging sleds or driving mules, burros, milk cows, horses or goats; a woman hunting her husband's murderer; Germans and Swedes who hadn't stopped off anywhere to learn English; a battalion of marching troopers showing the flag. A man mushed a herd of a couple of hundred cattle overland nine hundred miles to the Yukon, butchering the survivors beside Teslin Lake, but a wind blew up and swamped the scows he had built to float the meat the rest of the way. After a year or two, more Tahltans were passing through to their traplines again than white men; the abrupt quiet must have been stunning.

A good book called *Forty Years on the Yukon Line* takes up from there.* The relay men played checkers over the wire, or played poker with cartridges for chips. They cooked lynx stew and boiled raisin pudding in a dish cloth. The author writes a rhapsodic diary description of the wild's Eden face: Tedadiche Creek—Catch-'em-With-Your-Hand. It was so small you could step across it, and yet Dolly Varden spawned in it eight abreast at the end of May, crowded under the banks. He scooped out four hundred one afternoon with his hand, and skewering them on a length of wire, smoked them right there. Or, during a forest fire: "We began to meet dozens of porcupine waddling along the trail toward us, all in such a hurry they did not trouble themselves to turn off. Then we met a colony of ants, millions of them, stepping along at a brisk pace in a solid mass about a foot wide and thirty or forty yards long . . . Small birds also seemed panicky and were twittering and flying aimlessly around. We also met black bears who turned off the trail when they saw us and once in a while could hear the crashing of what must have been a moose."

After a lunch of moose stew, I read through the Hyland family diary, which terminates in 1917. It's hard to quote,

* *Forty Years on the Yukon Line*, Guy Lawrence, Mitchell Press (Vancouver), 1965.

being an unwieldy matrix of names and sharply abbreviated adventures. Willie Campbell is in it regularly by 1910, going off on jaunts, and Roy Callbreath's birth is recorded, the doctor taken downriver by Little Jackson. There's Little Jackson, Big Jackson, Clearwater Jackson, Pious Jackson, Monkey Jackson, and Groundhog Jackson. In the annual tug-of-war the residents beat the nonresidents, but the Indians beat the whites. The Hylands' Hotel served one hundred and twenty-two lunches one noon. The hunt for Gunanoot was on, and there was pleasure skating on the river, an occasional potlatch, plenty of action in court, and much reference to temperature and to the mail carrier's grueling trips. For elections he carried the ballot boxes as well. All winter people are leaving for Wrangell or arriving from there on the ice. A moose is run into a snowdrift and killed. A dog gets a nose full of quills. In the spring the wait for break up is palpable, the stir of the first steamboat's arrival and the rafts and canoes setting out. Barons and counts come to hunt in the fall. A frightful number of babies die, maybe half of those who are born, and many old-timers tip over and drown.

Mike Cole sent up for 3 Mos for giving whiskey to Mrs. Ah Clem. Big Emma gets into trouble too, fined several times for drinking, but has a low infant-mortality rate (Mrs. Ah Clem's is high). The Crazy Swede is dragged in from the bush with no clothes left and starving. There's Shakesville, where Chief Shakes ties up his canoe. Deaf Dan, Billy Fan, Packer Johnny, Taku Johnny, Chili Johnny, Long Jimmy, Dease Tommy, Bear Lake Billy, Dease Willie, Bear Charlie, Cigar Willie, Little Tommy, Little Charlie, Little Harry, do a turn. And Coomsinah, Tommy Cigar, Yoho Joe, Lame Dick, Telegraph Tom, Telegraph Jack, Juneau Jack, Willie Jack, Bummer Jack, Taku Jack, Casco John, Dandy Jim, Broken Arm Jim, Sambo, Johnny Quash. Also Ah Yack, Ah Clem, Ah Que, Ah Sing, George Jap and Frank Jap.

August 8, 1907: Painting yesterday and very warm. Opened Liard furs today and rebaled them—very good lot of martens and Beaver. Dennis returned tonight having hurt his leg. Pack train at Lava Beds.

September 10: Geo Hughes left for Sheslay to bring in heads for hunters—J. F. Callbreath going across river to prospect for new trail to Buckley. Lame Dick came in today had to leave hunting party—sick.

December 24: Dance last night. Dennis arrived this A.M. from Twin Creek—got Red Fox and Lynx. Dease Willie & McCabe & Taku Johnny came in today from Lake. Dance tonight.

January 6, 1908: Geo Campbell & Johnny cutting house logs—Pete, Little Bob & Taku Johnny went to Twin Creek to bring in Moose. Broken Arm Jim came in today.

January 10: W. Warnock left at 4 a.m. with mail for Atlin. McCluskey left for Nahlin to help repair cabin. Dennis left for Post with feed for Larry Martin. Geo Cox came up today and went back same day. Pat up in Court for assault & again dismissed with warning. Billy Hawkins came in today—No sign of Creyke yet everybody getting anxious now gone 36 days. Cartoona came in today. Lema Charles came in today.

January 25: Weather continues mild. Dandy Jim, Broken Arm Jim and Benny returned from Shakesville. Killed two moose.

February 3: Bear Lake John and boys left for Tahltan this morning. About two inches of snow fell this morning. A Meeting of the Hospital board of Directors held tonight. Decided to build two storey frame building on Gov. Lots near reservoir in block Six. Cost not to exceed $2000.

February 7: Dan Brown, W. H. Murray left today for head of Muddy River on a prospecting trip for about 9 Months. Dease Willie, Dennis & Ned Brooks have gone with them for about two weeks, their outfit weighs 1650 lbs. Brown Murray party returned today—too much water on ice in Canyon. 12 below zero.

February 22: Yoho Joe Coburn went to Salmon Cr today to see a couple of girls—Davy worked today hauling goods from lower warehouse. W Warnock and Geo Campbell came down from Tahl Tan tonight.

May 22: One of Jacksons horses broke away and went back to Tahl Tan this A.M. sending Pat for him with instructions to bring back Casco John's horse. Larry Martin came in today killed 2 moose. Broken Arm Jim killed moose across River.

July 29: Larry and Willie Coburn started for Dease this AM with 11 horses packed. Dennis started for Nahlin this A.M. to meet two mining experts will take them across country to Thibert Cr. are going to examine and report on Pike's mine. Packer Johnny & Liar Frank came in from Tahl Tan. W S Simpson & Family & Susie went to 6 Mile Creek today to fish.

August 18: Train left this A.M.—they snagged our horse and had to leave him this A.M. Baled up furs and addressed to Seattle. J. F. C. (Callbreath) train came to Summit today. Nettie and family came in from Dease yesterday and living in one of the New cabins. Shakes came up today. Geo. Campbell, Dandy Jim & Jimmy Hawkins started work on Little Dicks cabin today.

October 28: Geo Campbell returned from Glenora today—reports upsetting of Willis Hogalins Canoe in Big Riffle and drowning of Colonel Crogan a prospector—Adzit returned today only went as far as Wards, did not meet train. Ah Yick began work in restaurant at noon today. The Jap left on a hunting trip.

November 21: Little Bob & Benny left this AM for Winter hunt (South). Ah Clam went for meat to Little Sheep Creek. Ned Brooks & Dick went to Ranch today took 400 lbs grain for Troxel.

February 8, 1909: Mr. Lindsey went to 6 Mile today to work on Govt work. Billy Hawkins & Yoho family went to North today on hunt. Topsy and Coomsinah went to Summit for Ptarmigan etc today.

May 16: Billy Hawkins arrived with meat. Boys from the Nass with 166 beavers arrived late tonight as follows, Geo Achasa, Mat Richards, Little Charlie, Taku Johnny and Jimmy Hawkins.

May 29: Little Jackson, Bob & Lendecker left for range to round up horses and return to meet steamer. Slim Jim, Liar Frank and Little Dick returned from beaver hunt yesterday.

22 in all. Bought Coburn bear today—also Liar Franks & Slim Jims beaver.

January 12, 1910: Beal went to Tahl Tan today—Davy went to Twin Creek looking for Old Kitty—Ah Clam and Family and Rabbit Jim went trapping down river yesterday.

April 12: Lendecker left for Saloon this A.M.

Davy went out today to meet Packer Johnny

Pete went out for Beaver hunt

Lame Dick went back to Tahl Tan

Dease Willie shot moose on river in front of Drytown this A.M.

Lame Dick killed two moose on river above T. C.

November 23, 1911: Susie fined ten Dollars for being drunk and disorderly and M Pelkey (H Bay Cook) fined Fifty Dollars for supplying the goods. Very soft weather.

January 16, 1912: 10 below—a number of Bear Lake Indians came in today going to Tahl Tan. 9 Bear Lake Indians including 3 children.

January 17: Bought 3 Fox from B. L. William. Billy Fan went north today. 15 Below Zero this A.M. Willie and Joe Coburn came in today. Little Charlie left today for hunt.

January 18: 10 Below. Adsit and Dodd came in tonight. No moose. Albert George killed 5 Moose.

April 19: Putting up outfit for Pete Hanya & Billy Hawkins for Beaver hunt. Liar Frank came in today—is going to Sheslay.

May 29, 1913: Ira Day's train came in. Sammy Frank came in with horse load of meat.

May 30: Ira Day's train left for Dease. Griff Thomas went out with it for trail work. 2 white men prospectors walked up from Glenora, came up on gasboat Karen from Wrangell, 2½ days. Dandy Jim got 2 King salmon, first of the season. River dropping.

Hyland can tell me how most of these people met their ends, what their loves and antipathies were. The sheer abundance of information in him almost defeats questioning. He quits being bluff, and as if he were indexed, opens a page, his hospitable meat-slab face serious. In the evening we watch a storm move in a block across the end of the lake. The boats sit in a conversational circle around the wharf. Nine loons swim by close to shore, big white-and-black birds with long necks. When they cock their heads at the music inside, Lou puts the radio in the window for them. We look at some of the rock specimens, and Steele spreads out the Game Department's pencilled sketch of his and Cliff's territory on paper—some of the great peaks of the Coast system—basins and shoulders where nobody has ever set foot, let alone hunted. I begin smiling again: this bold, paper province, these many kings. He's smiling too, somewhat wryly, because such a havoc of landscape will support only bears and goats, probably plenty of them, but not the caribou and the scimitar-horned sheep that are the rage nowadays.

JUNE 23, THURSDAY:

A MOIST DAY. I can start a fire with the tan piece of paper from inside a shirt which has been to a Chinese laundry. Tomorrow's wood is stowed in the oven to dry.

Am with Henderson once again. Tonight we drove down the Iskut, down the series of quite disparate valleys it has cut, to the end of the road construction so far. The lakes that are strung together get much smaller and the river gets a little bit larger. The mountains shrink down to formless hills and relax from their duties of walling. Except that it was wet and glistening, it became like the Sioux country of the Dakotas, full of nooks and porpoising little ridges and unexpected developments—washes a Sioux might ride out of at a distance of thirty-five yards. There were rudimentary bridges over thrashing creeks with gravel bottoms. As the sun had come out, some of the hills were vividly green while their neighbors were still white with rain. Then the hills bulged and heightened to mountains, straightening into an orderly and imposing range on either side. When the valley grew fine and broad, they

[111]

gained a posh, lofty dignity. Instead of being cupped serviceably for catching the rains like the headwaters mountains at Eddontenajon, they were ranked as along a boulevard, where the gathered water sped on its way. The forest itself grew taller and vast. The low intervals of brush, the marshes, the pea-vine openings and meadows were stopped up. It was a lightless, impenetrable forest: it was the prototype forest which presents a mad sea-net of heaped, angular, tree-sized sticks as its face. You don't think of going in; you just look at it, turning your body sideways on the seat. The Iskut isn't spraddled into sloughs and jungle islands until nearly the end, so that it doesn't upstage its valley like the Stikine does, and instead of impressing a traveler as being the most voluminous tributary of the Stikine, it seems as demure and functional as one of its own tributary rivers would be. But the valley has high-flown dimensions that I hadn't seen since the railroad trip down the Skeena River—very bannery and grand. The crossing point of the Telegraph Trail has been obscured by a burn. Some time has elapsed, new growth is getting a start, and the dead trees have weathered a silver-gray.

A wee plane waited on a corner of a muddy air strip, as if there only momentarily. The construction camp was on a platform of mud that had been bulldozed on an outlook on one side of the valley. It consisted of a square of trailers, several cozy-looking, the rest dormitories. The mountains looped across the end of the valley in the distance, where the Iskut curved at right angles toward the west. Being closer to the sea, they were very snowy, and in the reaches between them many of the people I've talked to have trapped at one time or another. It all appeared so spacious that I could imagine the whole bunch of them making their trips and treks all at once without bumping into each other.

Bob Henderson's mission was a delicate one. Though he was pretending to have driven down to sell smokes to the men, he was courting the Indians on the crew who had worked as guides for him in the previous year. The hiring problems have made him obsessive, talking about squaws and whatnot every other sentence, and in the village when the children crowd around us to ask questions and wrestle, he spins the boys down so hard that they walk away rubbing their wrists and rear ends.

I went to find a maintenance man named Armel Philippon, who walked over the trail from Hazelton in 1934 and who has been known for this achievement ever since. He has his own trailer and stays through the winter, snowed in, as watchman for the machinery. Last year his wife and he used to snowshoe six miles to Cliff Adams's house and back for a visit every couple of weeks, but next winter the camp will be thirty miles further on, all snow, and probably they won't have even a radio. He's another fellow who came into the country looking for gold originally. It seems that everybody did. He was twenty-three, it was the Depression, and this was the blithe approach to the Depression. He had a companion about ten years older, a carpenter, who generally helped him along and once saved his life when he fell off a footlog into the Blackwater River and was being drowned by his pack as he hung onto a branch from the log, until his partner lifted it off.* They had driven from Vancouver to Hazelton in the first part of May in a Model T Ford. Having no money, they traded the car to the Hudson's Bay manager for $35 worth of supplies, and set out with fifty-pound packs, most of whose contents they soon threw away. They kept just the food, their two blankets and the rifles, and they ran out of food long before they were done.

Philippon was a city boy, so everything seemed touch-and-go to him, rushing along for six weeks—the benignity of the weather, the snowy passes which always lowered them into a warmer climate again before nightfall, the business of throwing a tree down and scaling their way across a cannonading creek as if they were steeplejacks climbing giddily. They hadn't a tent; usually they simply rolled in their blankets under

---

* It's a very short river, but barrels along. Jack Lee's brother-in-law also nearly drowned here.

a tree to sleep. Not only did they scoot through the gauntlet of grizzlies safely; they never saw one. They never encountered any game on the trail except for a few porcupines and grouse that they bagged for the pot with a .22. They met no other transients either, and by that day and age were treated rather as curiosities by the telegraph men. Naturally they'd hoped to prospect as well as hunt while they went along, poking into side valleys where nobody had turned off before. They'd hoped to find at least a souvenir nugget or two, and instead it was the best they could do to keep making headway on the main trail. If they saw goats up above on a ridge, they hadn't the energy to go after them. They were soon begging food from the linemen, gentlemen who were generous enough but were nearly out of supplies themselves, since June was the month when the pack train arrived. The rivers were dangerously high and the timing was bad for mosquitoes too. With no repellent, that was the worst hardship. When the trail was easy to follow, they sometimes traveled at night in the chill, or paralleled the trail to escape them, up in the snow. The Nass was the ruggedest going, a tangled swamp valley overlaid with wind-falls and braided with streams and bogs, a million mosquitoes, the trail an illegible mush.

He says that they liked the linemen without exception and that they were never allowed to starve. It was just that between these Samaritan cabins a lot of their meals would amount to small bites of hardtack prolonged, each nibble made into a mouthful. As he talked in the trailer to me, he got hungry remembering it, and went to the kitchen for something to eat. Beyond Ninth Cabin they were lost for two days after taking the wrong trail, so their hungriest time was then. But they slept well, and indeed by the end of the trip he had gained weight from the exercise and fresh air. Some of the best country they saw was in crossing the uplands of Sansixmor Creek and Yaza Creek and Slowmaldo Mountain, and the best and prettiest stretch of the whole event was when they doodled down Raspberry Creek at the last, after crossing the watershed that separates the Iskut and Stikine.

Arriving in Telegraph Creek, they felt proud and "saved" —in good shape but thoroughly awed. They camped on the bank, resting for two or three days. The townspeople brought them salmon to eat. They were still broke, needless to say, and since they had a tremendous momentum, they hiked on ninety more miles to the gold-panning area north of Dease Lake. The carpenter didn't remain, but except for periods in Vancouver, to marry and to see his children through school, Dease Lake has been Philippon's home ever since. There was plenty of company—somebody working on every stream. He became the veteran instead of the greenest. He's a slim, hardy man dressed in khaki, with a lean, gazing face—one of those slight godlike smiles that you see on an old figurine. Although his eyes are hollowed, it's a foxy, amused, humane face; it's a face you would want on your jury. Slim as it is, it opens as expressive and rich as a rich man's purse. His wife looks like an ordinary woman, like a nursing-home nurse. She's stout and short. The trailer is any Los Angeles trailer. As far as one can tell casually, she hasn't been marked by the life they have led, just as he hasn't been soured or crabbed in some manner because he didn't strike gold. Quite the reverse. He's the most serene man I've met here. He's marked with the exuberance of the search.

I asked a clumsy question. I asked if any of the telegraph men had gone nuts from the solitude, moving my finger beside my ear. For a minute he was a little disdainful. What I should have asked is why there aren't any hillbillies on the Stikine. I've yet to find a hillbilly, although Hazelton had a number of them—benighted, pale, bread-featured creatures from the Dust Bowl who peeked round their doorframes. They hamstrung their goats to keep them from straying, or tied one on each running board for the children to suckle from when they went on a trip. Isolation breeds hillbillies, but solitude doesn't. Solitude on a scale like this singes and sears. It makes for rapt faces like Philippon's and for a fire-walker's ambling aplomb.

Going home, Henderson and I saw a wolf. The first people who settle a valley discover that the animals are not especially nocturnal. The noon heat, not the daylight, is what they avoid. Bears and deer are grazing in the back pasture by five o'clock. Roadbuilders also find that in the beginning the wildlife enjoys the benefits of the road. It was a gray, tall, preoccupied, lost-looking beast with long legs, all of its bulk in its foreparts and head, and that mostly shag. It was within forty yards, sniffing, wandering along, glancing about as if confused by a scent, though not really intrigued. A jittery, gloomy creature, it was slow to notice us. Very rarely before, in the Mediterranean countries, I've seen such a harassed animal—a dog who was too big ever to be given or to forage enough food, who hadn't the smarmy quality of the other dogs, no fawning, no sympathy to offer, who was helplessly swift and perpetually gnawed and only too knowing and insightful. As soon as the wolf did notice us, it looked more directly at us than a dog. Its stance was suddenly galvanized, straighter than a dog's, rather like a phantom's, too alert to be true. When we got out of the truck, it left the road and sat down in the scrub a short ways off and looked in the other direction, puzzling distractedly over whatever it had been puzzling about before. For us, a loudspeaker might have been broadcasting twelve-tone music; this was a rhythm different from ours.

It's the fourth wolf I've seen. The last one was a two-year-old female on the Clearwater River in eastern British Columbia, who was shot at night on a jeep road because headlights were new to her. She kept struggling up on her elbows to face the rifles, and we ducked round our fenders as if she'd had a rifle herself and were shooting back. Her fur was in silver-fox shades and her head was larger than life. I stared at it the next day while she was being skinned. She had grim, snapping eyes set at a spellbinding slant, and a mouth like a bomber's undercarriage—like the bomb bay doors. At the zoo you can watch wolves mouthing their meat like a cobbler turning a shoe in his hands or a tailor handling a bundle of clothes. Oversized as it is, the mouth can be used as a pair of hands. Wolves' legs are long because they churn for a hundred-and-fifty miles in a line and then a hundred-and-fifty more miles in another line and then a hundred-and-fifty more miles, all their lives. Their shoulders are large because they fight with their shoulders. And their heads are large to contain their mouths, which are both hands and mouths. Their eyes are fixed in a Mongol slant to avoid being bitten. Nobody born nowadays will see a wild wolf. They are an epitome; one keeps count because they are so exceptional a glimpse. They brush by a settlement in their journeying and get shot because obviously it isn't possible any more to gallop a hundred-and-fifty miles and not brush up against a settlement. Not being as secretive and restrictive in their sorties as a mountain lion, they eat whatever is the right size and discloses itself. Nor are they all gloom and jitters. They present personalities so versatile that at some point they become a target for that reason too. The first wolves I saw were up on a rise playing like seals, arfing, nosing. Usually when they are sighted they are loping as trimly along as if they'd just loped around the world. It was a pastime of the old-timers to trace the back trail of a family of wolves during a snow-storm for some brief part of the distance to judge by the snow that was filling their prints how fast they'd been going.

JUNE 24, FRIDAY:

THE CREEK IS SILTY after the rains, so it's hard to get clear drinking water. We've been joined at the store by an admirable old river bargeman named Hans Anderson, who naps on the floor in the afternoon and cooks spam and powdered potatoes and hotcakes for us. Bannock and peanut butter for lunch. Bannock is a camp bread, a flat, round loaf made of flour, water and baking powder, with maybe a dash of vanilla for flavor. Bob is a good host, and we're a comfortable trio except that he's wearing himself thin from working past dark at a pace which a thirty-five-year-old man would have trouble holding to. He's learning to curse, so he does it too much.

I dropped in on Frank Pete this afternoon, the hunter Cliff

Adams spoke about. I'm always a little timider, I delay about going to see the Indians in these towns, and hearing so much talk about them from the whites, I keep wondering how they feel about us, expecting the familiar embitterednesses of white-Negro friction. But it's not like that. The sardonics are one-way so far. They trust in and seem to assume our good will. In Wrangell Judge Wing told me the Indians resented being barred from the Elks, but of course Eddontenajon hasn't an Elks.

The girls out on the roadside grinned and dropped their eyes as I asked directions. They walk there a lot. They're not picking weeds to eat; they're not on their way anywhere. They stumble and giggle and reel at the edge of the underbrush, back and forth, taking the air, and look so toothsome, so on a platter, that it's Caribou Hide all over again—courtship in Caribou Hide. Since the Caribou Hiders were a more fearful and primitive group than the Tahltans to start with, being hidden away at the head of the Stikine, they are happier about the new developments, like the highway. The village clangs with shouts, logs being split and visits paid. The ground is a litter of marten backbones, bits of bean boxes and cellophane wrappings, but all so recently tossed down that the smell of the place is still as though a windstorm had splintered a bunch of trees and left the butts scenting the air. Every house, every tent, has a cache alongside like a prayer platform, a ladder leaning against it, and on top generally a pile of mattress wadding or rags and nondescript hides.

The kids bicycled up when they saw me and checked on whether they knew my name. "How old are you?" "How far away you come from?" "Do you have a wife?" "How many years school did you have?" "Can you fly a plane?" "Can you drive a truck?" "What *can* you do?"

A boy of thirteen said proudly that he was in the third grade, though the Telegraph Creek kids would not have thought he was doing so well. And they laughed at my stutter when it occurred, but these kids are genuinely fascinated.

They stalk me with pretext questions to make it happen after they've used up the regular ones. They watch for the tricks I have, like switching a word. Yet at the same time they're exceedingly friendly; they think I'm a great addition, impressive indeed. Being made fun of is the other side of the coin. Everybody walks up with that winning and vulnerable openness, as if there were not a crook in the world—and nobody's seen such a thing as a stutter either, a difficulty which is not like a leg that's off or an eye that's gone. It's exasperating to be gawked at. I want them to get over their surprise, get used to it, jump into the twentieth century quick.

Frank Pete is a strongly formed middle-aged man with a straight back. He's short and his mouth is broad; he has a stubble beard and sloping eyes. At first he is somber and reserved with me. He's the tough Indian, the "heavy," going formidably slow, figuring out who I am. However, it's flattering to have one's words taken down. Soon he begins to talk in an off-handed flow, almost inaudibly, then emphasizing a word or two with the rather pleasing, melodious voice I remember hearing from a Mohawk I knew. He has the same bone-chocked face and dark coloring as the other man, and since many Mohawks were enrolled in the Hudson's Bay exploring teams, even reaching the Pacific, I wonder irrelevantly if he's a descendant of one of them. He's a Tahltan, not from the band from Caribou Hide. The reason he left Telegraph Creek, apparently, was simply that the game was gone. Another couple of Tahltan families did too, and live next to him in a line. The payments from the Indian Department are not to be counted on. When he's flat down to nothing here and can't buy the white man's grub, he can always shoot a moose, he says, while at Telegraph Creek it got awfully hungry by spring, but of course he misses the salmon runs.

"You have to be a good sneaker" to come up on a moose in June like this with the leaves thick on the ground. "When I want him, he gotta die, that's all." He smiles. We sit on a homemade sawhorse, boughs and debris to our ankles. Right now he's waiting for a plane to fly in to take him to a mining job in the Yukon: only a one-day job. Yukon law requires claims to be staked by individuals, so that the copper companies bring in people to sign their claim markers for them and the paperwork and then to sign over what they've just signed. Probably they come as far afield as this because somebody like Frank Pete isn't going to try to horn in with a lawsuit later on. He'll be paid $20, however, and will get in a thousand miles of flying for writing his name a few dozen times. In the meantime he's putting a tile floor down in his house. It's a two-story house, surpassing Hyland's and Cliff Adams's in size, but lacks the picture windows they have, has very small windows. For the present he lives in a white tent rigged on a log frame. He's got about nine children. ("Might as well say nine.") The whole time we talk, one little girl is doing her schoolwork with a vengeance at a table set in the doorway for light. His eldest son is going to high school in Whitehorse next fall, and makes a good haul every year from furs. He says the kids like school and are sorry when the two nuns who teach them leave, and he points out a friend's boy who has become quite a mechanic with model airplanes. A girl has been crossing in front of me at intervals, saying "Hello" or "Hello again!" She's a fine-looking, long-haired, big girl with an apricot complexion, in a suede jacket and department-store slacks. Having been off at nursing school for a year, she's the Bovary here, hopping mudholes in her nice shoes, hardly able to contain her revulsion.

Frank Pete tells me that sure, he's glad that the road is being built, but mentions as reasons only the kids and the fact that the hospital will be more accessible when they break their arms. Jobs, electricity, lower prices he hasn't thought of. He says the priest broke his collarbone and is gone for six weeks, laughing as if a friend had done the same. His brother Jack Pete works at an asbestos mine, and obviously he wouldn't be reluctant to move there as well and modernize. His cache is stacked with sheep and moose hides. He has a drying rack with forty or fifty trout hanging up. Because they are split, they look at first sight like oak leaves in the autumn colors, or else like the glands of big game cut up. He's also got some beaver balls tacked in pairs to the frame, which make the best scent material for practically any kind of trapping. ("What are they?" I ask. "Balls. Beavers' balls!" he repeats, laughing.) Beaver was the staple meat of the old-time trappers in season, but he finds it too greasy. He likes groundhog better, which hasn't been eaten much for the last twenty years but was dried as a staple for the winter when he was a kid. And porcupine is tasty, except that the animals are so handy and easy to kill that you try to conserve them. "You're glad to see them; you run over and kill it. We tell the young guys, don't you kill the porcupine—awfully handy when you're lost and when you need them and just have a stick."

He watches me writing this down, as light-mannered now as he was heavy before, talking softly. Wolves he dismisses as a danger, by which he means that they run if one has been shot. Once he was challenged by a pack of five, and once, with his uncle, by seven on the Stikine ice. In each case he was disillusioned to find that the sled dogs ahead of him were utterly terrified, turned round, tumbling over themselves and scrabbling right back up the harness and over the sled and against him, hampering his actions and aim in firing, which got him mad. Worse yet, in the spring on the trapline, the dogs, if he brings them along, will start chasing a grizzly, when he isn't after a grizzly at all and may not be prepared to deal with one. In May this happened. He was on a creek in a cutbank where he had no space, and the grizzly naturally turned on the dogs, so they wheeled and rushed straight back to him, with the bear close behind. He sold the skin to the doctor at the asbestos mine for $65—the doctor, he says, "jewed him down."

We get onto the craft of trapping. Bears he hasn't trapped, and it's illegal; bear traps aren't even sold. The old people said you could put the set on a bear trail unbaited, the trails are so regularly used, and there would be a wail as if you had caught a human being. Marten and muskrat are equally unsuspecting. Muskrats keep a hole open in the ice just the size of their bodies by crawling in and out, where you can catch them quite mechanically without bait. During the summer they establish a path over the beaver dam at the end of the pond, which works just as well. A marten trap goes on a stump or in the low crotch of a tree, whittled wider to hold it, and you hang a scrap of rabbit skin or beaver meat on a stick next to it. For mink, the trap is placed on a flattened log on the bank of a stream and some beaver scent is sprinkled around or a piece of meat left. Otter are attracted similarly. And lynx are caught in the thickest forest growth close to a lake, with beaver, or rabbit, or any meat pegged over the trap, pine needles scattered over the trap maybe, and sticks poked into the ground in a natural-seeming sort of way so as to form a barrier, giving only the one entry. Fisher, although they are fairly rare creatures, come into both lynx and marten sets.

The beaver-ball smell will draw beavers too, needless to say, but the usual bait is nothing more than a poplar stick fixed at the edge of the water so that it can't be pulled in deeper unless the beaver swims up to the trap. The trap is about three inches underwater and is located a hundred yards or more away from the beaver house to prevent the kits from being the first caught. The other important element in placing it is that the chain doesn't allow the animal to climb ashore once he is caught, because if he gets his paw in position to gnaw he soon gnaws it off. It's easier to arrange for him to flounder and drown when there is a little ice remaining to hold him off shore and complicate matters for him. Anyway, the rivers continually rise and fall overnight in the spring, which may drown him. On the other hand, if the trap isn't left high and dry and entirely useless, the water may cover it so deeply that the beaver's feet float safely over when he approaches and the man can't even find his trap the next day. Marten and fisher, although they are not equipped with teeth like a beaver's, may also chew a foot off to escape, resting dazedly between bouts of the pain, whereas a lynx will lie down immediately and surrender himself if he is caught by one toe. He will deliver himself over whole in the trap, fastidiously, and then be untamable in captivity.

Foxes have a more conventionally brave spirit. Being highstrung, susceptible animals, however, they freeze to death very fast once they are immobilized, so that fox traps don't need as frequent attention. Coyotes and foxes are quite alike. For both, shreds of the bait meat should be scattered all around to excite the animal so much he forgets his caution as he gobbles them up. In the center is the main chunk with the trap right on top of it, and he gobbles closer and pounces. This won't do for a wolf. The bait is tied three feet off the ground to catch a wolf, in a narrow space between trees where he won't have much room to dodge about. Two or three traps are used, each attached by several feet of chain to a stake that will pull out of the ground and drag behind him when he flings himself outward to get away. Otherwise, with a weight of a hundred or a hundred-and-fifty pounds, the chain might break. But it's very difficult, nevertheless. The youngsters are with their clever parents. The likeliest chance of overcoming the assembled braininess occurs when a pack runs up to circle the bait all at once, each afraid that the others will snatch it, snapping and vying and smelling the smell.

When I get ready to leave, Frank Pete goes on talking as if to himself: about his pride in his children, his impatience for the big plane to come soon. A relaxed well-knit man, he's not really very nostalgic. His trapping ground is Ealue Creek and Lake; he points behind Ehahcezetle Mountain. The map shows a remote valley which at its head through a funnel pass gives onto the Klappan River, and neither will change very soon. He's been telling me about Cold Fish Lake, where the Walker ensemble hunts and the caribou are still as plentiful as poplar leaves. He's too independent to be hired by Walker, though, and too old for the highway foreman to take a particular fancy to. It's June; he's jobless; he sees others bringing a fistful of money home while he's still dragging in loads of moosemeat. In a gush I suddenly feel sorry for him, talking to himself on the sawhorse alone, like a man out of work.

JUNE 25, SATURDAY:

As FOR ME, I'M very brisk. It's a cold profession, this new one of journalism. I skimp on and rather snub everybody near my own age, even a founder like Tom Black, as not germane. Towards the older people I'm full of affection, but am all questions, all smiles and no give. They know nothing about me when I leave and I know a great deal about them. In Telegraph Creek the day after somebody had poured out a notebook full of stuff to me, we'd meet in the store and nod but not bother to speak—which, oddly enough, was apparently what he expected too. My novelty has broken the ice for me, plus an occasional city-slicker effort at ingratiation—the business-lunch grin. And I've put myself in people's hands, which usually works. At first they draw back, but then they move forward again. Also the Kennecott helicopter pilot was a help, since all of the pilots are respected here, as the dog-sled drivers used to be. He was a Negro from San Francisco who took me to be a fellow exotic and rolling stone.

I've been too busy and happy to be lonely, and I must say I've missed neither friends nor family, other than my former wife, whom I haven't seen for two years now anyway, and have been missing right along. Sexually, instead of her, at night I visualize the English girl I lived with in Greece, whom I haven't seen for nearly a year. She was a lean, dreamy, athletic blonde, born during the Blitz and frozen at the age of nineteen, it seemed to me, though she was five or six years older than that. She dreamed of love and being rich, mostly, and when we went to Izmir from Samos and lived it up, riding in horse-drawn cabs and so on, she crossed her tawny long legs and turned as creamy and smooth as a queen. The populace lined the curbs as we passed. She was loyal and sweet to me, but

towards the end of the period we became choked with um-
brages and unable to speak to each other except on the politest
level. She ran away to another island on a night boat at one
point, and after anguishing in uncertainty, I finally went to the
police, imagining her death was on my head—I saw us as the
petrifying snake and the bird. They thought that I might have
murdered her and put a detective on my trail until she came
back. Even so, as wordless as we grew after that, we made love
better and better, my penis as big as a surfboard underneath
us. Whether as the snake or not, from my window I watched
her sunbathe and swim much of the day.

Of course these Indian girls are too vulnerable to fool with,
so I have only the past to keep me company in bed. The girl in
New York I've been involved with lately looks like a composite
of several movie stars of the 1950s. We talk easily. She
understands men and women-to-men delightfully, seeing them
through a man's eyes whenever she wants to, although she's a
woman's woman. In any quarrel we hear about she will side
with the woman immediately, and yet understand more of the
man's position than most girls would who would side with
him. She's a bubbler whose every fifth bubble is acute and
astonishing. She drinks tiger's milk and eats avocado. She's
open and gentle, though she has gaveling glamor, eye-popping,
clamoring, redhead glamor for an evening, and when you tell
her she's beautiful, quickly she turns her head so you can't see
her and want to. Yet she sometimes reminds me of the divorcee
boutique proprietress in a town, who is hard indeed to attain
but who is attained, who is loved a little but not a lot, and
whose lively, innocuous life gradually begins to unravel. I've
scarcely thought of her; I've been surprised.

People here hunt in their overalls. Along the Alaska Highway they put on expensive camouflage suits designed for the
last war and sold in the sporting-goods stores, suits which
would be suicidal in Maine, where red is worn down to the
very pants cuffs. I've been nipping along in front of the bull-

dozers, asking questions that soon won't be asked at all—about meat-eating and wild wolves and bears—a dabbler's questions that to me are fun. I haven't stayed long enough to get very personal or to follow anything up. As a result, I remember well only the people I've liked, such as Judge Joel Wing with his fluttering manner, slapping his forehead when he was confused for a name—the kind of manly, effeminate bachelor Sherwood Anderson cut heroes from. And John Ellis swirling up-current into his Shangri-la in that urge for total possession which we whites share. He marked on my map every cabin he'd found on the river for a hundred-and-sixty-five miles, so that it's been an index for everyone I've talked to since. I remember Lou Hyland jotting letters to her friends, one ear cocked for the hum of a plane. Telegraph Creek, of course, took my heart with its leaning brown church, its boat landing in front of Hyland's old store, and the trestles built daringly over the river for a garbage dump. I remember Alec McPhee standing above me in his garden, against the hillside, bent in the wind like an oyster shell as he looked at his beans.

I'm reminiscent because I expected to leave today for Cold Fish Lake. Hans Anderson and I waited around all morning for Mr. Walker, "the big boss." Hans hollers "Yo ho! Yo ho! Yo ho! Yo ho!" out the door at mealtimes most endearingly. When you come running, he has a pot of water boiling and he shakes a white powder into it and in almost the same motion spoons out the "mashed potatoes." We do have plenty of canned butter, which helps. I love his yo-hos, and he's flatteringly sure that Henderson and I sneak out every midnight to the girls at Eddontenajon, while he's snoring on a mattress on the floor with a coat thrown over his head. He has a barrellike back, a doughy squashed face and a pointed nose like a character in a fairy book. His accent is Germanic crossed with baby talk. Though his home is a trailer in Watson Lake, he drove down in his old truck for a break in routine after the numbing Yukon winter, not intending to stay. But having seen the spongy soil that you sink into, the trees, the clearings of horse feed, he's settled in; he's planted potatoes—you get nothing but stones in Watson Lake. His history has been a hard one: immigrating as a boy, going broke on his farm during the Depression. He sold the farm for $15 an acre, collecting only the first $15. It's now in a suburb of Victoria. After that he reached Lower Post, in itself an achievement then, and mined, batched for himself, cruised the rivers and started a store which his partners squeezed him out of once it got profitable.

Hans stiffened, nervous about satisfying the boss when he arrived. He stewed some dried apples and prunes as an offering, shaking in plenty of sugar, and went and sat behind the wheel of his truck, where, as owner and operator, he felt his most prepossessing. I wanted to hug him, but catching some of this apprehension too, I stopped reading and swept and neatened my cabin. Sure enough, around noon the big Grumman Goose swung overhead like a coasting bird, banking superbly for its landing. Walker, a gracious Briton, appeared and asked me to wait until Wednesday, please, before I come to the lake. He has the slack old-boy cheeks, the fresh complexion, slightly snaggly teeth and hanging flap of white hair that make Englishmen pleasant to see. Hans made a hit with him. They talked about tough winters spent in the bush. Hans had to eat out of the dogs' pan plenty of times, and Walker told him that if he never exactly did that, he had certainly eaten out of the frying pan. With a great smile of relief Hans began splitting cordwood to prove he felt vigorous. The chips flew uncomfortably close to the rest of us, so we broke up.

JUNE 26, SUNDAY:

TODAY WROTE A STORY called *A Fable of Mammas*, starting by flashlight at 4 A.M. I woke with it in my head from a snatch of a dream, the dream having arisen from a story by Sherwood Anderson which I read last night. It's the first story I've gotten from a dream. Always before, the fragment dissolved in two minutes when examined, the notion that it was any good being as much a part of the dream as the idea itself. The Anderson story was *The Triumph of a Modern or, Send for the Lawyer.*

JUNE 27, MONDAY:

GLORIOUS, BLUE AND BALMY. Caught a ride this morning to Eddontenajon. The mountains stood close and steep, with silver runnels and pockets of snow and passes going off in every direction, as if the country were still full of sourdoughs and mystery trips. Plank bridges have been laid across a creek that bisects the village beside the church, which is another log cabin. On the low hill backing the whole, a cemetery is already getting its start, picket fences around the few graves. I walked up and down, pretending to have business to do at the opposite end from wherever I was, practically sifting the place through my hands like a miser. The cabin foundations sit edgily on the ground, as though on an unbroken horse. Initials are cut on some of the doors to tell who lives where, and fuzzy fat puppies play in front, next to the birch dog sleds which are seven or eight feet long and the width of a man's shoulders, weathered to a chinchilla gray. The grown dogs sleep in a fog of hunger. Swaying and weak, they get up and come to the end of their chains, like atrocity victims, hardly able to see. Snowshoes hang in the trees, along with clusters of traps. Inside a cabin two women waved to me from their beds. Never picture the mountain men of olden days as Hercules types who lived with forest-sylph squaws. The typical mountain man was probably a short fellow who had the slender physique of a marathon runner, while his wife was built big as a bumper crop; when they went to bed he climbed happily on.

Alec Jack, dressed carefully in a neckerchief and first-quality jeans, was advising the new priest about an addition to the church porch. He's the councilor of the village and lives in a cabin with blue cupboards and blue window trim. He's a Tsimshian of the Wolf Clan, a nephew of Tommy Jack who I knew in Hazelton, but brought up at Bear Lake, ten days' journey northeast from there. A white draft dodger snuck out to where they lived during the First World War, hid with them and taught an old man of the band to read and write English in his spare time. He was the only white man Alec Jack saw in his childhood. Later, when he was gone, the government paid the old man a small stipend to teach other people to write their names, and a priest would come out in the summer months to help in a general way and to run a store for them. The fur traders had stopped visiting the lake before that, and when the Father stopped coming too, in 1926, they felt exposed and alone. They made a laborious migration to Thutade Lake at the head of the Finlay, summered and fished for char with some of the group from Caribou Hide, and when winter set in, continued to Caribou Hide itself, which became their home for the next twenty years. It was considerably farther from the white towns than even Bear Lake had been, but the collective population gave strength and permanence to the settlement.* Its inaccessibility put it on the maps and gave it a cachet—it was a place you could say you were from. If simply to demonstrate that he could, the Indian agent in Telegraph Creek would trek out by dog sled once in a while. He was English and honest and kept no mistresses. He was abrupt

---

* The Bear Lakers were quite a controversial group of Indians forty years ago. In Hazelton, as on the Stikine, nobody thought them overly formidable, although they were renegades who had even managed to put together a dialect of their own from several separate language stocks. But in Fort St. James they were considered a serious proposition. Bear Lake Charlie, for instance, supposedly shot a Prussian-type trader in the shoulder when he began to get on people's nerves. Besides Bear Lake Charlie and Billy and John, some of the other notables were Plughat Tom, Pierre John, Jimmy Blackwater, Thomas Abraham, and "Peter High Maddon," who was Gunanoot's friend. Whenever a white man disappeared in their country, the Indian-haters to the East would ascribe his death to one of them. The whites who were living with squaws usually disagreed and said the fellow must have fallen through the ice on the Sustut or blundered into a bear trap and frozen in a wet snow, since these greenhorns were cannon fodder anyway. The squaw men were humbler souls than the Indian-haters, as a rule. However, their influence was ameliorating. Nowadays, when the white men are neither haters nor squaw men, the Indians meet a clipped, cool attitude.

[129]

and arbitrary in his opinions, a bit silly, but since he hadn't the power either to help or hurt anybody, his visits provided amusement and boosted the sense that Caribou Hide was a significant town. The missionaries operated a two-grade school in the summer and showed up at Christmas as well. An airplane landed with staples once a year, besides which Hyland Post, only twenty-five miles away, offered some rudimentary trading facilities. So they took the hardships in stride. Often they carried their furs three hundred miles to the summer sales. They were skookum Indians, tough Indians, cohesive and free.

Then the game got hunted away. The exodus of itinerant whites for the Second World War was another blow to morale. In 1949, as Alec Jack says, they "decided to live on money instead of caribou." "To make it easier for Ottawa" to look out for them, they combined all the bands—the original bunch at Caribou Hide, the Klappan River Band, the Sheslay River Band, the Bear Lake Band, the Dease Lake Band, the Telegraph Creek Band—into one band called the Tahltan Band. "We put our dialects in our back pockets and just use English now. The women are just like a lady now. They bake pie and cake. The children don't know the inside of a tent, just cabins and houses like the whites. They go to Whitehorse to improve themselves." His small granddaughter sits on the sofa sucking a cornflakes box. Alec Jack himself is a balanced, affable spokesman, accustomed to talking to whites in the forms of address that they understand. He gave me coffee and walked me around with a rolling step, an energy muted and milder than mine. It's always like this—like being on a subcontinent set aside for a while, to be in an Indian town. If I were a wolf and I went to Tasmania, I would find other wolves, muted and marsupial and different from me.

The old people are living in tents until the rest of the village builds cabins for them. Kish-koosh I saw at a distance across the creek. Nobody can talk to him any more, but in his heyday he walked in the snow without socks and his feet kept so hot that they melted the snow in puddles behind him. You could tell which tracks were Kish-koosh's tracks. Alec Jack paused before several stovepiped tents, saying no, she won't be able to help you—the trouble being that the person had gotten so very old. We visited Dogan Dennis, eighty-five, "chilly all time," who lives with his deaf older brother. They have a plank bed and a couple of blankets. Dogan raised Bear Lake Billy's children after Bear Lake Billy was killed, so now the children take care of him. He chomps and grinds his few yellow teeth continually as part of the effort to keep himself warm. He has dark flush-pink skin, gray shoulder-length hair, and the goatee and drooping mustache of a ravaged old Mongol. One eye has said good-bye to his head bizarrely and the other has turned a blind navy blue. By contrast, his brother Jimmy sees so well that his eyes point off in different directions. Although the tent floor was clean, my breath was knocked out by the smell. It curled, as violent as a fire, lifting my hair, quite panicking me, and seemed to be not so much that they didn't bathe as it was the smell of digestion failing, of organs askew and going wrong.

This pair palled together in the Hylands' diary, took out the English earls on hunts, and watched the Gold Rush from the vantage point of Caribou Hide. The first white man had passed through in their grandfather's day. He wrote a wonderfully eloquent, lonely account of his summer which is a volume of the Hudson's Bay Company's Archives series.* It hasn't a dot of punctuation or a capital letter to interrupt the descriptions. At that time the Sikanni were starving, muddy, drowned sufferers living almost entirely on snared groundhogs, led by a single still-competent old chief. Interestingly, the Dennises refer to this starving time too, though they claim later on the

---

* Samuel Black (1780–1841), *A journal of a voyage from Rocky Mountain portage in Peace River to the sources of Finlay Branch and north west ward in summer 1824*, ed. E. E. Rich, assisted by A. M. Johnson, with an introduction by R. M. Patterson. London, Hudson's Bay Record Society, 1955. Mr. Patterson has also written excellently about the Stikine.

situation improved. The Sikanni got hold of some guns, hunted better, penetrated successfully to the salmon country and allied themselves by blood to the river tribes. In his account Samuel Black described pillar edifices like ruined "temples" in an uninhabited valley, not rediscovered since, but neither Dennis can remember any snippet of what the religious beliefs of the Sikanni were like. They say the white men came from Hudson's Bay, "and the Indians lun away, and white people leave food for them and go away on a raft and the Indians come back and see food, so when they come back the Indians know not to be scared any more and don't lun away, so then they stay and trade." They traded black fox and tanned lynx. A gun cost as many beaver skins as could be stacked flat on the ground to come up to the tip of the barrel—maybe sixty skins. It was a long-barreled, black-powder, scatter-shot gun which was loaded with a rag on the end of a stick. "Many, many beaver, too many beaver and shotgun no good—no work good and no good when work, either, so now they feel guilty and try to give little of it back with old-age pension."

The talk comes out in a jumble of mumbles and ejaculations. The priests have always been useful friends, and "now rest of white men too, now always good friends with white man," says Dogan. "They teaching us, you know? They kind of teaching us. We good to them, they good to us."

"They don't cheat you?"

"Maybe they do, but we don't know. Maybe we cheat them too with bum beaver skin. Tell 'im it's good, but it's no good. I was big trapper before, I got good eyes, I got dog team, I go around with my brothers and trap with dog team. But I never make much money with furs. I make $280 with furs one winter; sometimes only $50 or $80 or $105. Spend all money in Telegraph Creek and got no money when I get to Caribou Hide. Now I die any minute, I'm all in, they have to feed me now, I'm very old, I die any minute now. I quit trapping 1936 and I quit hunting around with gun and I quit dog team, I kill most my dogs. That's all I can tell you now. I have to quit."

When Alec Jack and I leave, the Dennises start talking in singsong Indian. For lunch Dogan feels his way with his cane to the cabin of Bear Lake Billy's son, Belle Nop, whom he raised. Since old Jimmy wasn't in on that he isn't included and has to fix his own food. Alec Jack shows me a cache belonging to one of the younger Dennises where there's a white billy's hide and a grizzly bear skin from the Klappan valley, which is only about a week old, heavily salted to keep until fall when some despondent hunter will buy it on his way home. The claws are the length of my fingers, like ivory, and the skin is still fleshy and wet on the inside.

I talked to a young man from Telegraph Creek who's moved here to live with a woman he likes. She and a friend were doing their hair in the doorway, and he had a fire going, shielded by strips of canvas, with brush piled around for fuel. On the scaffold overhead a batch of pink trout was drying. Pieces of meat hung down, a hole punched in each and a rope strung through. Some rib cuts were drying too, but mainly the fire was roasting the head of a moose, kept in its skin so the meat wouldn't burn. It rotated steadily at the end of a wire which he wound by twisting from time to time. The eyes were closed, the hair was blackened and sometimes afire, the antlers were gone, the ears had been cut off to feed the dogs, yet it was as recognizable as a moose is in life—as at peace as a comic strip, humorous moose. He said the head would feed his family for a meal or two and that the body would keep them provisioned for the whole summer while he was away on a job. We chatted, watching the head revolve. He was self-effacing, mustached, a soft-edged fellow. Last winter he chopped firewood for the school and trapped beaver, mostly for the meat, because his father was a half-breed, and not being on the Indian rolls, he wasn't allowed to sell furs, at least not directly. Confused by the sight at first, I asked what the head was for. He laughed bashfully. "They eat it," he said. "The Indians eat it." Actually, he shot two moose, two buddies who had gone wading together yesterday at 3 a.m., but gave one away.

JUNE 28, TUESDAY:

WE WERE KAROOMING DOWN the unfinished road last night toward the highway camp on what was to be another business visit for Bob Henderson. Going about fifty, we went into a skid, then another worse skid, and hit an embankment, luckily at such a slant that much of the force of the truck was expended in spinning around to point in the opposite direction and in flipping over onto the roof. Neither of us was injured badly, Bob not at all. I found myself lying on the roof, which was now the floor, looking up at him, in his driver's seat, upside down. He asked how I was, extricated himself quickly, and got out through the back door, which had popped open (it's a delivery-type truck). Off he went, I thought into the woods to recover his temper, since he was near tears. Instead, with the presence that marks him, he was going for help. Like most people in an accident who have broken their glasses, I immediately began to search for the parts, only later looking for the exit, thinking of fire. The air was bristlingly dusty. Sand from the road, powdered eggs, tire chains, Bull Durham tobacco, leaking oil and paper money were strewn or spattered everywhere. The last skid had been one of those slowly unrolling, inevitable-seeming emergencies. Having considered the likelihood of a smashup several times lately, I drew up my knees in order not to go through the windshield, and after denting the dashboard with them, rose out of my seat like a ball and fell on my head halfway back in the truck. My arms drew in to protect themselves rather than protecting my head. We would have faced a twenty-mile walk in either direction, except that the highway company foreman had been out fishing. Bob brought him back. I was wandering up and down, coughing and chuckling in shock. A long time was spent in transit and in righting the truck with a winch and chains.

Today I'm shaky, limping, a band of pressure around my head. Morbidly we've been discussing how the bush planes fly in during bad weather in case of a serious injury, circling the mountain fronts to find a low pass they can squeak through, preferably along a waterway, because if the clouds do close in on them they can only go down, never up. They land if they must, since without instruments, with limited fuel and a mine-field of brutal mountains around, *above* the cloudbanks they're as good as gone.

JULY 1, FRIDAY:

PASSED A MISERABLE TWO days lying in my sleeping bag with a log at the end of the bed for a pillow. No electricity to read by; unmerciful rain on the walls and roof; dreary fears as I real-ized my head had gotten banged worse than I'd supposed. It's one thing to boast to yourself how many hundreds of miles you are from such civilized amenities as a doctor when you are well, and quite another when you are not. I shivered; I felt as if I had on a constricting hat; I couldn't yawn. The spam and powdered potatoes were not to be stomached. Hans, ominously kind, spoke about friends of his who had died after some delay from blows on the head. The covers of the men's magazines in the bunkhouse were a gory slugfest. "Love is what matters. Love is all that matters," I muttered as in a delirium, thinking of the wife divorced, the years misspent. Though the weather remained too soupy to fly, there was the question of where to fly when I could. When I mentioned Whitehorse, Hans said to steer clear of the Yukon, for heaven's sake. It was a boneyard up there if you were sick. Finally the highway company offered me a Samaritan seat on its grocery plane flying south to a town called Smithers. Bob siphoned a half tank of gas into the truck (the usual mouthful of gas for breakfast for him), and we drove the same route.

All my hurts hurt, I was woozy and cold, but it was a dramatic flight, winding between the mountains for an hour and a half in rain and hail in a wheeled plane which wouldn't be able to land until the end. To begin with, the muddy runway didn't want to let us take off. Then it became a matter of *now* what's he going to do? what's he going to do *now?* The pilot was a stocky smooth man in his thirties, new to the West, who kept his finger on the map the whole way.* Besides me, a mining geologist was hooking a ride. He looked like Clark Gable. He had charisma—no suitcase, just a pack, a grin, a matinee idol's mustache and an ageless, swing-along vigor. He'd walked overland from a field camp the day before, and he looked as though lots of people were worrying about him back home; he looked as if he busted up hearts and mountains equally adeptly. Since our route was the same as the one I've been asking about, I couldn't help peering outside and getting engrossed. Like the Telegraph Trail, we followed the Iskut down to the dog's leg it makes, crossed several passes to the Bell-Irving River, crossed to the Nass, to the Kispiox and the Skeena, and we were crucially dependent upon these valleys because the ceiling was never more than a thousand feet. We crawled along above the trees, surrounded by smothering banks of clouds and the bases of mountains whose tops we couldn't begin to make out. We would fly to the head of each valley, where it seemed too narrow to turn and go back if we were wrong, before an exit appeared—a sort of high trowel-shaped chute. Carefully we'd hitch our way around and up into this opening, having to climb, brushing the lowest clouds, for a minute or two almost flying blind. Again, we'd go right to the head of the tributary, with the valley sides closing in—a mountain megapolis—until the next pass showed through the mush, a series of interstitial creeks and upper basins. The mountains were crudely cuspidal, the rivers green. The lakes were black, in strange, disorderly Rorschach shapes. Looking down, I wished I could bless the rivers. Thin as they were, they were what gave us our passage through. The pilot was tense, the geologist jaunty, and I, whom they'd left prematurely for, didn't feel it in me to do any fancy surviving if we were forced down.

An hour and a half of this cliff-hanging went by. There

* Later in the summer I read in the paper that he had crashed.

[1 3 6]

were many successive valleys. The map, extravagantly eclipsed, came to life. Underneath us was an absolute maze of twisting bogs glutted with snow and rain-forest growth, as gorgeously wild as the cold air was cold. We crept along under the layers of clouds, which always just seemed to allow us our necessary few hundred feet of altitude, sometimes only barely, when to see was like trying to breathe with a hand clamped over one's mouth. If there was a tear of blue somewhere, I wanted to tug on the pilot's arm, but of course that wasn't for us. I'd conceived of high headwater country as being fairly dry, like a hilltop is in the East, for example. But these watershed saddles were sopping—a flux of snow-water marshes.

At Hazelton at last, we flew over the railway line and checkered farmlands and logging roads. At Smithers the air wasn't chilly and the soil wasn't spongy. Taxi drivers were loafing by the telephone, spitting through their teeth—the guys who double as school-bus drivers. "Troubles?" they asked at the desk in the hospital, but I struggled and got a good doctor, who was as exhausted as I. We went through the tasks of examining me like two dead men. Then the pills, the clean silverware, the nurses checking with flashlights all night long, the dozen attentions. Back to the world of women! Suddenly it was all women. It's not that there aren't any women in the bush; it's that they're so muffled up. I won't soon forget the easement of falling into that bed.

[VI]

In Hazelton and
Flying North

AM READING *Pickwick Papers*, which I once thought egre-
giously trivial. One is always a fool disliking a classic.
Like disliking a nation one visits, it's the result of a blind spot,
which goes away and leaves one embarrassed.

I'm staying in a plaster-and-plastic motel, getting back the
use of my knee. I watch TV and bask in the shower. Smithers,
founded fifty-three years ago, resembles a California town
three years old except for a few pleasant relics. This is elbow-
grease country, this is the young man's land of which we hear
mention, where all the young men one could hope for are busy
with loans from the bank, getting in on the ground floor,
scrimping for the bonanza. Six years ago the Hazelton-Smithers
highway was a corkscrew dirt road where old men sat sunning
in front of the homesteads they'd cleared, their children having

[1 3 8]

gone south to greener pastures. Now it's three straight lanes, and the pastel lunch stops being put up are set back to allow an expected expansion. Cars go by with canoes on top like New Year's hats. The nature displayed is human nature—there is always that. After some seventy-five years of pioneering in the valley, the stage has been prepared for money making.

Yesterday I drove to Hazelton with an English girl, a freckle-faced, spunky, runty type whom I picked when I left the hospital in preference to a girl from Manitoba, although the latter was much sweeter and took poetical strolls at dawn. I wanted the British astringence and the seven-seas stuff—the brother in Hong Kong, the mother in Cyprus. And I made a mistake. The girl is on a seesaw with lesbianism. She lives with a hefty Australian butch who drives the neighborhood roads at eighty if we go to the movies, suffering frantically, and she is herself changeably contrary. But she's appealing, too—breezy, sleepless, tough on herself. The saving fun for the moment is just in the fussing, the courtship, going through the time-honored motions that get nowhere.

I was afraid I'd be spotted by one of the people I'd known in town who would ask where my wife was. It didn't happen, however. The tiny pre-fab shack by the river where we lived looked suitably dingy. All of the buildings we lived in look dingy now, whether in New York or here, and we slept in atrocious single-sized beds. Skirting past, I winced as some of my arrogances of the period came to mind, but mostly the memory was of two people living together like two ticking clocks: unaware. *I* was, anyway. I didn't even realize I loved her, which naturally made her feel inadequate to the job of forcing me to realize. The shabby house gave me pangs. Without wanting to stay long, I hurried about town to see what I could. For one thing, the museum has gotten quite grand, with decorative masks, headdresses, eagle-beak rattles and dignified ceremonial garments of which the Tahltans have no equivalent. Outside is the big totem pole the kids used to climb. When I lived here, the manager of the Royal Bank branch was helping establish the place, in lieu of a scout troop to work with or a charity fund to direct. Unfortunately, he was in competition with the owner of the gas station, who also had founded a "museum." Each of them drove out to one or another of the sites on Sunday and searched for relics scattered through the grass. The gas-station fellow kept his discoveries only until he could sell them to tourists. They probably didn't last long after that, as he said, mocking his rivals from the committee.

I was struck by how much like Telegraph Creek Hazelton is. There are lopsided churches of missions that failed and went home, and ghostly, ramshackle novelty stores with antique lettering on warbled windowglass. Or *Lee Chong's*, *LAUNDRY and BATHS*. A few sled dogs still roam between the eccentric log houses and haphazard gardens. The cemetery with its wax flowers and infants' graves is up on top of the same sort of nettly bluff standing alongside the river. Although the road leading into Hazelton is a clamor of jerry-built housing and government compounds—Forestry, Hydro-Electric— the inner village, ringed by the Tsimshian reserve, has been left unaffected. The senior Indians sit on the street corner instead of wandering rootlessly around, as they do in Smithers or on the Alaska Highway. Nobody runs over their feet if they stretch them out. Most everyone carries a dash of their bloodline, and they can consider the town is theirs. Their houses are either blue frame or log brown, while the old-timer whites', tilting idiosyncratically, are painted red or are whitewashed. On the beach traces of the old steamboat landing remain, beside the rig for a bucket-seat cable.

The Skeena is a remarkable twin of the Stikine. It's a spiky raw river, a swift silt-yellow with a great deal to do, yet managing somehow to leaven the town with history and leisure at the same time, as perhaps every river, by the nature of rivers, will. Speeding by, it's so raw that you wait for it to switch its course while you're watching, or to sweep a floating mastodon by. It's so new you feel like a gazing explorer; yet

Map of the Skeena and Finlay Rivers, and Surrounding Area

the town on its bank is made to seem ancient and wise and tried and true.

The helicopters land and take off with that peculiarly concentrated jet-age whine combined with an old-fashioned drumming which has become the identifying sound of all of these settlements, however. The horses that used to graze free down the street are fenced into buttercup fields, growing fat, not like the snake-necked, flat-flanked bush horses. After the houses and pastures end, a thick cottonwood woods runs alongside the river to a sand point, full of well-beaten paths through the hazel bushes and full of children. An adult must creep and stoop, but the paths are centuries old. The logs on the ground are worn like benches, the trees written on. An especially attractive family, the Sargents, have dominated Hazelton since riverboat days, when they had the *Inlander*. They are still represented by a son who operates the principal hotel and store, a fancy, luxurious, graceful structure architectured into the village with understatement. He has a penthouse he lives in and an excellent restaurant downstairs. He's a silent, haunted-looking, inconspicuous man who fixes the kids' bicycles on the patio on the fine summer days, kids from far and near. He soft-foots along, carrying most of the Indian band on his credit rolls like relatives down on their luck—immense sums; I remember the banker agog. Like Steele Hyland, he's an heir who has relinquished the wheeling and dealing in lumber or silver ores to the new entrepreneurs. Instead of a toolshop and forty machines, or instead of keeping a hundred wild horses, he has his booklined penthouse looking out on the mountains and his crabmeat supreme. He flies a plane once in a while, and his wife is the mover and shaker of the town.

My friend and I missed in our aim whenever we tried to speak pleasantly to each other, but were overly accurate if we leveled and fired. Both wearing prissy ironic smiles, we bumped north fourteen miles in her red sports car to the Kispiox to see the totems, a good many of which have been restored. They've been put in two rows. The very top figures—

bears, ravens, porcupines—poise themselves uneasily on their perches, peering off as if they had been asleep when it happened and don't know how to climb down. They're like cats who have gone to sleep under the hood of a car and woken up after the car is in motion. Other larger totem poles lie bedridden in the grass, patiently grimacing, too old to restore. They mark where the snowplow should plow and they furnish the children with elevated paths. The children have gotten blasé in the past six years—not a head poked out of a window for our benefit. The village is spacious and clean, with white farmlike houses and barns. The Skeena slides over wide gravel bars along one side and the flossy Kispiox cuts a square channel on the other. Eighty log trucks a day go by now—200,000 board feet of lumber. A handful of eagles continues to patrol the salmon runs, but the moose have been drastically shot off. There are twice as many whites and twice as many hunters, so that it looks like another green, God's-country valley, like the upper Hudson or upper Ohio—nothing paganly tumbled or tangled about it.

We said good-bye, she and I. I hitchhiked fifteen miles further in a log truck, being somewhat ungracious to the driver. I've gotten snotty about how long the person I am talking with has been in the country. Most of these young knuckleheads I ignore. Coming from a world where everyone is young, where any old man on the street is virtually a freak, the great thing is to be where a man's achievements can be guessed at pretty well just by his age. I was hoping to see Jack Lee again, and even my bushy-haired host was interested in that.

Lee answered the door. "I remember you, but I don't know who you are," he said with a smile. He's sallower, hollower, and his wife Frances looks bigger and more competent than ever. The garden is like a flower show and the vegetable garden like a state fair. Wet green fields spread to a pond five hundred yards away. "Look at all the dead horses," he said. When he whistled, the sleepers raised their heads; those awake went on yanking grass. Horses eat forever, eat twice as much as a cow, he says. He has a hotbed where he starts his cabbages and tomato plants with horse manure—cow manure doesn't heat. When he retires he's going to live up on the Duti and the Kluatantan in the summer, he says. He still has his phenomenal woods-stomp to cover the ground.

We talked rapidly, catching up to date. They were brimming with their guiding successes and I was asking questions about the demise of the game. Last fall through field glasses Frances was watching her son in snow costume hunt high above her on a slope. He shot a mountain goat. A snowy, man-shaped figure, it rolled and dropped, slamming and bowling over and over, rump over head and head over rump, down, down, as if it were he who had fallen. Jack has been hunting the very head of the Kispiox lately with bow-and-arrow clients. The river is so fish-rich it becomes a sort of bear kingdom, though at the same time you can actually hear the earth-moving equipment at work on a part of the highway that will connect through to Eddontenajon. The machinery pounds in the distance and the bears promenade, mostly grizzlies, grizzlies two to one. There are so many bears his description sounds as if a bear had climbed into a tree in Central Park and concealed himself, taking note of the people who ambled by. Big bears, little bears, laggards and hungries. There is a fairy-tale surrealism to it. Last year the party of hunters was strung along the river in different trees miles apart, so that instead of ambushing a solitary animal, each of them meekly witnessed a series of set pieces: Papa after youngsters, Mama intercedes; Fatty tires of ants' nest; shy lad loses female. Jack had a mean bear under him for a while, whimsically destroying the fish. It would half kill them with a gentle bite and paw them. Straddling a log, it patty-caked the surface of the water. Another bear napped nearby and finally woke up, tripping on the windfalls as it went off drowsily into the brush. Strollers strolled, frittering the day away. They greeted each other or dodged aside. They whacked the rotten logs and licked the grubs. Upwards of twenty bears.

While I was with the Lees their garden was visited by several families new to the valley who hadn't had an opportunity to plant a garden of their own as yet, though Jack wasn't sure why in every case. We went for lunch to his mother-in-law's, who lives with her brother, who dropped in for Christmas nine years ago, had a stroke and has stayed. Dinner was three vegetables, roast beef, rolls, potatoes, salad, milk, saskatoon berries with cream, and pie and tea. "Sit in," they say.

Marty Allen, the other man I'd wanted to see, was next to me. He's her other son-in-law and may be the northernmost farmer in our hemisphere. He was telling me what he'd said to the Governor General of Canada when the Governor General inspected Kispiox, and what he'd said at the most recent wedding of the Wookey family. The Wookeys are the Snopes here. His own wedding was marred when the bull they'd been given pulled the ring out of its nose on the way home. His wife's puppy, tied to the wagon, got its rope twisted in the wheel and almost choked. Although the ride between farms was day long, they used to do it every second week then. Now, with their trucks and cars around the yard, he says, they never bother stopping by unless it's to borrow something.

I was made much of—this idea of my having come four thousand miles to lunch again with them after being in Norway and Spain. The conversation frisked easily. Marty is a burned-faced fellow with sloping shoulders and a Roman nose, an Alberta nose. When I was in Hazelton last, he was driving his eldest daughter seventy miles to her piano lessons Tuesdays and Fridays. She's seventeen now, not quite ready to accept a steady boyfriend, but pouring coffee for the lonesome loggers who show up, and pestered by their pinching. He took me to his house afterwards, where I fell for his blond daughter, ten, instead. She was up on a black mare, whizzing around, directing it with digs of her little big toe. A rope looped about its nose for a halter. She hauled herself up and down by two handholds of mane, and they flickered across the yard like a pair of fish, trembling and fluttering. The boys were enmeshed with an improvised sawmill resembling a Ford, surrounded by sawdust and leaking oil. Every few minutes it went up in flames and they took off their coats and beat them out. Mrs. Allen, a serene, squared-off woman with attractive small features, was cooking fifty-three cans of salmon that the Kispiox Indians had given her in exchange for the beaver meat which her boys turn over to them in the spring and the steer tripes Marty gives them.

Marty, flattered that I'd remembered him, was ready to open the gates of his memory for me: how he'd finished the war in Holland on a burial squad, marched across the George Washington bridge with twenty thousand other Canadians, and headed for the Yukon to make his fortune. He wound up in Whitehorse as a mechanic instead. One night his partner and he got drunk in the Legion Hall. They sniffed the cold air, and squirrels were selling for a dollar a skin, so they quit. They came south to the Skeena and trapped in the Groundhog Range, priding themselves on making the one hundred miles home in a single day, putting the tarpaulin up alongside a tree and catching an hour's snooze, perhaps.* His partner counts fish at the head of the Babine River every summer in a lean-to, living the rest of the year on the government rations he hoards. But Marty bought the ranch of George Byrnes, the man who had been the packer at this end of the Telegraph Trail, working a huge string, until at last he went crazy and dug a grave and killed himself at the edge. He was "bushed," they call it. They named one of the mountains after him.

So was I bushed. I was enjoying the Norman Rockwell sing round the piano in the next room, the larder of cakes, the

* This Groundhog Pass could be a killer after a snowfall. Two Indians were taking fifty-six horses to Caribou Hide for George Byrnes to winter them, got a rather late start, got caught in four feet of fluff and had to shoot every one.

spoonfuls of cream like liquid marshmallow, the round family table. Even more than the Lees', the place was loud with visitors and unofficial orphans—a logger with a hook for a hand, a dried-out drunk from Santa Barbara. Lee is the old-timer, but Allen is the valley's chief citizen. Like any early settler, like the people who built my parents' house in Connecticut in the first part of the nineteenth century too, he built right next to the road. The traffic was horses and wagons, perhaps twice a day and the contact was welcome. Recently, though, when the road was regraded, the supervisor obliged him by bending it to go around in back of his property, out of sight. Tom Black, in founding Eddontenajon, has begun with a house site a hundred yards back.

I was interested to hear about my friend who agreed to walk me over the Telegraph Trail and who would have made it, with or without me. He "seemed to be worth so little that I thought we ought to take him out and shoot him," according to Marty. Then at thirty-three he advertised in the *Free Press Prairie Farmer* for a wife, signing himself "Black Beard." He said she should be able to live on lynx pie and skunk stew and he got a good many answers, including one from a girl from a family of eleven sisters. He went east to look at the others as well, but stuck with her. They've broken a plot of ground a dozen miles beyond here and are living on turnips and moose meat. Their food bill last winter was $5, for the baby's Pablum and orange juice.

Chasing the kids out, arranging himself on the settee for an interview session, Marty kept wanting to see me write things down. After all, when somebody is the northernmost farmer in Canada, it's about time! On the other hand I was relaxing for a change. The household in its prime of life, the civilized hustle, delighted me. Though there wasn't plumbing and though the original log-house walls were barely disguised behind paneling, it was more like Connecticut than Telegraph Creek. It's odd how superabundantly I exulted on the Stikine, and yet how flatly my preferences are here. I'm like a person whose passion is the violin, who haunts all the concerts, yet doesn't attempt to play himself.

Marty dangled facts before me. He walked me about the garden, where Swiss chard, pumpkins and pole beans were growing—anything you can think of. The harvest season gets too wet and cold for crops on a commercial scale, but the only limit on the number of cattle he raises is the acreage that he can keep in hay. Nearly half the year they're out on their own in the burdock and wild June grass and the timothy meadows of the old homesteads. Besides his main hay cutting, a second growth has time to spring up a couple of feet before he mows it for silage. It steams and ferments all winter and the cattle are crazy for it.

For most of us now, simply to be on a farm is exhilarating, to be let in on the humble logistics of dealing with eggs, to walk past the sheds of tall red machines smelling of greenery. The details of making a start seem intriguing, as the finances of putting a dry-goods business on its feet do not. In the Rockies in 1960 I had seen a gaunt family of five and a humpy miscellaneous huddle of animals passing the cabin where I was staying on their way to homestead land which was across a bridgeless, strong river, beyond the skimpiest road. My wife and I were boarding with a woman who was living on goats' milk, principally, with her young son. I remember her tugging those goats, morning and night, on the end of their tethers, and doing the wash for the town, but of course she was quite an established citizen compared to the tattered outfit who passed.

Marty began with several horses left over from the Byrnes' pack train, then bought an old tractor, a baler, then an old car, then an old truck, then another tractor for his wife to use. He borrowed $20,000 and paid back $30,000. "Isn't that a corker? Lots of people have moved in and moved right out again; had a little hard luck, you know." To avoid lengthy rotation schedules he needed to buy fertilizer also. Some of the swampier patches took years and years to clear and sow. He'd get the worst of the brush off during the winter when the ice had brittled the wood, but the beavers would flood out his seed afterwards in the warm weather. He sold cedar poles to the telephone company and balsam and hemlock logs to a fellow located in the Empire State Building. By last fall he had worked up to the point where he mustered sixty-six beefs to butcher, "long yearlings," eighteen months old, including the heifers who hadn't managed to get themselves pregnant. He takes the meat door to door, cut and wrapped, at forty-five cents a pound, though his regular customers buy in quantity. He can tell what he's giving them by the way that the hide comes off. Tough beef is tough to skin; good meat announces itself with a hide which practically skins itself.

I wouldn't have wanted to be the death of a cow, but he was killing an infertile animal anyway that afternoon, so I watched. Since I'd just inaugurated the highway between the Skeena and the Stikine with its first injury, and since I was revisiting a house where I'd known happier days, my mood was suitably sober. In fact I felt as if I were watching a quite random death, as if the rifle at the last moment might swing towards me. I noticed from how the farm dog slunk around that he did too. My memories of marital twists and follies ran into memories from earlier still, which for silliness put even my marriage into the shade.

Judging by the situation in the pasture, the whole lot of them had been tipped off. Besides the victim, the heifers as a group bounded into a poplar woods as soon as we entered, while the cows with nursing calves kept perfectly placid and quiet. With the heiferlike lope which farmers develop, Marty followed the fugitives, his face beet-burned except underneath his large nose. I got into the truck again in the premonitory silence. When he had driven the runaways back into the field, they bunched for self-protection. He walked around and around them with a pump-action short 30–30, resembling a light BB gun. When he scattered some hay they separated hesitantly. As the others left her, the cow fixed her eye on me over her shoulder, while he took aim. He shot her below the ear in order "not to kill her too dead." She fell as though axed, without any bull-ring delays, and he dashed and cut her throat quickly with sudden professionalism as she lay stunned—a small, exact man, instead of gangling and lanky. With apt, jerking, upward motions he sawed the hole until it gaped, as if he were crouching, tying a swift knot. Then he drove off the rest of the herd. They'd bolted at the shot, but had turned and come back, lowering their heads to look lingeringly, whether from fellow-feeling or out of curiosity. The heifers bounded into the same woods, but the cows who had calves were calm and unresponsive. When he was shooing the others they didn't consider that his advice applied to them. "Yes, you too. On you go," he said, friendly.

The cow lay in shock, sometimes conscious, sometimes anesthetized. Her legs pumped, and he squatted beside her throat, superintending the flow. If she stopped threshing he jabbed her feet with the knife or else got up and manually swung her legs with a kind of comradely sympathy, like helping someone to finish a job, giving his attention to her hind legs as well. None of the other cattle were anywhere in sight. Once they left us there was a finality to it. The relationship that exists with them is such a strange one. They live with us: we live off them. They were deciding not to know. The cow on the ground groaned and gasped, pawing from the horizontal position. And yet it wasn't so much an act of suffering as of dismay and regret—all was over. Because she ignored Marty she seemed to me remarkably impersonal, but the pawing was redolent with woe and sharp frustration—all was dissolved.

I still wasn't convinced that this was the end of the deaths for today, that this wasn't the first of a chain. And the dog skulked subduedly, swallowing, feeling exposed in the open field, full of his own mortality, though he was smiling, too. He licked his chops rather guiltily, so as not to arouse or offend us. He was waiting to lick the grass where she now lay, but he was also afraid of being shot. I was thinking that the event had become irreversible; we were stuck with it. If we should change our minds, however much we might try to save the cow, it was too late. She kept rallying, fighting for air through the hole in her throat, her face a contrast of red and white, but it had gone too far.

When she was dead, Marty severed her feet and head and hung her from the fork lift of the tractor by her ankle tendons. He began to loosen and strip off the skin, mainly by pushing down on it with his elbows. Opening the body, he sawed through the brisket, handling the organs familiarly, turning them over, examining the uterus to confirm that she had been barren, and let them slide down on the ground in their dull, various colors. He was gently respectful about this. He might have been going through an old person's last possessions; the sense was the same. A neighbor boy rode up, kicking his horse close to the pile of organs, and tried to make him smell them. He told Marty his sons had caught three big salmon, and he laughed because the cow's bowels had moved when she was shot, and at the dismal-sounding exhalations from her dead lungs. Marty chased him away, saying he was insulting the horse.

Cutting carefully, he reminded me of the bush professionals working on a moose, with the skin spread out like a table. The tail was saved for soup; the liver and kidneys were placed on the skin, which was inside up. Globs of fat were put aside for suet for pies and cooking lard. The rib cage looked like a red accordion. Nothing of life or remembrance clung to it, though the flesh on the steaks continued to twitch. The impression was of a burden surrendered, an assignment completed—the stomach left for the crows to peck. Onerously, the body was sawed lengthwise and left to hang. The skin was dumped in a lump on the head. And that's where the cow remained, on the ground as a Hereford-colored wad of hide and a meek head upside down, reduced to the size of a newborn calf. I thought of the pulverizers that convert an automobile to a modest bandbox of scrap. But its character as a cow did remain. It was like a costume taken off, tossed aside, that contains more of the character in the play than the actor does as he disappears. The character lies there behind.

I've forgotten to mention the Fish that flies over Smithers from atop a pole in a Chinese man's yard. He's had it since the New Year, and it's a great, fat, elongated Fish, more of a fish than all these caught salmon.

July 9, Saturday:

Have resumed. Took a night bus to see the green dawn. It was a five-hour trip to Vanderhoof, past countless long lakes and steaming ponds and shaggy, continuous forests hooded in fog or Easter yellow where the sun hit. Occasionally there were a couple of late-sleeping houses in a cleared spot, with high-roofed hay barns and red horses wading hock-deep in the wheat grass, as if they'd made mischievous use of the night alone. Against the forest, both the barns and houses looked like toys, except that the barns were surprisingly large and the houses surprisingly small. Every farm had several of each, where some pioneer had labored and stewed, marking time until a town formed. The fresh joy of traveling caught me again, leaving behind the garter snakes and down-to-earth voices, the swimming, the baseball, the traditional temperate summer of Smithers. I'd had plenty of those.

Vanderhoof is like a prairie town in its dusty flatness, although the names on the signs give it a boost: *The Lucky Dollar, The Green Parrot Café.* Guests moseying into the hotel remove their boots, so I waited for seven or eight hours in stocking feet before boarding another bus for Fort St. James. Two Babine Indians were with me, named John Joseph and Herbert, who had been hired by Mr. Walker to replace the defectors of Eddontenajon. They both were drunk, but Herbert more than once was nearly put off the bus for telling the driver he drove crookedly. Herbert was tall and erratic-looking, with a gap in his teeth where he had been punched. John Joseph was happier in appearance, shorter, and less tousled, but also less warm to me. In their hair and physiognomies, even the garments they wore, they reminded me of the newspaper Vietnamese—of the wide world we read about and don't see. I was glad to elude them, however, during our wait for the plane in a cocktail lounge which discourages Indian customers. I talked with a diamond-driller from a magnesium mine, one of the few Frenchmen I've met in the West. It's something of a puzzle why the French have dug in their heels in Quebec for the last hundred years when the bulk of the continent was explored first by them. Paddling from Montreal, they were down on the Arkansas, for instance, long before the Virginians got there. This one is a black-locked youngster wrapped up in the dangers of his job—the pitch of the ground his rig is set on —and his hopes for a divorce with low alimony.

Fort St. James is an historic trading post which has expanded lately. People go to and fro lazily on errands, a melded winking population of sneakered half-breeds and booted whites. Three Norse-looking buildings remain from the old set, which have squared timbers and a vertical log standing at each corner instead of a cross-hatch of ends. *Squared* log timbers— maybe I can't convey the effect, but it was like a cultural explosion after the round-log walls that I'd seen. The steep, sophisticated roofs are shingled decoratively, and the original chinking has lasted a century and a half, being a sort of a white cement instead of just moss and mud. One building posed wearily on stilts in the field as if it were herniated and ready to give up.

I got a bit lonely. My British friend had given me a generous send-off, raised sweater and all, her nipples like obstinate, dumb little heads in my mouth to be knocked about. Unexpectedly we'd drawn close as I was about to leave, really concerned for each other. Rumpled, limping because of my knee, I'd tiptoed away. I wrote to her in the lounge, thanking her. Too many departures. And I'd done her no good. She'd needed an honest talk with somebody, and at one point she'd needed me to say outright what was wrong because she couldn't force the words out, and yet was quite frantic to have them said. But I'd lacked confidence and had evaded the subject with ironies.

About 6 P.M. we got into a Grumman Goose (John Joseph and Herbert in back with the freight), and taxiing belly-in-the-water like a speedboat, climbed with the thrust of the grimacing engines. The pilot, Merv Hesse, bulged his lips as though he were biting a tennis ball, reaching up, reaching down, for levers and switches. He had the stick in the crook of his arm and wrestled it back as if he were playing a sailfish. Wearing fitted dark glasses and large earphones, he talked into the radio. Though the flight was of no more intrinsic importance than the rest of the flights I've been on, because he is one of a handful of illustrious pros, immediately it seemed very different. Nobody knows who's the best of them because they each fly their own territory, but there aren't many pleasures that beat watching somebody do what he's exceptional at. I guess it's a masculine pleasure, the pleasure in excellence. Not until the climb was finished did he turn over the land, which was a far-reaching expanse of evergreens with swirling patterns of lighter-colored deciduous trees. The lakes shone like salt pans, cloud-spotted lakes of great size. The flat forest began to be varied by mounds that built into landforms gradually and then into mountains.

At Takla Lake we banged down in a belly landing to refuel at an isolated reserve, exiting through the nose hatch past the emergency raft and rations. The proprietor is a chuckling Hylandish man who supports himself by trading furs, selling staples and keeping the biweekly post office. He has a trim home painted beige with Venetian blinds, plus seven other buildings on the property and a stylish houseboat, all beige as well. The pier is spade-shaped, itself a production. A traveling boat was tied up with an outboard on it that could have shoved a liner to sea, and a horse at the edge of the lawn scratched his rear on a thicket of underbrush. The Omineca gold country is behind here.

We were supposed to pick up two other Indians from the

Babine band who had wanted to come across country by the connecting lakes and portages instead of around by bus and plane as we had. But they hadn't shown up, and Herbert too wished to desert—his suitcase was held as hostage. A local leader arrived, a zestful man with a fisty dark face and recessed, close-set eyes. His hair was cut in a circle from the crown of his head. Obviously admiring Hesse, who flies in his village's supplies and mail, he hated to argue with him, but when Hesse said they were stupid undependable Indians, he observed agitatedly that Hesse had appeared a day earlier than planned. Hesse was mad. We boarded again. Bullying the stick against his chest, he zigzagged into a masterful, fantastic takeoff, changing direction while under way.

Now the mountains got serious, trending northwest in parallel ranges. The ceiling was high, and on every side was an absolute primevalty for as far as we could see at seven thousand feet. It can never have been any emptier, because the handful of trappers are gone and even the Indians have been sucked south and centralized. We flew for an hour and a half. We went up the Driftwood River, a valley the shape of a shoebox, the forest so thick that the tributaries showed only as snaking, special upshoots of trees, until we came over a dumbbell-shaped lake. Next was Bear Lake, where Alec Jack used to live. It's a narrow wild-looking lake with snow on the shelves above it and shallow alpine puddles on the caribou-grazing benches higher still, just underneath us. The mountains around were like modern war. There wasn't one that couldn't be climbed and there wasn't one the climbing of which would count for anything. Chains of them extended on in laughing, awesome serration to the four skylines, not a hero among them, just a fierce mass of tire irons and short knives.

At the outlet of Bear Lake we followed the Bear River to the Sustut, a wider, lush valley juiced with fertility. We were flying at peak level in a grander, more orderly fashion than on my trip last week down the route of the Telegraph Trail. We were seeing everything, the snow smothering the rock and the rock bashing free of the snow. The peaks were a tumult of rock and snow—not beauty, but an unspeakable tumult, like electronic jamming. The beauty was at the lower elevations— the majestic rug of the forest and the brief, apple-green plateaus at four thousand to five thousand feet. The forest was so complete, lapping up the bordering walls of the valley and curving with the Sustut, that I would have moaned, looking down on it, if I'd had time to moan.

Swaying and bucking as on a life raft, we scraped over a further series of ridges and peaks. This was the highest flying we had done; we were way up with the snow so that the cabin was cold. But the sunlight washed the whole sky a milky blue. Everywhere, into the haze a hundred miles off, a crescendo of up-pointing mountains shivered and shook. A cliff fell away beneath us as we crossed the lip. The lake down at the base of it was oil-green. We passed over a glacier—blue ice nestled into a saddle. There was no chance to watch for game; the plunging land was life enough. It was a whole earth of mountains, beyond counting or guessing at, colored stark white and rock-brown. To live is to see, and although I was sweating against my stomach, I was irradiated. These were some of the finest minutes of my life.

The Mosque repeated the Sustut: a forest goosed with verdancy and curving lithely. Crossing the Mosque, we joined the valley of the Skeena, which, even at this remote upper end, is trenchantly troweled. In succession, short creeks arc off on either side, grassy and green, to the ponds at their heads. There are burns and green forest, burns and magnificent forest, everything washed in blue milk. Surging irregularly upward again, we squeezed over a new sequence of mountaintops onto the Duti River; then onto the Kluatantan; then to the headwaters of the Spatsizi. The Skeena's source valley was just on the west, shaped like a cereal spoon, underneath Gunanoot Mountain, and the Nass's was a skip beyond that. Then promptly beside us on the right, on the east, lay the Stikine's beginnings, with peaks the gray of volcanic ash and its source a sopping, unprepossessing valley too high to have trees, containing three or four oxided, winding ponds. Even the mountains that muscle together around the head of the Finlay seemed close and plain, a little southeast, as if we were seeing all the world at once. We rode an updraft over still another few barriers and twisted down the Spatsizi from near its head, past precipitous, green-colored, sawtoothed peaks that appeared to mount higher and higher, and over a maze of small muddy sloughs. In a side valley was Cold Fish Lake, quite incredibly high, right at shoulder-level among the peaks. Forest spread everywhere now. The shorelines were gracefully indented, and we raced in low over most of the length of the lake, alighting at the last moment, as if we were going to shoot up on shore. Instead of a banging on the belly of the plane, this time there was a pretty whir-flutter of water and air, like the sound a flock of ducks makes when it lands. The lake, in fact, was full of ducks; when we landed they took off.

On the dock two mild Englishmen in their sixties were waiting for us. We unloaded the crates without many words and we ate. In the cabin I'm in, a grizzly skin is pinned to the wall like a spread-eagled moth. I should probably note that I'm allergic to it.

[VII]

The
Spatsizi Country:
Jim Morgan

Yesterday, showers and fog. Today, shifting weather. Up here the blunt Arctic is never far; one lives on its sufferance like the villagers on the slopes of Vesuvius.

I've described Mr. Walker before: thin nose, long upper lip, oval, fragile forehead, fresh skin. After a public-school education he came to the New World as a buyer of grain for his family's business. When the Depression hit, he moved into the Bella Coola valley, five hundred miles to the south of us, to farm and to trap. A refined unleathery man, he must look less like a guide than a lot of his clients do. He's the gentle sort too, who is attracted to people who have an apparent weakness, so that my stutter endears me to him. But since he's an aspiring author, it's quite a trick getting anything out of him. He thinks that to tell me a story or two would be like drawing a map to a mine. Since part of the reason I'm with him, though, is because he had indicated that he was going to talk, he's embarrassed and apologetic also. He's a good conscientious man, a dangerous enthusiast and optimist who often entraps himself by the commitments he makes in advance, as now, when he hasn't enough of a crew for the crowd of customers who are coming next month. Being somewhat the same, I sympathize.

Mrs. Walker is a fitful, formidable woman best avoided, a Victoria lawyer's daughter whose twenty-six seasons in the bush have further stiffened her back. If no opposition is offered and if she's in a decent mood, she can be enjoyable, however. As with an American Brahmin, the simplest way to her esteem is by showing a taste for nature—friendship through flowers. We've been into the woods together, looking at larkspur and stonecrop, bluebells, chickweed, alyssum, saxifrage, cinquefoil, bedstraw, kinickiniks, columbine, forget-me-nots, anemones, gentians, phacelia, penstemons, lousewort, ragwort, arnica, twinflowers, and the alpine rose bush. She pointed out labrador tea, which the Indians brewed or else smoked, and the juicy mossberry which they chewed for thirst, and the soapberry that they beat to a froth and then sugared to eat as a tonic. All this profusion exists in a sample acre or so of currant bushes, junipers and lodgepole pine, while the lake alongside has lake trout up to twenty-five pounds.

Although I won't be able to do it again, I persuaded them to talk with me for a while last night in their cabin; I suppose it was partly the spirit of hospitality. I was after a sense of the homestead era, just as I was in Telegraph Creek. The Bella Coola River was less of a thoroughfare than the Stikine and remained virgin into the thirties. Shots with the Indians were still being exchanged, and an annual cooperative cattle drive took place from Anahim Lake across 250 miles of open range. It was a good place for waiting out the Depression. Nobody had any money, but everybody had plenty of food—apples, vegetables, salmon and moose. People rafted their hay crop across the river from the opposite fields and fished in earnest by rigging fish wheels. They wore flapping, homemade buckskin shoes, and the solitary old-timers up in the mountain meadows cooked an atrocious slop for themselves in the lard pail for supper and didn't come down more than twice a year, pulling the human language like a sticky taffy out of their mouths. A man would bring along a couple of cows to trade for flour and baking powder and tea and dried prunes. He'd have carved a flute to announce himself; he'd be blowing on that, and have flowers behind his ears and a crook swinging from his arm, and a shaggy dog trotting behind. If the storekeeper couldn't make change for the difference between the cows and the flour, he wrote out a money-order of his own which people honored for hundreds of miles, carried for years and endorsed to each other when the occasion arose.

Everybody had some kind of project going, whether it was a scheme to farm beaver or an experiment to plant clover and bluegrass up in a cirque. Others prospected, or maybe explored for the straightforward excitement of making a map, hiking out constantly and becoming remote and wordless as they encountered more and more country that nobody else had seen before. When airplanes were first heard of, one man began hollowing out a cottonwood tree in order to build his own (he'd already built everything else); he bought a propeller and engine to attach to it, until the aviation commission stepped in. Another man was a Seventh Day Adventist who locked his daughters in the attic whenever a stranger called. Once they were nubile, he thought they ought to be worth some money. He priced them at $1000 each and succeeded in getting it. The oldest went into the bush with her husband for ten years, producing three children before she came out. Then she was afraid to appear, lest her relatives see how delicate and pale her babies were, though of course they weren't that at all except by comparison with the Indian children they had been with. When she did emerge, it was 1940 and the new mail truck happened to be parked at the Walkers' house. When they looked out the window, this lady and her three tots were crawling on their hands and knees, peering between the wheels.

As in Telegraph Creek, marriage was a momentous problem. A fellow wrote to England for one of two sisters to come to him, but when he went to Vancouver to meet her train the wrong one stepped off. There wasn't the money to send her back, so he married her, never entirely sure *which* of them he had really asked for.

Once again, the portrait is of a champagne exuberance in the air for a while, the gaiety of a brand-new country and of forthright types sifting through, already in their thirties as a rule, confident, formed. The Walkers cleared a plot about fifty miles in from the sea, in order to escape the worst winter drenchings and yet be sheltered from the interior cold. They stump-farmed and boarded hunters. The valley walls went up eight thousand feet, but it was a spot with abundant sun which the Indians had used for rest cures, where warriors and sickly youngsters had convalesced. The original settlers, living on the edge of a boundlessness as they did, were a peppy Columbus-like crew instead of a collection of Tugboat Annies. But since no gold rushes occurred to flush the valley with new blood, it turned hillbilly soon; Walker speaks of those abrupt, eight thousand-foot walls shutting the place in.

Whatever the personal squabbles were, he and his wife pulled up stakes in 1948, selling their place for a song. As he says, the first settler never makes any money. It's the third or fourth owner of a piece of property who does. More Indians than whites turned out to wave them off, and with the help of two Indian boys they drove their herd of horses over a stitching of obscured trails clear to here, taking most of the summer to do it and using old maps and notes from surveyors' journals, frequently guessing their way along for many miles. It was an epic trip, and naturally, like the trips over the Telegraph Trail which Armel Philippon and Alec McPhee described to me, it was a zenith for him personally. It's worth money too, as he says, so although I spread out the relevant maps as temptingly as I could, he wouldn't go into any of it. Mrs. Walker was still less inclined to talk, not having been in favor of my visit to begin with.

They mention Caribou Hide in terms curiously split. In contrast to the litter and drunkenness of Eddontenajon, it was a village spotlessly clean and self-sufficient. No store tins or wrappings in front of the huts, no welfare payments corrupting the soul. It seems a shame to them that the Indians weren't left to themselves with their crafts and skills and their pride and their honesty, rather than being decked out as inferior white men. On the other hand, two old women had died of malnutrition shortly before. The entire village was flattened down in a semistarved state, although the Walkers had passed plenty of tracks of game hardly a day's ride behind. Indians give up quickly, they say. Indians haven't the resolution, the imaginative force of a white man; they just lie down and die.

Samuel Black, writing in his journal in 1824 about the precursor village to Caribou Hide, said somewhat the same thing, as a matter of fact. He wasn't finding much game himself, but he noticed a distressing limp fatalism in the Indians of the area, who were facing starvation. They weren't numb senseless stoics, by any means. They were wretched and worried enough, but if there was any determined resolve to survive, it was more likely the man would lie in his tent motionless, conserving his energies to the very last on the chance that an animal would stray down the trail, than that he'd go out and hunt relentlessly. This was perhaps only partly an attitude of "God's will." We whites, after all, have a penchant for forced marches and the like because we believe we have somewhere to go. We have outposts to reach and cities beyond them, whereas the Indian was starving at home. Black also wrote absorbingly about *missing:* how one could starve when surrounded by game just by *missing*, going out and getting a shot and then missing. He recognized that mental factors might apply, that one presumably could court death in this way, and he observed that the Indians seemed even more susceptible to such quirks of the mind than the white roustabouts of his party. It was rather jittery waiting for meat when he felt that his hunters were missing compulsively.

But he gave everybody a new lease on life. The tiny village packed up, babies and ladies and all, and accompanied him north for two or three lyrical days, through a country composed of stony narrow defiles of fir and buckbrush, with troops of groundhogs whistling on both sides of them. The groundhogs had never seen an enemy before except wolves and lynx, so that whenever the travelers stopped to relax and smoke and loll in the brush, talking in pidgin Cree, they harvested baskets of groundhogs like fish from the burrows around by setting nooses—a chorus of other groundhogs whistling meanwhile, chaffing them. Black, who had been something of a desperado earlier in life, a ruminative Blackbeard type, unbuttoned and unwound with the venerable Sikanni chief as he rarely did. At the Chukachida, finally, the going got impossibly rugged and swampy again and the Indians gradually dropped out; only the whites pushed ahead. They didn't turn back till the Turnagain River, where they wrote the date and Black's name on a tree and, giving up on their aims, headed south for the Peace River system and home.

The Caribou Hiders packed up and followed the Walkers too, if not quite as instantaneously. Camping at Cold Fish Lake, they hunted with revived conviction, starting to sweep the hills of game. Since Walker was in the game business, it was partly in order to get rid of them for his sake that the government resettled the band at Telegraph Creek. Those were lovely green years, when in effect the land was handed over to him and the men of the band gained regular summer employment in exchange; he stuck conscientiously to the obligation, probably sensing it more than they did. He and Alec Jack would ride out on exploratory sallies. Alec Jack told him the Indian names for the dominating massifs and led him into the various hideaway basins the villagers knew of, where they expected the game to be. The exploring itself was a long task, and the present dislike the villagers are showing for him is especially baffling because they did genuinely like him then. He would bail them out of debt at the Hudson's Bay Store every spring, and Alec Jack still keeps a photograph of Walker beside his kitchen table; yet, like most of the others this year, he won't work for him. It's a familiar story from other colonies where less gentle people were involved on either side. The Walkers aren't wrong to suppose they were popular once, but they're unable to realize the ambivalence of their own reactions. Boys remain "boys" a very long time—so long in fact that now that the highway has come they've suddenly lost all their men; they're left with a bunch of untrained youngsters for guides who truly are boys. More than they would have in the old days, I'm sure, they make fun of the Indians to me: of their pronunciation of English, as if they were Chinamen, of their darkie-like changeableness, their limber-limbed promiscuity, of the hours they choose to knock on the door, the way they turn up to work without adequate clothes, the candy they want, the queries they have.

We all eat at a single table with hearty loud ease-making efforts from the Walkers' end and a sobersides silence from the two rows of Indians. There's an "art" to handling Indians, supposedly, of course. They're "children" and yet not children at all. They're trusting before they're resentful, but once they're resentful the cause is lost. From early on, they're trained to spot movement across a great distance, so that for catching sight of an animal they're like nobody else. They have an intuitive brilliance at hunting, but not the tenacity or the discipline that they should have. They may locate a trophy ram that nobody else could have found, and then lose him because

[1 6 4]

of not taking the sort of dogged delight a white man does in battling a tactical problem. And as interested in animals as they are, they don't have a taste for logic, either; they don't study them, so that sometimes they're quite uninformed. For instance, cougars have materialized in this country lately during the summers, coming up the Nass and Skeena valleys from where the logging activity has begun. It's a new territory for them, sparse in the deer they eat, cold and snowy. It's a retreat; the old-timers told me they'd never seen them here. But Walker has stalked to within forty yards of one, guiding an archer client, who missed. The cat dashed up the mountainside, while coveys of ptarmigan exploded in regular progression ahead of it. An Indian, he thinks, would have seen the tracks or the animal itself and assumed it was only another lynx.

He speaks of them with a kind sympathy, however, which will be missing when the mines and the logging camps open up and a red-neck contempt replaces his mixture of feelings. Every morning he's on the radio attempting to recruit a crew. It's sad to hear. Both Walkers seem really to believe that their operation is finished now. They feel tired and old and keep trying to rouse themselves, remembering how they used to be. The friend who is staying with them, a wan fellow who went through three bouts with pneumonia last year, increases the *fin de siècle* atmosphere. His appearance would remind anyone of the statistics about bachelors dying young, and at tea he enumerates to me the coincidences of life which have irredeemably shaped it for him.

Hunting is changing, besides. The guides who by government assignment control the site of Caribou Hide have airlifted in a jeep to facilitate things. Other guides employ helicopters, skipping across the mountaintops and touching down if they see a trophy. The practice of firing "simultaneously" with the client is growing also, to ensure that nobody misses. The kill, not the stalk, has become the central experience. The talk is about measurements; everybody wants to get into the record book. It used to be that the competition was between a man and his quarry. Now it's between man and man. People don't write and ask, "Do you have sheep and bear?" They want to know if Walker thinks he may have a sheep with a fifty-inch curl somewhere in his area. And as money spreads and more is expected of every vacation, people drop in for a quick week's shooting, instead of the old-fashioned sportsman's leisurely month, the fellow who tented and roamed at a dignified pace, enjoying the open air, seeing three dozen acceptable heads before picking out one to stalk and to kill. The delight of a hunt should be the stalk. The kill only puts a period to it, Walker says. The kill gives it a necessary point but adds nothing. Much mention is made of camera hunting, but the customer who can afford a big-game hunt isn't that good with a camera. He wants more, anyway; we all want more nowadays. Life is short and we all want much more. There are many more of us, and so, doubly, in order not to feel drowned, we each want more.

July 12, Tuesday:

The pleasure of fiddling with fire. A fire is air. Building a fire is based upon having a feeling for air. A boy named Paul, a sixth-grader next year, has taken a liking to me. He whistles like a whippoorwill as a signal of greeting and runs wherever he goes, bursting into a sprint. As a grandson of Dogan Dennis, he is Bear Lake Billy's great-grandson.

The horses were shod today and Mrs. Walker apportioned supplies for the hunting caches. Her husband was patching spark holes in the tents and repairing the generator which powers his radio. He's an extraordinary man, indeed a visionary, who still stakes himself lovely plots of land wherever he goes. (If it happens to be on their territory, his rival guides pull the stakes out when they find them and send a protest to Victoria.) He's a shy, charitable, interested man close up, more likable than at a distance with his hiring problems and his jealousy of his competitors, whereas bold Mrs. Walker is more likable at a distance than at close range. I'm afraid that I'm not doing justice to him. It's a peculiarity of mine that unless I like somebody considerably, I'm liable to lavish whatever fairness I have on people who are decidedly different from me, like Frank Pete or Steele Hyland, whom I have nothing in common with. Besides, as I mentioned, Walker skips away when he sees me coming, as if the map to a gold mine were printed across the front of his shirt.

The cabins and tents are set in front of a grassy, flattened-off mountain where the caribou gather for love play in the fall, hundreds of them in sight at a time. Across the lake a series of rhythmic high ridges and draws leads into a complex massif called Nation Peak, where the clouds stir about. Everything is immediate and close, timberline being only five hundred feet up. Through the spotting scope we've been watching nine goats browse on a steep slope. Above them are several specks in the snow which are probably goats lying down where the flies will leave them alone. The basins where Walker and Alec Jack explored fifteen years ago lie behind. They'd climb and stumble upon thirty-eight, thirty-three, forty-one Stone sheep rams convocating together in a hammock-shaped cirque and get that quizzical innocents' stare which is only seen once.

I walked up the caribou mountain through an old burn, with the willows and aspen head-high and lupine and yarrow and fireweed growing. A few spruce were left alive on knolls and in hollows which the fire skipped by. From the lake, the line of mountains across the way looked like a row of elephants' backsides, but when I got higher they mounted and took more imposing forms, less rounded and climbing more, linking the valleys hanging between them with the valley under the principal peak. The valley of Cold Fish Lake itself is headless, emptying at one end into the Spatsizi and at the other end into another tributary of the Stikine. The winter trail from Caribou Hide, which the Indians ran with dog sleds, went along the bottom of it on the ice, while the summer trail was up on the high plateau I was climbing toward, where the walking wasn't obstructed by brush.

It was hot. The game was napping. I went down into the forest again, picking out numerous tracks of moose. A moose's two toes are straighter than a caribou's, like two half moons joined. A caribou's foot, in order to aid him in snow, bows out like two quarter moons. In a couple of other places I found bear tracks in the mud, smudged over, and also a short series of wolf tracks, which are bigger than a coyote's and longer in the foot than a cougar's or lynx's.

An enormous added dimension is given a country by its game—to watch for a file of caribou weaving on the skyline (six were seen this morning) and to tremble for grizzly. No combination of stunning scenery can make up for its loss. Of course we pacifists who go into the woods without guns owe our safety to those who don't. It wasn't long ago that an English Indian agent named Harper Reed and one companion encountered what he estimated as 150 wolves on Cold Fish Lake. The wolves, in one of the winter assemblies they hold, were engaged in herding moose, but they curled round in a sickle-shaped line to face him instead and began to press in, like Khartoum. He was terribly pleased.

I sunned for a while on a bluff. A perfect reflection of the opposite mountains was combed into the lake. The moss was so deep that my elbows and knees sank in a foot. Though most of the trees were white spruce, they looked like the gamut of evergreens because the raw soil withers them before they grow very large. The roots grope out of the ground; the needles change. I watched a blue grouse peck about. A caribou swam across the lake, buoyant and tireless all the way. She was a pretty bleached tan with two-pronged antlers in velvet, and she splashed in the shallows like a filly, muzzling the bugs off her rear. The animals all get elated, sleeping, waking irregularly when the days are as lush and long as this. They have more noddling about to do than they can find time for. It must be particularly joyful for a flustery creature like a caribou. Vulnerable animals that they are, they're soon to die. When I lived in Hazelton the last ones there were being killed. The previous winter some Tsimshians, out for a weekend, had discovered a remnant band of sixteen in deep snow and killed them all. Caribou give up the ghost very quickly, as if suddenly coming unstrung. Whether shot or speared, they spill out their blood lavishly, unlike goats and sheep, who bleed and die with great reluctance. When I lived on the Clearwater River, which is further south, they were already remembered as a sort of a vanished prize. Because of the tall flair of their carriage and their superb, airy antlers, they'd been the biggest game. Their herds had defined the wilderness, moving along, eating the drooping black lichen on the low limbs of the trees. As a matter of fact, one settler told me that he had chosen the valley for its caribou. He was hiking through looking for ground to homestead when he climbed a side ridge and caught sight of a band of twenty-two in the meadows on top. Like most such people, he was no youngster then, but watching them, he felt as though he had never been so happy or certain about a decision before. And now he was surrounded by strawberry fields and cream-giving cows. He lived in a cabin floored with halved logs that the whole valley held dances on, and he had a housekeeper caring for him, so the loss of the caribou was small next to that. Because of the logging, even the lichens were gone. He was smiling, not tolling a bell, but he was remembering the talk—how silly and giddy caribou are, how simple to kill, how they mill and fool and join the pack mules, how they won't run away if you raise your arm until they know why you are raising your arm. I've been hearing the same. It's like a bunch of buffalo hunters talking about their staple game, or the malicious gossip about the Indians at Eddontenajon. When it stops the herds will be gone and the Indian settlement will have become a museum piece.

A ring appeared around the sun, meaning rain. When the ring is around the moon, they say you can tell how many days the rain will hold off by counting the stars inside the ring.

About ten, as the sun set, the lake turned to mercury and the mountains acquired stately proportions. The Walkers were working at building their umpteenth cabin, nailing purlins to the rafters. They intend it to be a "hideout," off by itself on a pretty cove, as opposed to the main camp on the lake and the overnight cabin at the opposite end or the camps that they keep at Hyland Post and Eddontenajon. Goodness knows how many more they built at Bella Coola before they even arrived in the north. And yet as they kibbitz each other they might be putting a wing on a house in Bryn Mawr. It's not the people who are so different here, it's the events, the mode of living, a most ancient mode going back to when the Greeks landed in Sicily or the Danes settled in Iceland. Each mode of living is a choice, and so we have one less choice now.

JULY 13, WEDNESDAY:

SCOOTED DOWN THE SPATSIZI to Hyland Post today by plane, the lazy man's way. I flew with Danny Bereza again, the mail-run man who originally took me from Telegraph Creek to Eddontenajon. He's a chattery, prim, preoccupied guy, and he popped through a pass from nowhere, materializing magically over Cold Fish Lake. The noise was stifled in drizzle and fog. The plane seemed to pause in the air, the size of a dragonfly against the mountain, before plumping down. Bereza was stuffed up with a cold and the plane was crammed to the roof with canned goods, fertilizer, horseshoes, lick salt, blasting powder, though this was only one errand of many for him. He expected to work twelve hours by nightfall and to fly something like nine hundred miles. My first feeling when we shook hands was pity. The sky was so soupy that although maybe today he'd be lucky and find enough holes to complete his trips, it was hard to imagine him getting through the rest of the summer. Once we were up in the air, however, the view was different. For every cloud there was a hole, at least at our level, and some of the clouds were no worse than fogged glasses to look through. In such extravagant country a plane's speed seems slow. We jiggled along as if we were sitting in a simulating machine, hitching up, hitching down, when the wind abused us. These headwater valleys tip and slide in a primitive fashion. Down is where they're going, but not very efficiently. They aren't canyons; they're rudimentary scoops between heights of ground. You look across at the rock strata above timberline and at the terraced, sparse forest below, and the ponds, sloughs, myriad streams and river braidings straight below, and part of the world is very wet and part very dry. Being so close to the head of the Spatsizi, we could see upriver to the last curve. The river wound like a willowing, picture-book road climbing to a castle, and it seemed as though all the world's secrets were hoarded just there, just beyond, just out of sight in those mountainous rocks. The impulse was not as much to go right away and see and gloat as it was to delight in being so near. Thus it is that a man who has become a millionaire overnight first balances his checkbook in the morning with his old funds and pays his phone bill.

I had too many sights going by. The valley enlarged; the mountains flattened into broad buttes which were spaced at leisurely intervals. We passed over chains of minute natural meadows in the waterlogged, spraddled-out forest. I was watching, absorbed, when directly ahead a parrot-green oblong presented itself. It was a great surprise, a glorious swank little festival rip in the forest, as green as a banner. It was the green of new timothy hay, fervid and strident and hectic and loud. I could hardly stay in the plane. It was like a piece of green carpet; I thought I could simply step down. The river was the only place to land, so we banked down onto a bumpy slim strip between abrupt bends. The braking action of the current made it possible for us to land there, but we struggled to taxi upriver against it and even to hold our own. Finally we managed to park in a tiny slough that was narrower than the wingspread of the plane, and two people scrambled down to where we were. One was a vacationing high-school boy named Rick Milburn, and the other a wolfer and explorer, fifty-six, bearing the appropriately anonymous name of Jim Morgan, he being the last of a breed. An Indian boy seventeen, Jim Abou, had flown in with me to join them.

I was immediately taken with Morgan. He's a slender, abstracted, slightly built man with nothing to say at all. He's a gazer. He might be watching the woods or he might be watching motes dance in the air. He looks frail and tenacious; he looks like Walter Huston and Gabby Hayes combined and brought real. Or if you could plug a history book into an electrical socket in order to bring the illustrations to life, he would be one.

Danny Bereza roared off for his next rendezvous in a spray of rainbows, barely evading the wall of trees. Since he works with mineral geologists principally, he doesn't say where he flies. We carried the sacks of goods up to the cabins and supped on moosemeat and strawberry foam, a pudding of Milburn's that failed. During the evening I hurried about, seeing where I was, a horse-kick of happiness going inside. It was another gleeful arrival for me. It seemed like the finest arrival of all, it seemed as if this were the center of things. The chipmunks were climbing the dandelions and eating the seeds in the summer's full frenzy—the sun wouldn't set—chittering, eyeing me appraisingly. The woodpile bulked bigger than the cabins did. The fences were so new that the poles still had more bark on them than some of the trees—the traditional first fence, the snake fence, which squanders the cleared trees in a zigzag course end to end and atop one another like clasped fingers, but standing eight feet high.

The river, which rises or falls according to whether the sun is shining on the snowfields, ran too fast and muddy for the trout to be able to see as they fed, so they swam into our little plane-parking slough. With a stick, a short bit of line on the end of the stick and a tatter of moose at the end of the line, I caught two Dolly Varden and two Arctic grayling. The dollies are delicate, spotted, cannibal fish; the grayling are hefty, long-finned fellows, more bluff and gregarious. Then at eleven o'clock Morgan set fire to the outhouse, since it had gotten chock full in the course of the year. It blazed up impassionedly above the river as if the fire relished its fuel, a regular fanfare announcing our presence to the creatures around. A crow would need to fly for a hundred and fifty miles to reach any other clearing like this.

JULY 14, THURSDAY:

I WENT FOR A walk in the morning along the creek which ascends behind Hyland Post. The path is a modest game trail between tumbled windfalls, both on the ground and overhead in the form of crossed swords that you duck through. The moss everywhere is a triple-mattress bed sprinkled with cones and ground pine. Higher up, I came to some breaks in the forest with dry forageable grass, and also a soaking fern bog full of black and red birds and fed by a spring, the ferns growing over my head. The mountain face was a blunt backdrop. The mosquitoes and biting flies settled on me to stay, being accustomed to animals that can't slap, but they were too numerous to slap anyway. White tufts of caribou hair had snagged on the trees. There were lots of hoof marks cut in the moss and piles of droppings left from the months when the caribou had wintered at close quarters here, accompanied by wolf-family turds. I was forever peering up at meadows I hadn't the energy to reach. The caribou and wolves mostly range high in this midsummer period, but wherever I crossed any mud I saw fresh moose and coyote tracks, or a dead log a bear had smashed open, looking for grubs. It always takes me a while in grizzly country to get over my fear of grizzlies, and this was the real Red Riding Hood forest, the trees topsy-turvy, fighting for sun, the ground rank and murky with primeval plants. The boulders and pines were affected with giantism; the ungainly terrain traveled in heaves; the creek caromed and plummeted too crudely to have carved a bed—it fell through a series of gashes. Each ascent snicked a snip off my heart and left me still looking up at a mountain wall with another meadow showing on top. The deadfalls that were caught on the living trees creaked in the breeze. A cloud that resembled swirling steam swallowed a clump of trees above me.

I saw a deer, of all scarce and unlikely things, bounding to keep me in sight as it fled. It looked like a jackrabbit in the supersized landscape, compared with the animals I was anticipating. But its feminine grace gave it importance. People here have a sheltering feeling for deer; they're so helpless after a snow, like conies before the wolves. They will shoot a moose for meat instead, although standards got rather general for the old-timers who were out in the bush alone. When somebody did shoot a doe, seeing that fawn-skinned, small womanly body stretched on the ground, he must have swarmed over her with his knees and hands and practically made it with her then and there. Maybe not. One of the contrasts I've noticed between the actual wilderness and the wilderness which writers incorporate into their books is the absence of sadism here. Sadistic images seem to abound in wilderness books, and yet all these people whom I've been meeting are quite free of that. With few exceptions, there's hardly a whiff as they talk.

Returning at noon, I had to cross a field of buckbrush which reached to my chest and head. It's so tough it's almost impenetrable, and is sometimes called hardtack by ranchers because of its poor food value. The leaves turn a brilliant red in September and are cup-shaped, so that they hold a rainfall and drench anybody who walks through. I was remembering Cliff Adams' experience in this same field two years ago, when he was chased by a mother grizzly. He was working with a friend who was carrying the rifle they'd brought along, but who wasn't within sight or hearing. He kept yelling, "Shoot the damn bear! Shoot the damn bear!" as he ran for his life, and from the distance he'd hear that Commonwealth query, "Eh? Eh?" He kept turning sharply as though he were trying to escape a bull. The mother broke off the pursuit, however, and went back to her cubs. When she did, conservationist that he is, he started to yell to his friend, "*Don't* shoot the bear! *Don't* shoot the bear!" Just at that moment the man caught sight of her at last. BANG. (Missed.)

I'm the type who in the army wore combat boots with my civilian clothes on weekends, but when I was on duty I had gotten myself the sort of a job for which I wore ordinary business shoes. This was a combat-boot crossing, though.

I finally got to the Spatsizi, which was like home. It swings briskly by the three cabins, bending symmetrically out of view in either direction as soon as it can, as if to say, get your glimpse, this is all you will see. It's already a fuliginous rich yellow-brown, and from forty to sixty yards wide, like a not very miniaturized Stikine. The ducks use it for a flyway, hurtling below the treetops at tremendous speed. A Canada goose flew by, having come up from heaven knows where, Acapulco last spring? And in the midst of his rocketing, he saw me from the corner of his eye. He stopped flying—he nearly collapsed in midair from surprise—and emitted a queer, flabbergasted *awp*, as if he were thinking, *Here?*

JULY 15, FRIDAY:

THE AIR MATTRESS IS an ingenious invention by which one sleeps on one's own hot breath. One blows it up at the end of the day. The idea causes me funny dreams, as the bells of the horses do when they graze around the cabin at night. Church bells, buoy bells. Or during the day you look out and see the window completely blocked up by a brawny brown body. It's there like the side of a ship. The ground seems to slide slightly to the side; you feel that you live in a Lilliput house. The horses keep us company for their own entertainment, because the fences are only drift fences, fences which suggest to a horse that he stay where he is, but which eventually end, so that if he insists, he can go around. Morgan's hours are such that I'm short on sleep. He's up with the morning sun cooking hotcakes with cowboy music on. Rick Milburn, who's officially the cook, is unable to get up quite at that hour. He was a cook in the Boy Scouts last year and has written on his hat, "Eat if you dare." It's a broad-brimmed Mountie's hat and reminds me of the summer of 1953 when I fought forest fires in California in a First World War campaign hat and a Second World War battle jacket. Rick is a chubby, effective fellow, and Jim Abou is also a good worker. He has a long, unformed Tahltan face with drooping Japanese eyes. He wears a crew cut, a cowboy's jean jacket, and a hat with the brim tied into the proper shape. He saunters. Scabbard and all, he carries his rifle everywhere because his father was chased by a bear in these woods last spring. It chewed up his father's hat.

"If you throw your hat at a grizzly, of course he's going to tear it up," says Morgan, who never carries a gun, whose one fear appears to be death itself—death working out from inside the body. He's afraid of his cough at breakfast, but he toils fourteen hours in the sun, ripping the buckbrush out, with that judicious delight that hangs exactly between laughter and tears. The battery which brings us our cowboy music is the tractor battery, in fact, and about the time he is re-attaching it, I am brushing my teeth, rocking on my heels, standing on the edge of the low river bluff.

Across the river an aspen and lodgepole pine forest spreads spaciously to two mounded, leveled-down mountains with grassy green tops. A wide area is opened up. Several streams tributary to the Stikine join together nearby, and scattered along their valleys are swales of the natural bunch grass, a grass that grows only a few inches high and cures uncut in the sun to a kind of hay which is not very nourishing, but nourishing enough. This wideness, these swales, are why we're right here. Horses don't browse off the trees as moose and deer do, but they are able to paw down through as much as a couple of feet of snow in order to eat. No matter where they may have been brought from, they put on a sufficient coat to survive the winter temperatures, if they are healthy and grown. If the wolves chase them and test them a bit, just as they test the caribou bands, they survive that too. The wolves are simply seeing how they run, who is sick, who is shaky and lame, like a farmer planning his butchering. So the key to whether they live until spring is whether they are able to feed: abundant grass, a shallow snowfall.

During the twenties Steele Hyland's father heard about the special beneficence of these valleys in regard to snowfall from the Caribou Hiders, who passed back and forth. Since the wintering range at Telegraph Creek itself had been preempted by the Callbreaths and others, he was sending his horses north at the time on the Telegraph Trail for more than one hundred miles to an open spot now marked on the map as Hyland Lake. It was all right except that it lay at a grueling altitude, exposed to the storms, and his herd was outgrowing the limited grass. He took his wranglers' advice and sent the whole bunch of them east instead to the Spatsizi, twice as far. The Caribou Hiders were glad, since they could trade in their own neighborhood, and the place was named Hyland Post. But shortly afterwards, it was abandoned because of a silver thaw that killed a lot of the horses. A silver thaw occurs if a warm maritime wind blows in the middle of winter, melting the top layer of snow—a Chinook wind, it is called. It may feel as pleasant as spring, but the water, with nowhere to run, refreezes disastrously as ice, which defeats the horses in their pawing when the weather reverts to winter again. Mr. Walker, who took over the land later by paying the back taxes, is having Morgan plant timothy in order to keep a hay crop.

Last night, it turns out, some of the horses which are going to be needed for the hunting season swam the river and made their way up the opposite bank for five miles or so. They reached the Dawson, a hasty boulder-bed creek that swarms in in several fingers like the front of a narrow flood from the south. They roamed up the scrubby valley of the Dawson into the choppy interior country behind and above: four stallions, two mares and two colts, some shod, some unshod, some only shod on their front feet. We went after them in the boat in the midday heat, tying up at every bend in the river so that Morgan could look for a sign. They had split into two groups, complicating the search, and had left the riverbank and come back again. He read the tracks and touched the broken blades of grass to see how much time had elapsed since they'd passed. There was every kind of track, otter, muskrat, coyote and moose, as well as a cluster of washtub-sized holes in the bank where a grizzly had dug for roots. We met three otters, and the squirrels we saw were eating mushrooms, sitting up, holding them in their paws like big toasted buns—mushrooms that were bigger than they were. We discovered a dried moose leg wedged into the crotch of a tree where the moose years ago had caught it and broken it. He had died and been eaten, everything but the leg.

On the Dawson we couldn't use the boat any more. We waded and hopped. It was all rather like *The Wizard of Oz*, unimaginable, jungly, fantastic country that had its own logic and that, except perhaps for a man named Dawson or an occasional Indian like Alec Jack, we were the first human beings to see. We watched the ridge tops; we looked into the glades with their gray-green foliage; we stepped round the litter of boulders in the bed of the creek. The valley was so new and strange that I wasn't even particularly nervous. It seemed that if we met a bear he would not take exception to us, but would go on about his business wrapped in motives and notions unknown to us, like the streetsweeper humped over his broom one meets at dawn in a foreign city.

Evidently the horses were headed for the blue sky itself—for the wild-flower meadows way in and back, on the shelves of mountains we could hardly make out. As happy as everyone was, Morgan and I decided to let the two kids make the walk. He wanted to do other work and I was lazy.

We did indulge in another bouncing boat ride, however. The Spatsizi is too young to have cut out a proper channel, but drives along, perpetually overrunning its banks, sometimes in regular corrugations of current like frost heaves on a road, and sometimes in flat dizzy whorls, or a surface composed of a thousand popping points. It hops over the bigger rocks, forming glassy slick nubbles, or else reverses its engines, boiling and bumping backwards for several feet. The skiff is very narrow, powered by an outboard motor and built like a tapering surfboard to skim. Morgan steers standing up in the rapids to see as much as he can. He's supremely experienced, easing and skidding between the snags and sandbars, his face pursed like a persimmon, and a riverman's twelve-foot pole in his free hand. He's a small-chinned man with an unassertive nose, a large upper lip, and curly hair snipped inexpertly. He looks like a canny country boy, except for his overall frailty and the fact that he never moves abruptly.

Since the Caribou Hiders didn't go in for canoeing much and the gold rush crowd considered the upper Stikine not navigable, he is probably the only man who has ever explored the river to its source—until it simply hasn't enough water to float a boat—as well as these far-reaching tributaries. But he hasn't been on the lower river at all, just as the rivermen at Telegraph Creek—Gus Adamson, Wriglesworth and the McPhees—have never laid eyes on what we are seeing. Working for the Forestry Branch, he's been employed quite precisely as an explorer, that galvanic word. In fact, that's why he is here working for Walker. Last year, when he had finished exploring the unsurveyed parts of the Stikine, they had nowhere else that was as raw to send him, so he wanted to stay on the scene. He didn't try to involve himself in writing the reports or drawing the maps. He was the technician; he was the guy who went through first. He says he would go out alone for a week at a time, preferring as a matter of safety to be alone on his first passage through the stretch of the river he had set for himself, and after solving the riddles and scouting a way around any emergency situations that might be presented and seeing what there was to see, he would call on the radio for a ranger to come in by plane and would take him and show him what he had covered.

He is what he does. He's a difficult man to convey on paper because he's got nothing to say for himself. He's like Willie Campbell. He's the very best, the obscure common hero. He's the man you want to see mountains named after, and yet he leaves it at that, he's antidramatic. Answering my questions is not even much of a chore for him because he doesn't connect up with them; he lives on a wave length of silence. When we're in the skiff, he drinks from his hat brim, dipping it in the river, and he moves through the muskeg and brush using none of my lunging motions, but with small ministeps. He splits firewood with a few quiet taps with one hand, holding the axe head. He keeps a blaze in the cook stove throughout the day, though our weather is up in the eighties, and he also wears long underwear: let the temperature change instead of him. He holds up his pants with suspenders. In one shirt pocket he carries his cigarette papers and in the other his bug repellent, which, like most old-timers, he seldom takes out. He has the same clear, extraordinary eyes as Armel Philippon and Alec McPhee, only more so. When these touch something they light on it. It's not that they're big; it's that they're wide. They've seen nothing they couldn't look at, and this not, I think, from innocence but rather because of all they have seen. Nobody has seen the whole world, but this is the quality of equilibrium with what one has seen. Of course a city man might need to go about with a half squint, if only to keep the soot out of his eyes. Morgan isn't a smiler. Like Creyke, like Wriglesworth and Roy Call-breath and Jack Lee, he's got swollen black lips that look as if they had been chapped for so many years that they're almost impossible to adjust in any comfortable way. It's hard enough opening and closing them, let alone trying to smile, and yet without moving his mouth, he's another blithe man.

We lunched sumptuously by ourselves on trout crumbed in cornmeal, and hot cakes with honey. I dug out some air photo maps of the upper one hundred miles of the Stikine so that

Morgan would talk. He did, just as dutifully as if I were a forestry official. He says there are two bad sections, one where the river suddenly is full of boulders as big as a house on every side which must be dodged somehow as the boat shoots along. The other is the canyon at Beggarlay Creek. In a narrow rock gorge which the photos don't show, a great whirlpool has formed. He shipped two barrels of water spinning around, and for a time he thought sure he would swamp and drown. Otherwise, he maneuvered past plenty of riffles, but had no enormous emergencies. He says jokingly that when they finally log in these parts, the sawmill people will be able to dispense with the peeler. If they just float the logs down the river the bark will be nicely stripped off.

While we ate I plugged away at him to make him describe the country itself. It's plateau and muskeg mostly, from what he said, with pretty sidehills, and mountains up on the tributaries. The rivers which entered on the right as he went down the Stikine were invariably clear-water rivers, while the rivers entering on the left, such as the Spatsizi, were turbid. The Chukachida and Pitman, both clear-water rivers, were navigable for a very good distance, fifteen or twenty miles. The Chukachida was deep and crooked and the Pitman was shallow and straight. On both, as he bobbed upstream slowly, huge, oversized moose were loafing along the bank—two or three dozen a day—which didn't even get up as he passed. Numbers of goats were down on the banks eating the mineralized mud, and they too merely looked at him, not so much curious as unafraid. None of the animals ran except the wolves and bears. By contrast, they were immediately cautious, though he thinks it was the sound of his motor which scared them off. He likes moosemeat better than goat, but he shot goat to eat because a moose would have been too much for him to eat by himself, and the meat would have gone to waste. Similarly, you don't get the discoverer's orgy stories from him that I've heard in the south, where a man in a quick hour's fishing hauls eighty-six trout from a single hole. As if he were bearing in mind that he was about the last of the discoverers, he caught his breakfast and stopped.

A few months ago Morgan visited Caribou Hide.* He says that the houses still have their roofs except where some tarpaper has blown off. Appropriately, he's been given this whole spread of territory as a trapline. It has lots of fisher, which are becoming extinct elsewhere, and lynx and otter, but not so many of the traditional furs like marten and mink. In just five weeks in the spring he trapped fifty-three beaver, selling them for $13.50 apiece, which is between the price for the skin of a kit and the price of a big "blanket" beaver measuring three feet by three. He doesn't generally bother with dogs and a sled, he goes on his snowshoes alone, because the country he trapped as a youngster was too steep to get into any other way and there weren't many moose for dog feed. He's prospected at various times too, and on the Stikine he found some intriguing bars that gave a good color when panned, where he wants to go back. When he was young, he hunted for bounty. He used to go out on the frozen lakes, pretending to be wounded, and flop around in the snow as the wolves gathered, to entice them near. More lately, the government has provided him with poisons and a plane. In a couple of winters he bountied something like two hundred wolf scalps, "until nobody else could make wages at it." The rivers and lakes become highways once they freeze, and he'd fly over watching for tracks and for kills. If there were tracks but no kill, he would land and drag a spruce to the middle of the lake and scatter his poisoned scraps there, because the wolves would be drawn to that. Everything died that touched the meat, even the chickadees, so he didn't like the work. The dead wolves froze solid. Since the hides are worth only $5 or $6, he didn't skin them, just took the scalps.

---

* In 1968 I myself spent a week near the Chukachida and the Toodoggone rivers. It was black-and-white country, very stark, with a few ephemeral caribou skittering through. But that is a subject for another book.

Like wolves, a wolfer himself is a sort of epitome, and Morgan, the last discoverer here, is also the last of the wolfers. Of course he has a brotherly fondness for wolves. The point is that there is a war on with them. If there wasn't a war they wouldn't be wolves.

I washed a pile of my clothes after lunch. He was out disking up the thickets of buckbrush. At tea I went after a biography from him, though it was slow going. He was born in Bella Coola. At one-and-a-half he was packed on the front of his mother's saddle for the three weeks' journey to Ootsa Lake, near what is now Smithers, but before Smithers came into existence. Growing up, he helped on his father's farm and would break and bridle-train horses for $5 a head, work he says you would get $100 for now. With his brothers-in-law, he trapped just about everywhere that his feet would take him. And he packed professionally on the supply trail from Ootsa to Bella Coola, which varied from winter to summer, like the trail that the Caribou Hiders used. In winter it took advantage of the iced-over waterways. In the summer it followed a high-ground, circuitous route that they called the Three Swims Trail because they had three unavoidable crossings to make. Worst and most circuitous of all was the One Swim Trail, for the late fall, when the rivers were not yet frozen but had become fearfully cold. When the original government surveyor for the area finally arrived, Morgan worked for him too. They climbed all the peaks, building rock cairns, and the surveyor, F. C. Swannell, would vanish for a week or more with only his transit and one sack of rice, a bag of prunes and a length of fishline. Morgan, a most unpresumptuous man, bided his time, raised a son who is now in the air force, and two married daughters, before he severed his ties and set out to do like Swannell.

A cow moose with her calf crossed the river in front of camp. She stayed protectively at its side in the rushing water, as black as a silhouette, humped like a horse which has been built up imposingly at the shoulders and reduced at the waist. At the other bank, when the calf paused in knee-deep water to congratulate itself, the cow strode ahead into the trees. While they were there, I had to remind myself that although they were neighbors, this wasn't a commonplace sight and I shouldn't keep on with the business at hand. But when they were gone, I couldn't believe it. I stopped everything and kept peering and staring, repicturing them, but seeing only the sweeping sea-net of trees.

Soon afterwards the horses showed up, having outdistanced Rick and Jim. They had started for camp on their own immediately upon seeing the boys, and they were sleek and shiny and wild after the torrential swim. They were tongueing each other's teats, chewing each other's manes, licking each other's cheeks, nipping each other's necks, going up on their hind legs and thumping down, and talking in squeaks and snickery nickers. They're snotty, small horses, smart little ironic barbarians, and a bunch of sexpots because nobody gelds them. They have long whiskers and bony blockheads—tough, bully heads, like bandit horses. All but the mare who had led them out went straight and unbidden into the corral. She stood in the gate teasing Morgan, feeling rebellious and clever.

We cruised upriver again to bring the two boys across. Everybody was in high humor now, and we stewed moosemeat and apples for supper. Morgan says beans are perfectly satisfactory and complete as a diet for him as long as he has the two kinds, white and brown. During the evening another heedless goose, flapping past, honked at us dubiously.

JULY 16, SATURDAY:

EVERY DAY WHILE I'VE been here a government plane has flown overhead en route to photograph new territory. It's a brave-looking plane in the fog, and since it's based at Steele Hyland's place, it has already crossed a lot of stiff country.

The Spatsizi Country: Jim Morgan

Along with the other advances, airplanes have made mapping easier than naming nowadays. Most of the features around the Stikine haven't found names as yet. Mountains of eight thousand feet are marked by a dot and some altitude numerals, or the names are bookish and stilted—Oxide Peak, Lunar Creek. The surveyors of forty years ago did much better because they were actually on the spot. Being men of good intentions, they were glad to incorporate Indian names on their maps when they knew them, or to commemorate a pair of white prospectors who were said to have wintered nearby—Harrymel Creek. Spatsizi means Red Goat, because the mountain goats rolled in the scree on the red sandstone bluffs overlooking the river until they turned red. Cold Fish Lake, according to Mr. Walker, had a tongue-twisting Indian name meaning High-Cold-Water-Lake-Where-There-Are-Fish. Sometimes the name was transcribed wrong, whether purposely or not, as in the case of the Toodoggone River, which instead of meaning "tough-slogging" was really called Two-Dogs-Gone River, the Indians at Eddontenajon say. Two dogs that somebody needed had run away there. Solomon Creek became merely the Salmon. Nipple Mountain became Knipple mountain back in Victoria, a minor change. It's an exceedingly accidental process, the naming of landforms and creeks; the name they end up with is only the last of a series. If no Indian accompanied the mapper, or if he wasn't unusually expressive, all the native names slipped through the sieve and were lost right then and there. Most of them were anyway, and so were the ones bestowed by the first sourdough in his gaiety to memorialize frights he had had—the freak storms, the goggly phantasmagorias he had seen, the encounter with a migrating horde of snowshoe hares, the fossil rhinoceros he found, the bear cub who toddled ahead of him on the trail wearing a red baseball cap on its head (a hallucination told me). At least the mapper spoke the same language as he did, but by the time the mapper appeared the fellow was already back home in Kansas City, deaf and dumb. Instead of

[1 8 5]

his memories, we are left with a name from across the coffee-pot—Gil Peak—or perhaps, if the mapper was imaginative, a mule's name—Big One-eyed Molly—or Uslika Lake.*

Rick and I rode into the bush this morning looking for a horse named Ace. The terrain is potted with grassy bowls an acre in size and fifty feet deep, and so many trees are laid on the ground in between that we needed to weave in 9s and 8s. We all reconnoitered downriver by boat in the afternoon, stopping and checking the clumps of footprints that we saw on the bank: always moose. It can't be repeated too often how incredibly new this river is. It might be compared to the Housatonic in size, but it simply isn't the Housatonic. It's stiff, bristly and resistant. The colors are primary colors. Everything is big and crude—the high sand cuts, the slivery, drift-piled islands, the blustery stands of spruce on the shore. The red sand cuts avalanche into the river as the river eats them. They get redder and the river gets redder. Demurely the Ross River joins, green from the glaciers it drains, and the waters hesitantly mix. There are hidden bars which the water accelerates toward. Hummocks of sliding water protrude. Snags snout upwards like alligators, muzzled in other debris. Morgan picks the middle, then the left side, standing up, cutting the motor to neutral to float over a riffle. A gravel creek comes in, which I call Gray Creek. The river swings on and on between scenes so concise and complete that they seem prepared. We've emerged from coasting in front of the mountains to a country of broken plateau with willow flats and hilly forest. As spectators, we continue smoothly, inevitably, around successive curves, finding other scenes set, as if just for our passage. At last the Stikine itself confronts us. It's about the same size as

---

* Captain John Smith, in mapping the part of North America which he called New England, named Cape Ann "Cape Tragabigzanda," after the Turkish pasha's daughter whose slave he had once been. Later, Charles I, for some reason, changed its name from "Tragabigzanda" to Cape Ann.

the Spatsizi, but *blue* and breezy up here, young and emotional, jiggled and studded and glittering. It's even swifter and more self-assured than the Spatsizi is, as exhilarating as a running sea, and, augmented, adds twenty more yards of width. The blue water brightens the sunshine. There are a hundred swallows flying and kingfishers, ouzels and other birds, even seagulls, mountains on one side and spacious forest everywhere else. The river goes along in major key. This is almost its beginning. There is no canyon yet. Life is easy for it; it's the young champion conquering day by day.

Ace was grazing close to the junction in a veldlike field of scrub that rose above our heads. We found his hoof prints in the waterside clay. Having ventured where hardly a horse had been before, and seeing us still able to trace him, he knew that there was no point in running. He went on nibbling flower heads, watching to be sure we were who we presumed to be. He trotted to the proffered oats, foolish and friendly—only allowing for his pride. The bargain was kept; after haltering him Morgan rubbed him affectionately and let him eat. The sky, the vistas in every direction, spread out so expansively that I found myself looking around for other people to appear —if not contemporaries, then perhaps the first handful who crossed the land bridge in tiny bands and sifted south to become Aztecs and Incas. With such a fine river bannering by, it was natural to think of them coming here.

Having caught Ace, we had the dangerous enterprise of swimming him back across the Spatsizi—dangerous for him. He was behind the boat at the end of a rope, his nostrils barely flaring above the water, though he had entered like a good trooper. When he climbed out he was polished as red as a ruby, panting and dripping. Jim Abou rode him home. The rest of us had some panicky moments because of fuel-line trouble, when we were suddenly adrift in the violent river. And there was a clapping thunderstorm. The whole world turned white. But Morgan reacted with competence, his face like a boy of eighteen, or like boyhood retrenched.

July 17, Sunday:

We are fogged in. I'm reading *Great Escapes*, a miserable, suffering book. The escapers are good at escaping, but are usually contemptible men. Much talk on the radio from Cold Fish Lake about the personnel situation. Walker can't believe that the Indians he has known for so long are actually deserting him. When it's not his bewilderment that we hear, it's the various mining companies communicating to their crews in the field by means of codes of digits, so that their competitors won't understand. Women read these lengthy lists, which go on for half an hour, the only female women's voices we hear.

On this rainy day I've made an inventory of Hyland Post because it has remained so characteristic in appearance, a sort of holdover.

The buildings lie in a close-set line on the river bluff. The old church is at the downstream end, used as a barn now, where an ailing horse can be nursed through the worst of the winter or a couple of colts kept and fed so that they won't become stunted. In forty years the walls have charred nearly black. The windows are boarded, the roof canvased over. The front door is scrawled with messages that were written in charcoal or tar, almost effaced, about trips people took to Telegraph Creek or Fort Ware, giving notice of when they hoped to return. Bones and scraps of caribou hide are strewn around. Four or five boxy cellarless heaps of logs immediately in back of the church mark where the settlement was: this at a time of nomadic confusion and famine for the Indians. A priest might come out for a visit by dog sled at Christmas, and as late as 1950 families went from these cabins to camp on the trapline in tents at 30° or 50° below.

The three later cabins in the row were built by the families whom the Walkers hired to stay with their horses, once they had brought them in. Each is unobtrusive and low, Indian-style, as brown as the mud itself, without even a protruding snow roof. The logs were matched carefully from an assortment of trees and chinked with earth, so that grass grows from the roofs, although they haven't been formally sodded. The windows are cloudy and small, aslant in their frames. The first of the three is used only as a storage place now, for grindstones, sledgehammers, pulleys, pitchforks, neck bells, packboards, axes and chain. There's a workbench with tools and a series of Catholic calendars with holy pictures. Outside is a sack of horse hair, an old dog sled, a heap of indeterminate gears and wheels, some barrels of lamp oil and gasoline and a few whittled boards in curious shapes for stretching furs. Next to a butchering table is a screened wooden cache with strips of smoked moose hanging over a bin of blackened wood. There's also a horse sled, and a frame for a weather station, partly equipped.

In the second cabin is the blackboard where the children who wintered here would do their schoolwork. Crates of all shapes are nailed to the walls, serving as cupboards, and outdoors is a cache for canned goods, another dog sled, another horse sleigh. Down the bank is a pile of enormous moose racks too big to believe, which would suit a museum, along with some ghastly, discarded, burned hides. The third cabin has the best appointments of all—more windows, more cupboards, tables, stools, bunks and a cooler for eggs. It's got two stoves, and rifles and books (the complete works of Gerald Durrell and Miss Read, *A Walk on the Wild Side*). A Father's Day card several years old is tucked in a niche, alongside a home-drawn Valentine. The walls are padded for extra warmth with layers of flattened cardboard boxes, so there's a give wherever you touch. It's crowded and homey with trunks and groceries, the cardboard seething with signatures, dates, drawings of horses and modest comments on the weather, but no dirty graffiti, oddly enough—mostly writing the Indians have done. A hand-drawn map of an area the size of New Jersey is pasted up. Different men have written informative hints on it, such as "good horsefeed," "swamp," "big valley," "meadows." Names have been written on too. Blueberry Creek, Deep

Creek, Little Cache Creek, Worry Creek. No unusual improvisation is demonstrated, but these aren't joking matters.

The whites who have lived here lately have started a bold new house some distance away and back from the river, not keeping the semimilitary arrangement of the rest of the post. It has a high roof and assertive dimensions; the logs are a freshly peeled yellow. There's an elevated cache full of cornmeal and flour, with a tarpapered roof and tin wrapped around the four legs to ward off the rodents. An older cache nearby is full of other stuff—a bunch of snowshoes, a caribou skin, two bearskins, rough-dried, one very large, a gunnysack filled with gooey bear tallow, the skins of two wolf pups, a large wolf skull, a lynx-skin stretcher, several toy airplanes, a child's plastic clown, and a stack of exercise books for children about six to nine, each painstakingly completed to the last page and graded by the mother, mostly with As. There's a beaver's hand lying outside in the grass.

I should also mention the flags, one in the hayfield where the ski planes land and one on the river to mark the plane-parking slough, which a pilot might not recognize otherwise. Though they're really wind socks, sown from white sacking, they blow with a spirit to match the river's wild rush, the tangled trees, the horses hobbled and hung with bells, the makeshift, zigzag fences, the stumpy fields that have just been knocked flat, still green with the forest's undergrowth. There aren't any house mice here, just chipmunks, no cats, dogs, poultry or cows, no National Park profusion of game, just these weird caches on stilts and the grass-covered cabins and the slough percolating with sixteen-inch fish.

And why am I so elated? Am I an antiquarian? It all adds up to whatever you make of it. I'm elated because I respond as I did on my first ocean voyage. It's as though the last bit of ocean were about to become more dry land, planted and paved. The loss would not be to us who have already sailed it, who have no wish to be seaman, and who can always go back and relive in our minds what we've experienced. The loss is to people unborn who might have turned into seamen, or who might have seen it and loved it as we, alive now and not seamen, have seen it and loved it.

JULY 18, MONDAY:

IF YOU MOVED MORGAN back seventy-five years, he would fit like a beard. He would not be a leader of any kind; he would be like what Joe Valachi called the "soldiers" of gangsterdom. He's fussy if crossed, but quickly forgiving, and right now he's in the midst of doing what I've been hearing everybody else tell me they did in the past. He's ripping the Arctic willow out, laying in a good wood supply, exploring a fierce little river and digging and timbering a garbage hole, which is set into the hillside to drain easily. If he has a mainspring it is curiosity, and yet, elusive and reticent as he is, when I corner him to make him answer my questions, he does so with lifeless dutifulness, as if we were filling out forms. The best description of him is the bare facts.

I asked if any of his friends had walked over the Telegraph Trail. He said one took twenty-six horses through to Atlin in 1934, losing only two of them. Any adventures? No, just a regular trail drive. I asked what he himself used to carry on his back when he went trapping from Ootsa Lake. He said a piece of canvas eight by ten to put up as a lean-to, and a light sleeping bag, an axe, a few traps, a .22 pistol to kill what got caught in the traps, or a rifle for procuring food on long trips. The food he carried would include baking powder, flour, rice, sugar, salt, tea, a little bacon or dried venison, and maybe a box of powdered potatoes or powdered milk. Scurvy takes months to develop, he said when I mentioned that. It comes from a limited diet of salt pork and so forth. A little lime juice brought along to mix with your tea will keep it away. The 30–30 is the ideal meat gun because it doesn't smash or hemor-

rhage the meat. The 30–06 was for trophies, with more powder behind the bullet, although nothing like the modern hunting rifles, which ruin half the animal in order to assure that
it's downed when it's hit.

In the winter Morgan puts dry grass under his outer layer
of clothes if the wind turns unexpectedly cold. Only a small fire
is needed at night if it's kept within reach and is built against a
rock that reflects the heat. The lean-to is faced parallel with the
wind, which generally blows up a mountain during the day
and down the mountain in the chill of the night. He stamps the
snow down on the tent pegs, so that they get encased in ice.
When we talk about trapping, he adds a bit to what Frank
Pete told me. Muskrats, for instance, push wads of moss
through the ice as it forms to preserve their air holes and they
can be trapped alongside these. Otter in a small creek can be
caught by fixing barriers of sticks which funnel them to the
spot where the trap is located. For fisher and lynx you build a
"cubby," which is a cat-sized hut, with catnip or greased
beaver castor inside, or a rotten fish. Beaver behave like a dog
going to a post if the scent of another beaver is put somewhere
around, so that trapping them is easier still. The main danger
in the winter is falling through the ice, which he says he's done
three or four times. Each time he went under a live spruce
after extricating himself, and built a fast fire from the protected litter of needles and boughs (he keeps his matches in a
bottle). There is always kindling under a live spruce, just as
there is always dry wood inside a dead tree, although an axe,
not a hatchet, may be needed to get it out. He packs an axe first
of all, even before a gun, and generally he lies low in brutal
weather, moving only if he has run out of food. The worst spell
of that sort was once when it was 30° below and he had to go
fifty-five miles in a storm. It took him three days because the
snow underfoot was so fluffy and soft.

It's been watery again today. We've greased and tarred our
boots, and here we are, two teen-age boys, one mild, accomplished, patient old man, and one dithering writer. Far from

being in a time machine, we're very representative, it seems to me: just the line-up that one would expect for the place and the age.

This afternoon a drowned coyote washed past with an ugly, foiled grin on his mouth, as if at the joke on himself. We chased him in the boat. In the evening I walked downriver, watching the sky clear. At the end of each island the current added a whine to its noise. The forest stood in a thick mad mass, an anarchy that I sneaked through.

JULY 19, TUESDAY:

I'VE BEEN WATCHING TWO horses romancing—rearing, cavorting around each other, so graceful they aren't to be believed. They aren't like horses at all; they nuzzle and flutter and flow in a *pas de deux*, spreading themselves like butterflies. They seem as at home on two legs as four. Slow-motion, and tall and curving, facing each other, they float for joy.

In the city when you go to the zoo the line between people and animals appears fairly narrow. To judge from the moods on both sides of the bars, the wonder is that the animals are kept separated at all. Dogs, too, become like their masters on a keyed-down scale, until they bustle about the whole day at make-work pursuits, since they haven't a job. But up here the difference is sharp. Even the horses ignore our existence, living by their own mirthful rhythms. It's not a matter of godliness or ungodliness; the difference is who is busy. I don't know who sleeps the longest hours, but we human beings are absorbed the entire day in setting the cook stove into a box of earth for fire-prevention purposes, or building a chute in the corral, or hauling firewood through the mud on a sleigh. Or else we're enjoying ourselves, which in my own case boils down to a business of standing, sitting, and standing up again readily, reading *Great Escapes* for twenty minutes or so, and busily strolling, patrolling around. The horses flirt at a slow and lascivious pace; the moose browse in the muskeg; some goats

[193]

and a grizzly graze on the mountain above us at timberline. Compared to us, if they're not nerveless, they're motionless. We're bowling 'em over—the chain saw is rasping from sunrise to dark—and they quietly browse.

A plane arrived overhead with supplies: brome grass and timothy seed, windowglass, tarpaper. However, the Spatsizi runs all in *Ms* and the pilot was afraid to land, so we followed him in the boat to the Stikine. Morgan steered, wearing a fish leader wrapped around his hat with the fly sticking up through the band like a feather. It's the same crumpled hat he drinks out of and which, when he's finished with it, he will use to filter fuel into his boat. The pilot was waiting for us. He was a husky fellow, newly divorced but excited to be in such country. The Stikine swung by, that clear breezy blue, flooding over its gravel bars in a crawling, silvery swarm of forms. The shoreline bristled with timber askew. I like Canadians better than I did in 1960. They seem less priggish and dumb to me and less anti-American (the change may be mine). Now they're almost too pro. He said, though, that he was glad a railroad was going to be punched through from Fort St. James to take this lushness away from the rich American hunters.

Speaking of bachelors' cooking, these are the recipes tacked on the wall:

Salad dressing (for greens of the field): ½ cup vinegar, 1 cup milk, ⅓ cup sugar, ½ tsp. salt, 2 tsp. mustard, 1 tbs. margarine, 2 tbs. flour. Mix, cook to boil. Bread: 2 pk. yeast, 1 tsp. sugar, 9 cups warm water, 11 cups flour, ½ cup melted lard, 4 tbs. salt, 1 cup dry powdered milk. Mix, bake. Hotcakes: powdered milk, powdered eggs, brown sugar, salt, baking powder, water. Measure by shakes, mix and fry.

[VIII]

A Gold Town—
"It's only the white men!"

JULY 20, WEDNESDAY. IN ATLIN:

ONE OF MY HOPES had been to go to Atlin, the town near the Yukon border at the head of the Telegraph Trail, or the portion of that which interests me. Just as for Telegraph Creek, I read accounts of the place, looked it up on the available maps, tried to visualize how it must be, and wondered if I could contrive to get myself there. Now, this evening, typically of this fine summer when every plan has fitted perfectly and worked for me, I'm in a hotel room on the main street.

Danny Bereza showed up on the Spatsizi this afternoon. He

was returning from a charter flight and Mr. Walker steered him my way, though it meant I would miss a pack trip with Morgan to supply some hunting caches at the heads of the Ross and Stikine. I've been watching such active weather this week, such smothering cloud banks move in and move out, massaging the mountains underneath them, that I'd begun to wonder what would happen to us on the pack trip when we got in between. The folds of the mountains do not awe me as much as the folds of the huge clouds do during energetic weather. I'm no outdoorsman, really, and I found that, if the truth be told, I would just as soon *imagine* the grandeur of the pack trip from what I'd already seen rather than undergo the pummeling rains we would be involved in. I eagerly jumped into the plane with my confident friend Bereza. We flew for a fantastic four hours. Linked with the flight from Fort St. James on July 8, this gave me a view of the whole expanse of northern B. C., some of it country that has never been seen from the ground.

The curving liftoff from the Spatsizi was itself an event—I mean, we succeeded. The shrilling, drenched green of the forest surrounding the post stretched to gorgeous red rocky peaks which stood behind everything. The various rivers wound back between them, turning a rain-gutter color. The peaks and saddles were striped with thick decks of clouds. Our own pass through to the Klappan, as we approached, appeared to be clogged with them even below the regular ceiling, but we plunged in anyway at a low level and throttled to a slow speed. We got so close to the ground that I could see single daisies. The walls on both sides of us weren't visible, but the clouds fortuitously blew a little apart, and Bereza hooked one hand in his belt, relaxing. We passed over an Indian platform cache. The ravines steamed. We crossed into the Klappan Valley, Frank Pete's hunting ground, which has more luxuriant trees and a gentler incline than the Spatsizi. It rained hard. Over the Iskut Valley at Eddontenajon we cocked in a steep turn and landed to pick up the government nurse from Telegraph Creek, who had been treating several of the villagers for flu.

Map of the Northern Sections

Some tourists stood on the beach in the downpour, bareheaded, just chatting, not taking shelter until we had left, in one of the manhood tests people enjoy. The nurse, who is abrupt and nervous at best, became apoplectic in the plane because I was getting a free ride. Bereza edged up into the clouds alongside Ice Mountain to scare her, and the poor woman clutched the back of her chair. "Oh, Danny!" she moaned.

Beneath us a dozen creeks chained down the mountainside. Again, and no tricks this time, we flew practically blind, seeing white and Irish-green, until, over Telegraph Creek, we broke into the sunshine finally. We spotted two moose by a pool. The aspen-and-jackpine plateau around the town ends in a hurricane ring of peaks, and we rocked like a ship, banking steeply into the gorge of the Stikine itself, to land on the racing river in front of the Callbreaths' hotel.

The nurse climbed out shakily. "Come on, mother," the Mountie said. "Move your big ass." He's a chummy man with a squeaky, bluff voice. It's his first month in Telegraph Creek, and after taking the census he was off on an orientation jaunt to meet his neighboring Mountie in Atlin. His wife, waving him off, was getting kidded about how she would manage the Indians while he was gone. The other passenger was the Hudson's Bay Company's district manager, who had come on his annual visit, a ponderous, doctorly man wearing the first suit I've sat next to in a long while.

We joggled downriver, climbed up through the canyon, and got over the high plateau, spotted with lakes and forest and purple patches of fireweed, north of town. The Tahltan River doubles back almost parallel with the Stikine to the lake where many of the salmon in the Stikine system spawn. To the east is Level Mountain, the prize hunting ground of the Tahltans. Appropriately, we watched a caribou galloping along one flank. The Hudson's Bay man caught sight of it first. He and I sat in back; the Mountie, as the V.I.P., sat in front with Bereza. We passed over a dry prairielike area, with the brown

Cassiar Mountains on our right and the snowy Coast Range on our left in the west. Then it was forest and watercourses again, a rolly, knobby, canyoned country splotted with lakes, while other mountains moved alongside, of a broader design—cone and mound mountains of no great relief, but lovely and green. For many miles the Telegraph Trail was clearly outlined, cutting from one short valley over a rise into the next, and over a rise into the next. You can pick out the switchback descents which the horses slithered down. Nakina Summit, Hyland Lake. Mountains were everywhere now, the original ungashed spread of forest with alpine peaks jutting up towards the coast. The lakes lay by the dozen in the artful patterns of a Calder mobile.

At last we reached Atlin Lake, a very large, complex lake ringed with low, jagged mountains and dark, Arctic-looking tree cover. The town has 160 people, about like Telegraph Creek, but it occupies much more space. It's on a flat and is the ghost of the rectangular tent city of 5000 people which existed briefly on the site during the 1899 rush.

A stealthy sense of relief overtook me at finding myself in a town again. I was exuberant too, as I've been at each of these arrivals. I've never come so far north before. The air is colder, the sand on the beach is a frostier color, the jackpines are blacker, the sky is wider and brighter. It's past ten o'clock and the sky is a powder-blue.

We were met by a slouching, tow-headed dock boy and by Mrs. Peterson, the inspired, fierce-faced woman who manages the little bush airline here. The two Mounties drove off together like boisterous fraternity brothers. The Hudson's Bay man embarked on the drive to Whitehorse. Mrs. Peterson drove Danny and me through town, which appears to consist of abandoned three-story hotels. Only one is still in operation at all, and we were the only guests. We were served a late supper by the haggard couple who own it. Danny grew up in the Yukon, but has been urbanized by several years in Vancouver at college. He wanted to be a poet not long ago, and enjoys disputing with me. He was proud of the prodigious day he had just put in. We both ate well.

JULY 21, THURSDAY:

POPULATION 160, AND YET it seems such a *town!* For one thing, the people are mostly white, and being 120 miles by gravel road from Whitehorse, a capital city of 4800, they have cars and the other appurtenances of contemporary North Americans. Like good gold rushers, they've been out and south many times; they used to prospect during the summer and then spend the winter in Seattle or San Francisco when the ground froze up. In Telegraph Creek the molding tradition was the Depression. The outside world was hungry, and it was a chancy business to depend on anyone else: better to trap and hunt and farm for yourself. In Atlin the people were geared instead to the factor of luck. A gold strike could come any time, Depression or no Depression, and otherwise the prosperity of the town was determined quite simply by the Treasury Department in Washington, which set the price that the mining companies were paid for their gold. The companies were forced out years ago, so you have this laughably beautiful site standing empty, with a Swiss panorama all around, the sky and the glaciers and the lake all pouring in light, fifty Swiss mountains across the lake, extending from here to Juneau, and the lake itself a remarkable, shiny, clear, capturing blue—one of the Greek blues, or a Ming blue, like a Chinese velvet. Name any famous resort and this is as pretty. Yet horses graze down the street; fireweed grows in the vacant lots; loons and seagulls swim up to the shore. I rattle about the town like a discoverer, tasting the mineral spring (like Tom Collins Mix), looking at the big beached steamboats, the *Tarahne* and *Scotia*. I sit on the bench in front of them with a death's-head Indian patriarch named John Bone. There are two surviving stores and I am the single visitor. The newest building belongs to the gold commissioner. Atlin means "Big Water." Some day soon it will mean Real Money. In the meantime it's laughable to stroll on the edge of the dazzling lake in the summer light.

There aren't many kids—a minuscule school, no government nurse. Everyone drinks and everyone's aging. The stoves are converted metal beer barrels, from which pipes convolute to the upper floors. It's a peaceful, resilient old community, and again, people are free about offering me help. You can nearly always count upon, even play upon, people's humanity, a quality separate from honesty. Immediately, though, just as in a city, I've been thrown on my own—I'm a stranger, as I never was on the Stikine. Being urban, I like this; I'm relieved. Don't let me escape admitting that I got rather scared in the bush.

I've been timid today about making a start at interviewing. I've walked around, watching the swallows who nest in the two steamboats, listening to my feet thump on the wooden sidewalk in front of the Royal Hotel, which is defunct and careening now, with an old jeweler's clock from the turn of the century posted like a street lamp outside the door. The dogs skirl past in their pack intrigues. In the Anglican church a list is posted of eighteen women a man may not marry:

1. MOTHER. 2. Stepmother. 3. Mother-in-law. 4. Daughter. 5. Stepdaughter. 6. Daughter-in-law. 7. Sister. 8. Sister-in-law. 9. Grandmother. 10. Grandfather's wife. 11. Wife's grandmother. 12. Granddaughter. 13. Wife's granddaughter. 14. Grandson's wife. 15. Aunt. 16. Aunt by marriage. 17. Niece. 18. Niece by marriage.

JULY 22, FRIDAY:

EVERYBODY CUTS HIS OWN hair and seems self-contained. As Jim Morgan said when I asked if I'd find anyone to talk to in Atlin about the past, "I guess there *is* nothing but old-timers there." Danny had the day off, and we ate lunch together in the dining room alone. Then he went to the Royal Hotel, which is considerably larger than ours and which he's just bought with part of his money from flying. I went to meet Walter Sweet, who is ninety-one. It's funny to think how bashful I used to be with old people. Now I'm the most comfortable with them.

Sweet lives in a cramped white cabin next to the road. He keeps his door open so he can wave at the cars. After eighty-five, he says, he deteriorated physically. He needs to rest two days for every day he works, "but a man over ninety years don't pay any taxes—hunting license, fishing license, I don't buy 'em." He has a sack of Gaines meal on the floor for his cocker spaniel and a doubledecker bed in the bedroom. His roommate has died. It's a bleak drafty cabin with canes and other mementos of his dead friend, an old Regulator wall clock, and a magnifying glass for his mineral specimens. He groans unwittingly as he stirs about, pouring two glasses of whiskey. His chest and back are swollen from age. He has a lengthened face, sharp jughandle ears, big hands, and he talks in a heavy, hard-breathing manner. You get a sense of the glamorless labor it's been, digging in streambeds for a lifetime. Mining is moving material. First you pan, he explains to me, or use a "rocker," a larger screening, shaking device, for as long as you can make a living at it. "Then you have to connive some kind of a washing machine—hydraulic operation." Finally, "heavy machinery," "capitalism." He used to have a good nugget to show to his guests, until he was fool enough to lend it out.

Sweet was twenty-four when he arrived, in the very first summer of the Rush. He's the only man left in town from that time. He and his pick-up partner were bound for the Klondike strike at Dawson when they heard about this one, which was closer. They'd walked up the White Pass from Skagway to Carcross (a former caribou crossing), and then turned aside, taking the sequence of boat rides and portages across Tagish and Atlin Lakes. The other fellow packed 115 pounds and

Sweet carried 90. They went straight to the first showings, which were at Discovery, six miles from here, and fell to work. Since then he's worked on dozens of creeks in the area, spending his money as he earned it. "Nobody else was going to pee my money against the wall except me." He became a foreman, but never a manager. "Only one man in a hundred makes foreman, and only one man in a thousand makes manager." He used to travel to Whitehorse by dog sled for hockey games, and he kept a boat on the lake, the *Gladys*, for freighting and fishing commercially, and a Model A at the other side for trucking on the portage. The partner, meanwhile, had saved his money, married his brother's widow, and bought a milk farm down in Washington State.

A bee flew in the door. Although he's got bug killer, Sweet carefully caught it in a towel and let it fly away. "They always go north. I wonder if that's where they live." He showed me a Valentine card from a pair of schoolteachers who once taught in town. "Happy Days!" they call him because of the salutation he has. He gave it again to me, raising his glass.

The discoverers of the Atlin goldfields were two partners from Juneau, Fritz Miller and Kenny McLaren. "Can't describe them, just that they were wonderful people. We just worked to make a living. We didn't ask people any particular questions." He unearthed a pile of magazine articles for me to glance through, however, and sat silently while I read, looking out the window, rubbing his wasted neck.

The history is the familiar one. At first the gold was so accessible that a shovel was practically a hindrance, but at the end of a couple of years so many people had poured in that the profit really was gone for everybody, whether he was a Guggenheim or a lonesome freelancer. And of course the first claims, in any case, hadn't been staked on the best of the creeks—it's a great stroke of luck if they are. People traded in claims and worked close to town because, whereas Telegraph Creek was a transport way point, Atlin was right at the edge of the strike. There was no need to wander for six or eight months or three hundred miles. By 1901 the whole apparatus of a community had taken root: a newspaper, three churches, three banks, three real-estate companies, a curling rink, an exclusive club. Men made as much money from the miners as from the mines. The heyday was short. Before 1910 these amenities were gone, and for the next forty years the little town hung in a roadless limbo, with only the hardy and preternaturally contented staying on. There was a benevolent storekeeper, like Mr. Sargent in Hazelton, whose name here was Schulz.* For long periods he singlehandedly prevented breadlines and carried the drunks and the needy kooks, the marginal types, the strangers who "arrived C.O.D." He'd give them a grubstake, and when months later they reappeared, needing their passage out, he provided that too in exchange for the broken tools. He gave any prospector the benefits of fraternity with the same breed of fellow who had established the town. The judge too was likely to pay a man's fine out of his own pocket, rather than send him to jail.

It was sunny and peaceful, reading about all this stampede stuff, hearing Walter Sweet wheeze. Just as in Telegraph Creek, there's no air of misfortune, no losers' saturnine mood imbuing the town, although no one who lives here struck gold at all, except flour gold and occasional pebbles, and most everybody who left left poorer than he was when he came. The gold was a pretext, obviously. The youngsters and summer soldiers were after adventure; the people I'm meeting were pursuing a life. If circumstances got grim, the idea that they were looking for gold was what kept them from feeling a fool. For the year-in-year-out prospector, the gold in the pan became simply a matter of wages, while he saved and prepared for the serious search that he had in mind—the determined visionary's search he may or may not have managed to make in the end, but which marked his face with the glee of his hopes, like

* Fort St. James has Mr. Lawrence Dickinson, a penetrating, gentlehearted businessman with dusty glasses, who arrived in 1911 as a surveyor's helper.

Philippon's and Alec McPhee's and Walter Sweet's here, with his "Happy Days!" When I was hospitalized in Smithers I heard a number of stories about prospectors dying, generally with their diaries beside them on the bedside stand. They were nearly as alone as if they'd dropped dead in the bush, but they'd expected that. It's a cheerful life and a fearful death. The diary—that last friend—was usually thrown out afterwards. Fritz Miller's was saved by the Board of Trade. It's very succinct because it ceases when he and McLaren made their big strike and entered upon a frenzy of work: "Saturday, March 25: Hole down to bedrock 5½ feet; *pay in one end of hole.*"

JULY 23, SATURDAY:

A FIRE IS BURNING up in the Yukon. The smoke has taken a day to blow south, but we have it now, a tang in the nose. The sun is coal-red. Danny's boss, Mr. Peterson, has already flown off to the fight, after attaching water tanks under his airplane's wings that are constructed to refill instantly, so that from dawn to dark he'll be able to be in the air without pausing, only touching down on the surface of a lake between bombing runs. He brings a boy along to fly him between the fire and the lake —he'll nap in the air.

Unfortunately I only had time to talk with him briefly. He's a solidly muscled, short man with the same headlong, seething concentration about him that lion trainers have. He's never still. He works constantly, gets mad, weeps easily. His wife is fiercely linked to him, as circus wives are—she with her inspired, gypsy face. The dangerous life puts an electricity between them. Peterson is no humdrum flier; he's been known to run out of gas in the air, even on takeoff, but his reactions are such that he lands safely. Once his tail fell off at several thousand feet and he fluttered down into a beaver swamp, incredibly. He's reckless and then as quick as a cat if there's an emergency. He liked the fact that I've come so far to talk to people like Walter Sweet. Like most bush pilots, he isn't a traveled man, and he didn't go and fly Spitfires during World War II; he's only flown here. In the north he's a famous man. He speaks swiftly and softly, as if life were short. I watched him lift off for the fire.

Atlin hangs like a locket from the Yukon; its affections and thoughts attach to there. Nobody has much to tell me about the Telegraph Trail, because the trail that they cared about was the seventy-mile trail to the White Pass Railroad. Of necessity, I've been asking more questions about gold than before, a subject I'm not very knowledgeable on. The warnings, the jokes I've been hearing in each of these towns were that I was going to swallow a lot of tall tales. That hasn't happened so far. Instead, the problem has been to try to evoke some glimmering of the magnificent truth from people like Morgan and Wriglesworth, who don't do any more talking than they can help. I would have been glad to hear lies, but if I've heard one or two from the lesser lights, they were only ascribing feats to themselves that their friends have done. All along the truth has obviously been so much taller than the tales I've heard that the tales have been kind of a shadow show.

I set out to talk to two talkers. Stampede John Stenbraten has been in on every stampede in his lifetime in the English-speaking world. That was his custom: when the news broke, to *run*. He lives in a little house down a lane by the lake with a middle-aged schoolmistress whom he married very late in life. She fended me off. I did get a glimpse through the door of Stampede John—of his fireball stance and gruff stare, as if nobody had ever jumped *his* claim. When I stuttered, he shouted in a rage, "I can't understand him!"

Robert Craft, ninety-four, is a busy man. He works in the power plant (we have occasional electricity), and also operates the town's soft-drink-and-candy booth in the front room of his cottage in the evening until ten. He says he'd die if he quit working; he works in order to keep alive. He was a mining engineer when he moved to Atlin in 1926, having previously been the chief of police in Timmins, Ontario. As a young man, he painted in oils and was a trick rifleman—he used to be able to hit a .22 shell thrown up in the air. His home is as cluttered as Sweet's is empty and bare. Watercolors are tacked six high on the walls, quite competent ones which he apologizes for, saying that it's hard for a man trained in oils to change mediums. His desk is littered with magnets and gadgets, rock specimens, invoices, letters. He's a square-set man with a strong-looking face and a toothbrush mustache, so hefty you'd think he was in his sixties, except for his neck. He's so businesslike and convincing, passing me nuggets and photographs of the claims he has had, I need to remind myself that while we are speaking of wealth, little kids are knocking on the door to buy Mars bars from him—he excuses himself for a minute.

Craft was in his mid-fifties by the time he arrived, but that still left him twenty vigorous years to hike the country in partnership with his son. He speaks with appealing excitement of all of the different creeks they staked and worked. Zenazie, Terrahina, Constellation, Union, and Packsack creeks, the last of which he discovered himself. Each paid at least adequately well—powder and 75¢ nuggets—but too many boulders were strewn along in the beds to operate easily. Dorothy Creek, which they named for a friend of his son, posed the same obstacles, though they loved it at first. Unawares, they walked up on it, and Craft's son, a good woodsman otherwise, dropped his rifle at the sight of five nuggets lying exposed on the ground. Turn Creek, on the Rapid Roy River, had fewer boulders and would have been profitable for them to work except that the altitude was so high the season was over before it began. The sluice boxes froze, and the lakes nearby were too short for a plane to get off with a load.

The basis of placer mining is that gold is a heavy element. It moves slower than the other gravels do when shaken in an agglomeration of them, and sinks faster when sluiced through a stream of water. It is found at the bottom of creek beds instead of loose on the slopes of a mountain. A claim can be leased from the government for twenty years by paying a $30 registration fee and by doing a certain amount of assessment work every year. When a man loses interest in the claim, he simply stops doing the work and lets it revert to the government again. Nowadays this kind of activity on the creeks is a thing of the past, except for believers like Craft. The gold in the gravels has been sifted out and most of the gold in the world is mined by hard-rock companies, who drill for it. Craft, who's been out everywhere within sixty or seventy miles of here, says, however, that a lot of small creeks he knows show no sign of ever having been worked at all. "A bottle of whiskey wouldn't last that long. They didn't get far, most of those fellows. They sat somewhere on a rock and drank up and came home." During the 1930s Craft and his son would be out six months of the year, dauntlessly roaming along, not bothering to stake the creeks where they worked because they'd stay only a couple of weeks and nobody else was close. He trapped a bit for the fun of it, the same way the trappers in Telegraph Creek used to prospect. The pleasure of going out first thing in the morning to see if something had got in his traps was rather like looking for nuggets, after all. "You're always looking for what's ahead." He kept a five-dog team, backpacking them in the summer, and he always earned back at least his grubstake. He speaks not of bonanzas, but as a technician, about what the problems were, getting up with an old man's conservative motions every once in a while to sell somebody a Milky Way.

For several years the Crafts worked a creek called Fourth of July. They weren't bothered by boulders, but it had been blocked by a glacier that had deposited a terrible mess of silt. They dug down through that laboriously, three or four feet worth, when they hit hardpan they couldn't dig through. Anybody with the capital for the proper machinery could go down fifty feet more, he says with a thrill in his voice, "and flood the market with gold." He grins, glancing at my face.

Mining's a slow game. He had to wait fifteen years for the people who'd staked Ruby Creek, where his son and a hired man are working right now, to give up and get off. After that, the past six or seven years have been spent in clearing debris off the claim, until at last they are just about down to where the pay ought to be. The creek is under an ancient volcano. Half of its loops were covered by an old lava flow, so the people before him missed these. The hired man works on the monitor, which directs the blast of water that cuts out the bank and does all the excavating. His son handles the sluice boxes, where the gold is caught as the water flows through, and Craft himself drives the bulldozer, pushing the talings away.

Ruby Creek is a creek with coarse gold—nuggets and flakes —much easier to collect than dust. For dust, they use magnets or mercury to pick the gold out of the sluice box. The old-timers sometimes laid moosehides down and let the gold catch in the hairs. Also, nuggets sell better than dust. A jeweler may pay $70 an ounce, twice the bank rate, for a suitable chip. So it's a peach of a creek that he's watched all these years, waiting to lease as his own. He and his son control four miles of it. Since it's at 4500 feet, the season is short. When the sluice boxes freeze, they come down and work for another month on Kenny McLaren's old claim at Discovery. They've got this staked too. The velocity of water on the creek prevented a thorough clean-up in McLaren's day. Only recently a man with money succeeded in turning the creek to one side, but he died before the rewards were realized. His relatives, who were oil people, let the claims lapse. Craft, therefore, is dragging a "dead man"—a heavy log—with his bulldozer over the newly dry bed, exposing the lower gravels.

He grins foxily as he gets up and sells an Indian girl a bottle of coke. You thrive as a placer miner, he says. No need to get rich. The gold you've washed out during the day is right there in your hand. You don't have to truck any ore to a mill. It may not be much, but you can walk into a bank or a bar and there it is, good as gold, right in your hand.

As for McLaren, he outlived Fritz Miller, staying on in Atlin to savor his fame. Twice he left town with $60,000 for a winter's fun, and the rest of his booty he spent on pack trains, looking for the location marked on the map which he and Miller had been carrying with them when they stumbled upon the Discovery strike. A prospector dying of pneumonia had brought the map into Juneau and given it to Miller's brother, but of course Discovery was not *that* site at all.

July 24, Sunday:

In America the old people are almost all women. In Atlin they're almost all men. It's odd.

The beauty of the nights cannot be exaggerated, with the sky dove-white and the lake beaming up light and loveliness at it. I can't go to bed; it's like a goose in the ass. I wander outside till my legs ache. It's like living on borrowed money that I'll never have to repay. Next winter, when these people are paying, I'll be back in New York.

I've finally met an angry Indian. George Edzerza. He's a Tahltan. He grew up in Telegraph Creek and remembers John Creyke and Benny Frank and Frank Pete as kids, Frank Pete as a little boy tagging behind the rest. He can't believe that Frank Pete is fifty-three already and weary of climbing mountains. Edzerza is fifty-nine and he's weary too. He's the principal guide here, looks forty-five, speaks fast and forcefully. He has a fourteen-room house that's the hub of the town's teenagers, with music going.

"Nothing for nothing. What's in it for me?" he asks right away when I want to talk to him; he wants to be paid. He's angry because he's discovered lately that his wife was cheated out of an inheritance of some size by an Anglican missionary, now dead. It's a mysterious story. Apparently, when the Englishman whom I've mentioned as having enjoyed himself so thoroughly in Telegraph Creek returned home at last, leaving both legitimate and illegitimate families behind, his relatives worried about doing right by the legitimate kids, especially after the young fellow died. Wondering how to go about it, they wrote to the missionary who was serving in Telegraph Creek at the time. He persuaded them to send the money directly to him, but instead of distributing it to the children he pocketed it, sending his own kids to college and so on. When he retired, the minister who succeeded him found out about the scandal but kept silent, seeing the dilemma as an insoluble one. He died too, however, soon after the first missionary, and now his widow, alone and sick near Victoria, uneasy about the knowledge she has, has spilled the beans in a long letter to the Indians. Naturally Edzerza is bitter. He's got plenty of children of his own, so what this means to him quite simply is that if his wife had received the money intended for her years ago, he wouldn't have had to go through the hard and panicky periods he has known, struggling to feed all those mouths. It brings to his mind a whole bunch of instances when white men have jiggered him out of his rights or his money, or done it to friends of his. For instance, he claims that he grubstaked the discoverers of the local asbestos mine but was cut out of most of his share of the spoils of that. And when he had his first outfitting business, he left his ten horses with his brother one winter while he went off to trap on the Coal and Nahanni rivers, above Lower Post. His brother was killed in a snow-slide, and a white man rounded up the ten horses and drove them into the Big Muddy River country where he couldn't trace them. He never saw them again, and the Mounties did nothing about it. His other brother died in a flu epidemic which raked the Tahltans during the Second World War, a time when Indian welfare came last on the government's list of priorities and there wasn't a doctor remotely near. He says the education which the missionaries gave him was deficient, that sharpers cheat him, and that he isn't interested in making friends with a stranger like me, only in dollars. The missionary who embezzled the money had been a great friend of his, as a matter of fact. They had traveled by dog sled here to Atlin for the fun of it, and down the Iskut as well. Ice Peak, the nine thousand-foot mountain that dominates Telegraph Creek, bears the Edzerza name (mispelled) on the map, so he's not the first member of the family with energy. The mountain looks towards another mountain on the Stikine which is named for the guilty missionary. I can picture the two eminences blowing storm clouds each other's way and glowering bellicosely. Edzerza's is higher.

Still, he is tempted to talk. We sit on the sofa on his sun porch while the kids in the parlor dance to rock-and-roll. They'll go to the university, he says. What rankles in him won't rankle in them. And he speaks of a number of whites with approval: the local priest, the Hylands, old Callbreath. Callbreath was a tougher, harder-driving man than the Hyland brothers, but he lived sixteen miles downriver like a loner, marrying an Indian woman, and he died broke, so that his children were left with nothing. Edzerza packed for him as far south as the Bell-Irving River on the Telegraph Trail, and packed to Hyland Post. Later he started his own little train, packing food to the gold camps on the Turnagain River and north of Dease Lake. He raised potatoes for the Hudson's Bay store; he guided the Nash car and Goodrich tire people. In the winter he trapped down the Iskut to Burrage Creek, which they used to call Sandbar Creek, and on south from there to the source of the Unuk. He built dog sleds for a living, too, charging $25. He got to be something of a specialist at that— someone else built the snowshoes for everybody. For his own team, he crossed Great Dane blood in with the husky, and employed a smart setter to lead them. The setter wasn't even hitched up, but it picked the safe path over the river ice and knew how to gee and to haw. Wolves weren't any good on the team because they would either attack him or rip up the dogs. They wouldn't stand being roughed up, and they're light-pawed, narrow-chested creatures. Besides, they didn't survive very long. If he was broke, he would look at them there in his team and know he could cash them in any time for the bounty. He says that for training a team you need just one dog who knows what he's doing, like the pinch of old dough that makes flour bread.

A Gold Town—"It's only the white men!"

Edzerza and his brothers used to chip copper along the Anuk, the site which Kennecott is developing now. In the same way, they explored the asbestos deposits as boys, looking on these as curiosities. "We took pictures. We thought it was interesting. We didn't know nothing about running and filing a claim and getting rich from it." When the Second World War started, he was impatient with life at Telegraph Creek and walked out on it. People "lay around in their rut. People forget there are other ways to make a living besides trapping, you know." The war brought freight boats to the Dease and Liard, as well as other opportunities. He worked on the rivers and on the construction of the Alaska Highway. He logged; he worked on a pipeline. He set up a store and restaurant at Lower Post. He was a carpenter, an outfitter. Then he shifted to Atlin in 1950, when the local guide, Nolan, retired. His hunting territory is 75 by 125 miles, much bigger than he would have gotten in Telegraph Creek. Also the mountains are lower and generally flatter and more open. The game is so approachable by road that he can take his horses and clients out in the truck in the morning and have them back with their trophies by supper. He puts them up at his own house, which saves him money. He doesn't care for the lore of hunting any more, just the business end. Besides, in all modesty, when I've talked to John Creyke and Willie Campbell, what can he tell me?

Edzerza says he uses his family for staff. He won't hire the local Tagish Indians. He has "a liquor problem" with them, and they smell bad; they're "dirty, backwards, sarcastic." Education doesn't improve them. They stick on the reserve, "no get-up," "bad acters"; he doesn't allow them on his property.

He was bored with me now, his crammed light-colored face turning sour, so I walked across town to the Tagish Reserve, "Indiantown." It's a collection of derelict shacks around the Crow House, a stark frame house with two tall windows and a diamond-shaped window high in front. The Wolf Clan had another house, the Wolf House, for ceremonials, until the

Indian agent tore it down, an act which the few citizens left here resent. They're so resentful, in fact, that it's hard to know what to believe. The kids look deprived and malnourished, unlike the Indian children I've seen everywhere else. Dirt-specked and -stained, they stand open-mouthed, clutching each other, unhealthily pale. They look as if they fend for themselves and don't manage too well. The couple of men of an active age seem like hulking nonentities. One holds the record for running the mail to Telegraph Creek—that endurance test —as the result of a transfigured three days early in his life. But he wasn't a regular carrier, and as far as I can find out it's the only outstanding thing he has ever done. When I approached his house he kept shyly sidling uphill, as some sort of a mental defective might, and his kids were too timid to be go-betweens. Maybe I'm being unfair, because they are sturdier than the other kids. They have round, very smooth faces and very small eyes, like Eskimos.

The Tagish speak a bastard Tlingit. It's not known for sure whether they began as a splinter Tlingit group or whether they belonged to an interior tribe originally and made satellites of themselves by adapting the Tlingit language in order to profit as middlemen. The trading route went from the coast at Juneau to here, 115 miles by trail, and then 75 miles further inland to Teslin Lake, where the interior Indians came. The interior tribes despised the Tagish, just as the Tahltans did, who met them along the Taku.

I'd been referred to Evelyn Jack. She was drunk and almost asleep, sitting with her husband at the kitchen table, with their kids in a silent row on the sofa behind them, when I found the house. She told the children to stay where they were, speaking with some ferocity, and accompanied me to John Bone's to translate. She's no relation, she said, to the Hazelton–Bear Lake Jacks whom I've met, Tommy and Alec. But she is kin by marriage to Taku Jack, a fellow known around Telegraph Creek during the first third of this century.

It interests me that Indians, in adopting white names, usually took the first name of a white chum, like Jack, Frank, or Pete, and used that, putting another name in front, because this is also what several friends of mine who have changed their surnames have done. They've chosen longer, more ornate first names, perhaps a name heard rather than a name known, and retained their own first name in front of that. But someone else's first name is transferable, and this is a blessed quality to a person starting off fresh. Last names are not. Several times here I've heard of fugitives who made new lives for themselves in the bush. They did the same as the Indians, or, in one case, the old first name became the man's surname and he pasted a serviceable "John" on in front.*

Bereza, that glamorous pilot, has been sleeping with one of Evelyn's friends, so she was in a flirtatious mood. She was wearing a trim white blouse and a dirty black skirt (the friend, a much softer, more vulnerable girl, wears flowered prints). When we met anyone, she said that I was her new boy friend. Despite her dissipated look, she still carries a certain residual handsomeness, with eyelids like poplar leaves in a round flat face, and stiff black hair. Her nose is straight and short and her mouth, wild and cruel, turns down at the sides like a turtle's mouth. She lost patience with me, however. When she asked if I'd give her money for acting as host I wouldn't, and I must have struck her as prissy and dull.

Bone's house is a sharecropper shack. The walls inside are covered with sordid green tin, along with posters of Turkey and Austria. The smell is a whack in the face, like acrid tobacco and urine. He's between ninety-five and one hundred and three, depending upon whom you ask—a gibbonlike, frail figure now, with black-rimmed glasses and a gray crew cut,

---

* As a more persistent inquirer, I heard a good many other stories of fugitives in 1968. A man who has killed someone is on his guard not to do it again. If, for instance, he shot a Negro in Texas and the friendly sheriff hustled him north, he lets his neighbors know about this item of history eventually. They smile a little and think him wild. But he lives as a solitary on his farm after that. Like a fellow who was once a drunk, he wants to steer clear of temptation. People wink knowingly at him when somebody who is disliked in the valley is murdered and slipped through the ice. "Actually I didn't do it," he says, with a rueful shrug.

his face a swarm of wrinkles and hollows. Our conversation got very discombobulated, partly because he's so old, partly because Evelyn was drunk and I hadn't paid her, and partly because of the smell, which practically lifted me out of my chair and set me outside. Evelyn all but fell asleep, Bone meanwhile telling her dirty jokes in Tlingit, telling her what he would like to do to her and chucking her under her chin. She was affectionate, laughing, letting him pinch her. She said she'd come in and clean the place up. He said he's not going to wear any clothes when she does.

The Gold Rush and his wedding party roughly coincided, and he told me a little bit about both, except that the messages didn't get through. He hunted moosemeat to sell to the miners and worked on the White Pass Railroad. Before the whites came, life was better for the Tagish (Evelyn emphatically translated that). They could trap all winter on the Taku undisturbed, and then they played and vacationed all summer here. Bone can remember catching sight of his first white men one spring at least twenty years before the big Rush. The whole Tagish village was living in tents on the Taku when six whites came poling along on a scow. They were after gold. They were single-mindedly heading upriver and they paid no attention to the Indians. They didn't even pause, but most of the Tagish were terrified. "Oh, they're going to kill us!" they cried, John Bone too. There was one old chief, though, who had been to the coast and had met the Russians, and he laughed and said, "No. No. It's only the white men." He waved to them as they went by to show that he could. Everybody smiled and grew gay and waved at the scow. The kids jumped up and down. "It's only the white men!" they yelled.

JULY 25, MONDAY:

IT'S A NATURAL THING for birds to do, but I haven't seen it before. They ride around on the horses' rumps, keeping an eye cocked, hopping off if a feast presents itself. Since what they're especially after is the horses' own dung, which is full of seeds, they couldn't be located better. Also they're safe from the cats up there. Atlin is such a civilized place it has cats. Eddontenajon won't have cats for years. In those raw, stumpy fields a cat would look as incongruous as a Chihuahua.

I can't get over the evenings—the balmy air, the late, late daylight. Life catches a perfervid quality, although nothing happens. The sky and the lake are the color of mercury; the moon is a slice of copper plate; the trees blow whimsically. The moments seem intense and precious. One could stay up all night and never get sleepy. Inevitably, I think of my wife. Instead of a marriage we had an extended engagement because I refused to have children and I kept doubting whether we should remain married, thus making it impossible for us to begin to be. I babytalked to her; I turned her into a child bride whenever I could, just as my father did with my mother. Of course she, on her side, was nutty too. Her crazy spells exhausted me; the first weeks of separation were an enormous relief. But it was a genuine love that should have worked, a love pretty much thrown away.

I've been told everywhere to talk to Norman Fisher. He's the Willie Campbell in town, the iron man, but so low-key I'm having a difficult time with him, or maybe I'm running out of steam. He's a reflective pipe-smoking gentleman with a markedly sweet-natured face, the toughness underneath, and a fit, prudent body, like an old athlete's. He ran the mail to Telegraph Creek for two winters before the First War. As early as 1902 he'd been in the Klondike, but by then "there were so damn many men you couldn't get a job if you cried your eyes out." He came south and worked on Wright Creek, finally buying one of the partners out. He lived in the low, snug cabin he lives in now and boarded at the Royal Hotel, never marrying, though he frequently wintered in San Francisco—in fact he does still. He fought in the War and returned to work on virtually all the gold creeks, one by one, finally retiring in 1949 to his present business. The sign on his door says *Fishing spoken here.*

Fisher has a crowded desk, and there are seagulls on the lawn waiting to be fed. On the map he points out for me the arms of the lake where the mountains fall steepest into the water and the mirroring effect is the best. I can't afford his boating rates, but he's been touched by my persistence in coming to his door (he's hard to see). At breakfast this morning in the hotel he walked up to me and laid his hand on my shoulder, meaning to ask me out on the water free. He has such delicacy that he couldn't say the words easily. I didn't help him because I didn't like his customers for today, an Anchorage bunch who were roaring put-downs at the next table. As we listened, he probably agreed with me. He stood in silence; he never did issue the invitation.

It was some fifty-five years ago that he carried the goods on the Telegraph Trail, so his being the "expert" in town indicates how little anybody cared to see Telegraph Creek. It was a pastime for him during the months when the creeks froze over. The pay of $100 a month was the same as for laboring at a sluice. He says he can't tell me about any hardships because there weren't any; it was just his favorite among all the jobs that he ever had. "You left here and you weren't bothered by anybody until you came back." The operators in the cabins kept track of his progress over the wire. They'd have dog feed ready when he stopped for the night and a hot meal cooked. He carried their rum. Sure, they were a bit funny in the head, but so was he. The isolation did nothing to them that the rum couldn't straighten out. One man was a composer, and Fisher packed him an organ over the snows on the sled. He reached Telegraph Creek in anywhere from three to nine days, depending on what he felt like doing, and would stay over at the gold commissioner's or else with the Hudson's Bay man. It was sociable all the way along the line, and the only difference between the two towns was that Atlin had mostly white people and Telegraph Creek had mostly Indians.

It was a 420-mile lark. When he felt sprightly, he started back, still usually managing to put in a couple of weeks of poker-playing at home before the next run. If he ever was caught between telegraph cabins at night he crawled into the pile the dogs made of themselves. He used six, one being a substitute running loose. He would set out the sleigh and harness, and they'd dash right to it. He had no lead dog, they were all good, all enjoyed it as much as he did, and he'd break in a replacement simply by sticking him in. The summits above the Nakina and Sheslay were sometimes hard. Snowslides raised hell with the trail. He'd watch the fires of the Indian camps, cozy below him, as he struggled down. Otherwise, the Dudidontu Valley was the only bad spot, a low area where the cold snaps broke the covering on the river and caused it to flood. He had already won his spurs on the route to Carcross, which was much more dangerous than the Telegraph Trail because it went mostly across the ice. With plummeting temperatures and terrific winds, the ice broke into floes. Once when the weather was fifty below he needed to paddle across ten miles of open water in a canoe. Another time, he had packed the mail on the backs of the dogs and was taking them through the bush around the lake because of the risky condition of the ice. They chased a pair of caribou, losing a mail sack, and at last, when he arrived at the outlet river with them, the raft was on the wrong side. He tied up the dogs, jumped in, swam across and brought it back.

As the years wore on, Fisher quit chasing a sled in the winter. He would catch the last boat out for the south instead, these autumn boat trips being the best sport of the year. They were drawn-out occasions because the crew of the *Tarahne* also was through for the season. On the other side of the lake the passengers would wait for them to put the boat into mothballs before proceeding to Tagish Lake, where the crew of *that* boat had to do the same. What with the drinking parties and the waiting around, it was likely to be ten days before they reached Skagway. Atlin was quite a city in its own right. It boasted three women taxi drivers and seven hotels, its own customs man, a tugboat just for hauling the saw logs, and caribou meat in the stores at 15¢ a pound. Now there isn't even a young fellow left to cut the winter's stove wood for these older folks who can't do it themselves. Some of them worry about how they're going to keep warm.

Fisher is ready to stop talking after every sentence, and yet he's really about the first person who has made me envy him for his time. His pleasures would have been mine. He's the kind of old man who listens smiling to everything, who has got the most to say and yet who's the least inclined to say it, not from vanity, but because he's at peace with himself, because he's long-lived. In any case, he doesn't take me very seriously. He doesn't expect a book will actually come out of my investigations; he's responding from paternal feeling. I asked to see his picture album, and he took out a snapshot of a crowd of well-wishers and cronies seeing him off in front of the Royal Hotel. The loaded sled is wrapped tightly in canvas; the dogs have surrounded Fisher and are nosing him eagerly. He's sitting on the board sidewalk, a swashbuckling figure in his tie and boots and high-crowned black hat, with an alert, military mustache. He's the center attraction. Everybody is happy.

I asked a lady this evening if Norman Fisher wasn't the most glamorous fellow in town at one time. She's a riverman's widow, a big, blowzy, rococo windbag of a woman who has certainly kept an eye out, but she didn't think so. She didn't make fun of him, but she said that he was too short and that he was a little aloof. Her thoughts didn't go back to him at all, but to people whom I'll never meet. So who knows?

JULY 26, TUESDAY:

THE POSTMASTER, A SCOTSMAN, hasn't been out of the district since 1934. The gold commissioner, however, is an admirably venturesome guy in a starched collar of the style current during the Gold Rush, whose eyes glint with excitement as he speaks of the north. He reminds me of the Anglican reverend in Telegraph Creek. He hasn't the physical gifts for a rugged outdoor existence, but he's got twice the enthusiasm needed. He wears boots in his office, slogging as if he had snowdrifts to cross. Year after year he sticks it out here, applying for extensions of duty.

The pie cook and fry cook in the hotel has owned thirteen restaurants and four hotels in the course of his life and lost them all.

Danny Bereza eats supper with me, chatting about the morals of the Indian girls ("No morals at all if you scratch their stomachs a minute"); also about the forestry supervisor, a rigid Seventh Day Adventist who won't drink coffee or go to the movies, but who kills, kills, kills—hunts like a fiend. After each thunderstorm he hires a plane with government money, to look for fires, supposedly, but really to spy out the game. Most of Danny's flying assignments are more confidential—geologists wanting to land in a slotlike gorge where the space is so confined that his pontoons are throwing back mud when he takes off. It's frustrating for him to keep so much to himself, not only the dangers that he surmounts but the flabbergasting scenery as well—eight thousand-foot walls of rock and ice, fabulous lakes where no one has gotten before and the goats run towards him to see what he is. Fresh from his plane, he walks in to dinner and sits down dazed.

I had lunch with Bill Roxborough, Jim Nolan and Charlie Gairns, three old-timers, and their wives at Nolan's house—or, more properly, they let me sit in. Gairns is kind of a foster son to Nolan, but Nolan and Roxborough again are men who have reached an age which makes it an accident, a matter of a handful of years, that I'm able to spend the afternoon with them. They're as frail as dry leaves, deaf, Nolan on crutches. Roxborough, gripped by his years, is the least animated. His father set sail from Ireland with the news of the Klondike strike. When he reached Skagway, though, the findings at Atlin were the latest thing, and like so many others, he veered here, getting in on the ground floor in a way that he couldn't have in the Yukon. He set up a roadhouse in Discovery called the Gold House, meanwhile mailing home nuggets in matchboxes until his wife had collected enough for the fare. In 1904 she and Bill, age twelve, arrived. His photographs, acorn-colored, show what the era was like—the different gold camps with a couple of dozen bald-skinned young bears ranged in front of a room-and-board sign. Roxborough and the others call off the people and try to identify which creek they're on. He grew up to become the town electrician. Earlier, he operated the movie projector, which burned ether and oxygen, for a druggist named Pillman.

The first car in town was a Renault, brought by a French newspaperman. After filing his story, he acquired a claim of his own and hired a friend from Limousin who was an engineer. The friend's fiancée came along also, and remains here still, very snug, very French. She got married to Mr. Roxborough after her lover went back to France and got killed in the Great War. The Renault was used to chase wolves on the ice. The Indians at Teslin Lake packed a Ford all the way to their village over the trail and drove it along a three-mile beach that they had. Bozo Fox was their chief. "All same as dogs," he called the Tagish, but after an especially acerbic dispute he came to make peace, dressed in feathers, accompanied by a small fleet of canoes. A canvas screen was put up between the diplomats, and knocked down symbolically when the settlement had been decided upon.

So many people popped into Atlin in those days, from any of a thousand motives, that the achievements of some, naturally, were not the amount of gold dust they got their hands on, but the memorable little houses they built and then left—curious, solid little pearls that stand alongside the streets, built by one fellow or another to please himself, which haven't a counterpart anywhere else. The Telegraph Trail was for another type of person: the desperate and destitute, the specialist, the stunt man. A California couple walked to the Aleutians. Two motorcyclists rode south from Dawson City in order to publicize the Chicago World's Fair. A man tried to ski all the way. A girl ran away from her boyfriend in Telegraph Creek and froze her feet in the snow. She had no snowshoes and she would have died where she lay if six inches more hadn't fallen and covered her from the cold. The isolated telegraph linemen had an awful time of it, provisioning the various adventurers who set out on the hike without enough food. A Russian woman named Lilian, who was about forty-five, caused the biggest sensation. She conceived of the Telegraph Trail just as the original entrepreneurs had, as a trail that was cut to go around the world. She started from New York to walk home, doing fine until she reached Hazelton. From there it became more arduous. The relay men in the cabins fed her and patched her clothes and bound up her feet in moosehide when her shoes gave out. They gave her a puppy, which died, so she skinned it and stuffed it with grass, continuing to carry it under her arm. She spent a winter in Atlin, cooking for a bunch of miners. Both Nolan and Roxborough remember her going down to the icy lake alone to wash her clothes. She was a queer 1920s character in a 1920s place. The next year she plugged on to Point Barrow on the Bering Strait. She is said to have asked the Eskimos if they would take her across in a kayak, but they refused. They fixed her a raft and helped her shove off. After that nobody knows her fate. It's hard to think of her surviving so much and not making it home. But she hadn't been talkative and she didn't write.

Nolan arrived on the Yukon River from Indiana in 1906. With his partner he built a raft, and they floated down to Dawson with one ton of food, a happy trip. They slept in grassy sloughs under a scrap of canvas. They ate berries off the mountainsides and caught fish and shot grouse. They negotiated the notorious Five Finger Rapids by the grace of God, coming upon an island below it that was littered with wrecked rafts and scows. Some castaway cattle were grazing there. At last they saw Dawson ahead of them. Lousetown was the bunkhouse district. They tied up and got jobs at $5 a day. Nolan knocked around, mined his way south, and finally went into the hunting business in Atlin, driving an outfit of horses over the trail from Smithers in the summer of 1925. Out of the herd of twelve he only lost one, and that was because the cowboy whom he had with him left a piece of rope on its neck during the night, and the animal got tangled up in the aspens. When he was past fifty, he switched businesses again, operated a payroll, and sunk a mine shaft two hundred feet down in the bed of Spruce Creek. He adapted a paddlewheel from the steamer *Scotia* as his overshot wheel for the surface part of the arrangement, and improvised everything else that he could. He's a bald, bulky man and looks like the hook-nosed, benevolent criminal who escaped from the hulks in the movie *Bleak House*. His wife looks like Lady Churchill.

Gairns, Nolan's good friend, is a big-faced, big-toothed speed talker who smiles almost continually. He's a man who has come through a lot of "tough shows," as he keeps calling them, and has learned that either you smile or you cry. There's another person like that in town, except older and more of a loser, who's covered with scars from all his mishaps, from his arms to his stomach, and is presently losing his savings in a motel venture which he has started here just a few years too soon. Whenever the poor joker opens his mouth, he beams. He has a gorilla queen for a wife; he serves her breakfast and supper.

Gairns's wife is a bright, kindly, frowning woman, deliberately ordinary, her eyes enlarged by her glasses. He has successfully pulled himself out of most of the holes he's been in. His father's leg was blown off in a dynamite accident before he was born, so that as a very young boy in Discovery he had to drag in the winter's wood for his family and generally "bite his teeth and buck into it." At the age of fifteen he went up above timberline and lived a whole summer on beans and bannock and prunes, coming home with a hundred ounces of gold. Nolan and he tell me about creeks they have panned together

—Coffee Creek, Feather Creek, Birch Creek—roughing it in the snows at five thousand feet. Gairns ripped the linoleum flooring out of the Nugget Hotel when Discovery was abandoned, and transferred it to his cabin to smarten up the interior. Outside, he banked snow against the walls as high as his arms could reach, for insulation, and when he came back through the woods to his wife at night, he would see the whole cabin steaming, enveloped in steam, it was so cold.

At the first autumn frosts, the ptarmigan flocked by the thousand. "They were so thick you needed to kick the live ones out of the way in order to pick up the dead ones." The thin report of a .22 didn't seem to alarm them, and so Gairns would go home with sixty-two one day and eighty-one the next day, hauling them tied to long strings behind him. He got so many ptarmigan he just ate the livers, he claims. He'd see moose as numerous as in a barnyard when they bunched up in the fall to rut.

Nolan was facing a hungry winter once, when he'd made no money to carry him through. He was out in the buckbrush and saw a moose and knocked it down; except it got up. He knocked it down again with a shot, but it kept getting up, and each time he'd knock it down still another time. When the smoke and confusion cleared, he discovered that he'd shot six. He went home and bent some old iron to shoe his horse for the work, and they pulled the carcasses to the house the next morning. He smoked some and sold what he didn't need. "Good meat, wasn't it?" he said.

"I never tasted better!" his wife says decidedly. "I put it in the pressure cooker."

Then the dog stories . . . When the going was especially rugged by sled, Gairns would run out in front of the team with his rifle and pretend he'd just seen a snowshoe rabbit, and they were revitalized. One time they chased a moose, though, and got away from him, sleigh and all, with $500 in gold dust in a sack. Luckily the sack didn't fall off. His lead dog was Bruce and his shaft dog was Bob. The rest of the dogs hated both of them because Bruce could stay at a quiet trot when they needed to shift into a tiring lope and Bob, at the rear, was a bruiser who ran as if he were just about ready to eat them up. Bruce would pull the kids miles on their skis, patiently running alongside whenever the ground sloped downhill, and ignoring the ptarmigan which burst out of the snow. When the temperature fell to sixty below, grades one and two stayed home from school. Even then, they were all right outdoors as long as they didn't start wrestling and breathing the cold air too fast. After they finished primary school, Gairns moved the family to Vancouver for a while. But his kids had ten years on the creeks and his wife was the only woman for a very great distance—never a moment's rest at the dances.

Nolan says that his friends who went to Vancouver to spend their old age have died off. The way to live is to stay in the open. When I asked, he gave me a quick, coherent account of the trail trip from Smithers. Before jumping off, he and his cowboy went to see Gunanoot in Hazelton to get some directions, though this was partly a matter of form; everyone did. Gunanoot had ripened like cheese in the role of a pundit; he was bored and didn't like whites any more. They took his advice, nevertheless. After following the Skeena past the Tsimshian site of Kuldo, they cut off on the Slamgeesh, avoiding several tricky swims and the swampy lowlands of the Nass country, where the telegraph line itself went. They twisted up Slowmaldo Creek towards the snowy pass that ran along Groundhog Mountain. For a whole day there was nothing but timber, no feed, so they needed to drive the horses through briskly. They saw Groundhog Jackson's coal discovery, with lamps and miners' clothes in the deserted cabins and signs of poking and tinkering. The worst section came after that, a mountainside covered with poisonweed, doubly difficult because the trail was almost erased. They reached the source of the Skeena at last, crossed to the upper Spatsizi and the Little Klappan, and down to the main body of the Klappan, where they were confronted by their first really formidable swim.

They'd missed the proper ford, so that the daring mare who by custom led the way everywhere was pulled underwater by the current. She came up and managed to get back to the bank, but naturally none of the rest of the twelve would agree to go in after seeing that. Nolan jumped on a horse, forced it into the river, and swam alongside it until it had reached the opposite shore. There's an *esprit*, a momentum to a trail trip, and the others did follow then.

The only gun was a Luger. The boob of a cowboy had shot away all of the ammunition at the various caribou they had seen. When a mama wolf prowled into camp soon afterwards while they were eating lunch, Nolan had to get up and shoo her away by waving his hands. At the head of the Iskut they met a big band of goats who had descended to browse and explore, but they hadn't a bullet for one of them either. No meat. They swam the Klastine and fetched up on the gorgeous Stikine Canyon. A Tahltan who lived at the ford wanted to lead the horses across one at a time behind his boat at the end of a rope, charging for each, but Nolan and the cowboy pushed them all into the river as soon as the first one was well away, and they swam freely, saving him money. North from Telegraph Creek, the trail became easier and better defined because it was mostly plateau and because they were following the telegraph line again and the route of the regular mail run. They were home in a week or ten days.

[I X]

River-Gray,
River-Green

WEDNESDAY HAS BEEN THE focus of the week for me because of the mail flight to and from Telegraph Creek. Off we go again in the Beaver, Danny Bereza and I. We're so heavily loaded that the pontoons had to be specially pumped. Even so, they are half under water and we take off by brute strength. Danny does a fine act of twirling dials and switching switches while we climb into the rain. There's a courier nurse aboard. She drove down from Whitehorse at dawn with a Tahltan baby who has a cleft palate. The baby is on his way home to Casca with the palate still unrepaired, but it must be admitted that a lot of money has been spent by the government in transporting him back and forth. The mail is packed to the plane's ceiling, leaving just enough space for me to hunch doubled up in the freight compartment, with parcel post under my knees and parcel post over my head, looking down through a window as if I were in a glass-bottomed boat.

An outfitter has asked us to radio back if we spot his horses, so we watch for them for the first few minutes, passing over some sidehills and a mineral springs, stained iron-colored and dirty green-yellow. The creeks are gray with rainwater. As always, the landscape defeats description. We see the steep crossing point of the Telegraph Trail at the Nakina River, with a dab of meadow and some cabins surviving and lovely bottomland loops farther on, sinuous fertile meadow. By a mysterious pact that seems to exist between the clouds and the Coast Range Airways, they are always just high enough for us to sneak through the passes. We see a flock of geese swimming on a pond, and a long beaver dam, and a moose in a lake. The Stikine plateau is carved by a series of canyons, the greatest and grandest and reddest of which holds the Sheslay River. At its head are the remnants of the old Sheslay telegraph-relaying station. By the time we fly over the Tahltan River, in the tumbled country behind Telegraph Creek, we can look down on several other deserted cabins, mottled and ruined, the roofs a splinter of timbers as in a shipwreck. Circling above the Stikine, we squeeze down into the gorge, which seems hardly as wide as our wingtips, just like last week.

I helped unload the mail sacks and liquor. The Mountie helped with the liquor. Since I was here last, the Tahltans have voted to make their reserve wet, so there is nothing the Mountie can do except to come down and see whom the bottles are addressed to and whom he can expect to have trouble from. Otherwise, the principal news is that a rockslide has blocked the Tahltan River, preventing thousands of salmon from spawning. A government helicopter has flown in to try to lift them over it. In the meantime, the Kennecott Company helicopter has been shifted elsewhere.

People have been telling me that I ought to visit the Klondike, since I'm so near, but I've been eschewing that advice.

Better to go back to Telegraph and keep my summer consistent. Besides, as I've mentioned, the gold country is 1920s in spirit, and I prefer the 1930s. My own growing-up years were the 1950s, a grim muzzled decade which I refused to be bound by or to have much to do with. I had strenuous, old-fashioned summer jobs which paid $14 a week. I hitchhiked for thousands of miles, crossing the country six times, on each of the major highways, and even rode the rods for a bit. I got to know coal miners, sheepherders and cannery workers. I fought forest fires professionally, and got myself fired from a job at the World Jungle Compound, a zoo in Ventura, California, for climbing into a mountain lion's cage. I acquired the hobo's aloofness; I find good-byes easy to say, believing that we are alone to begin with anyway, and that the good-bye only returns us to our original state. At prep school and Harvard I hoarded back copies of the *Daily Worker*. I attended meetings of a Trotskyite cell in the theater district in Boston, and then perjured myself when I entered the army by signing a statement that I never had. So Telegraph Creek with its 1930s atmosphere is like home to me.

The Callbreaths are out of town. I'd be out of luck for a bed tonight if it weren't for the two McPhee brothers. I climbed the familiar series of terraces, and there were Dan's two tall sled dogs and his little black bear dog in the yard. It was like old times for him, taking a homeless man in. When Dan and his wife ran a restaurant here, they gave away more meals than they sold, Alec says. He himself, though—he'd curl up under a tree on the riverbank if he was me. No, no, Dan says, I can't do that, I'm not like them, I'm out of my element here. Both of them are drunk because Dan's grown-up son, who boards with him and regulates him, is on vacation in Fort St. John. Whenever he goes away Dan brews up a hundred bottles of sweet beer. (He brews a hundred bottles because he *has* a hundred bottles.) We sit together on the chairs upholstered with beaverskins, Dan dryly humorous, his name stenciled on his spectacles, which tilt at an angle of forty degrees. Alec is accustomedly buoyant, with yellow-white hair and round blue eyes. "Am I drunk again?" He sings us a song:

> Oh, if I owned the Western Union cable,
> And took Mr. Woolworth's daughter as my wife,
> And owned all the stocks in the Wall Street stable,
> Then I think that I'd be satisfied with life . . .

Dan is the only socialist in the area, so he says that for thirty-six years he's "thrown away every vote I've cast." He worked on a flounder boat in the Aleutians once, and Alec is quizzing and pestering him on how many feet make a fathom. "Come on, quick, tell me what it is!"

Watching me scribble notes, Dan remembers that he had a partner one time who could write shorthand, only Dan didn't know it. For a month or more they prospected along and his partner, a thoughtful fellow, would drop little notes on the trail, notes to himself that he'd finished with, and Dan, picking them up, thought there must be a Chinaman traveling ahead of them. Then, because we're having a party, he remembers a birthday one of the riverboat captains had. The McPhees gave him a haunch of moosemeat, one of the ladies present gave him a scarf, and somebody else a rice-grain gold nugget. And a girl was there, maybe a bit drunk, who hadn't anything handy to give, so she gets up and pats her honey-sweet ass and says she'll give him a piece of that.

The walls are covered with dog-team photographs, and there's a yoke and two pails hanging up for carrying water from the Stikine. I can see Gus Adamson out the window, and Wriglesworth's house, and A. J. Marion's steep snow roof: all these old *walkers*, sustaining each other now. When one dies, they will all suddenly feel fragile, they'll all be ready to leave and look for an old-age home, but as long as they can look around and see one another they feel okay.

Dan visited his daughter in Calgary last July and found it almost impossible to take his usual sunrise walk. In the first place, the city fathers had neglected to put sidewalks on most of the roads. And he couldn't get up and out of the house by six o'clock. When he did finally find an appropriate time, he was stared at like a giraffe by the motorists who were streaming by —he with his nimble mountain-man's stride that devoured the miles. There's a euphoria that walking over a mountain range brings. He came up behind a bull moose on his way into Telegraph once and gave it a whap on the rump. The moose could have kicked him in half, but instead it practically jumped out of its skin. Another time, on the Scud, when he was trapping marten, he picked up a low spruce limb and a grizzly crawled out of a hole underneath where it had been sleeping. For half a mile they walked side by side, each watching to make sure the other didn't attack. Dan came back the following day and shot it for feed, but it was such a fat bear that his dogs couldn't make any headway, they couldn't dig in their teeth at all.

"No, they don't like that yellow fat," says Alec. When he lived down by the Katete on the Stikine, he was watching a bear in front of his house who was groping under the bank for frogs or crayfish or muskrats or whatever. It ignored Alec, and he reciprocated by ignoring it. But this was a really weird bear; soon it turned and lurched towards the house like a drunk gone beserk, or as if it had gone blind and out of its head. It hit the door with its paw, and Alec had only just time to grab hold of a gun.

Alec ticks off some of the other rivers he's been on, a fabulous list: the Jennings, the Sheslay, the Inklin, the Sicintine, the Kawdy, the Dudidontu, the Duti, the Parallel, the Kluatantan. One summer he went out for 105 days, prospecting north in a circle to the Rancheria River, where he was too late to get in on the actual strike, but stayed to shovel a few hundred dollars in flour gold. Heading home, he stopped near Dease Lake to help some friends make their clean-up before the fall freeze, working for free, although even the fellow's wife was picking up nuggets under the dam that they'd fixed.

The fall rains had put a strain on the dam. It was touch and go whether they would lose the pocket of dust they had trapped, but they succeeded in getting it out.

"You don't want nuggets, especially. What you want is rice-sized grains if you're working a creek," says Dan.

The Hudson's Bay man has sorted the mail, so we go down to check on that and to look at the Indian girls on Front Street, with their black shining hair dangling around their shoulder blades. Dan's wife and Alec's girlfriend (the one who fell overboard into the Stikine and drowned) both came from Front Street. The kids are up in the second-floor windows, straddling the sills, and the women stand watching us in the doors. Dan says somebody offered to sleep with him for a dollar but he doubted that he could still get it up so he just loaned her the dollar instead.

Noticing me back, the Hudson's Bay man asks, "What do you have, some sort of gold mine here?" I laugh and say no, thinking yes.

Dan fries us a pan of corned-beef hash. "This is turkey to me, you know, a man out of the bush." Some home brew is spilled on the floor. Even there it smells pretty good. The recipe is to take ten gallons of warm water, ten pounds of sugar, five pounds of malt, two yeast cakes and stir and let sit for seventy-two hours. Then bottle the mix if you want to preserve it, or if you like foaming beer. Otherwise finish it all within fifteen hours.

Dan was a deputy policeman for a while. He was left in charge of the town and let all the jailbirds out for a moose hunt. A guy from the Boundary walked up with a sled load of booze which he'd been working on most of the winter. He needed the money badly, so Dan helped him sell it. He and Alec were also the town's gravediggers. We talk about various burials. They were slow with their hole sometimes and the funeral party would fidget and wait. Dan's wife died lingeringly of cancer; first she was hospitalized in Whitehorse; then, when the charges increased, in another hospital in B. C. The trip south in a jalopy, transferring her, was the most horrifying incident in his life.

Both McPhees are very much easier with me now that I've been off and made the effort to return. They're convinced that I'm serious and that I like them. I've never felt quite so immediately at home. In the evening we strolled next door to look at the skiff Mr. Wriglesworth is building. It's twenty-three feet long—a five-day job—all finished now except for wrapping the ribs in a plywood veneer, "the same as putting a shirt on." He's planning to paint it peacock blue.

Dan's Indian father-in-law was a notable guide. While the light held, he showed me an album of photographs from a map-making expedition up the Nahanni River to Fort Yukon in 1928. And he talked about his own arrival in British Columbia in 1911, prospecting for sturgeon. He remembers the herds of thousands of seals he used to see in the Aleutians, and the caribou on Ice Mountain—five thousand migrating slowly past during the autumn of 1933.

JULY 28, THURSDAY:

NEEDLESS TO SAY, I love this town. Atlin has the blue lake, the Swiss view and the swish-swash historic hurrah of the Rush, but it isn't niched into a worn river bluff like Telegraph Creek. While I brushed my teeth by the pile of dog sleds in back of McPhee's, a hummingbird zipped and hovered beside my head. Dan has insomnia. He was weeding his potato patch, whistling softly, by five in the morning, teasing his bear dog.

The bear dogs! . . . What are there, two or three left? McPhee's once belonged to a Hudson's Bay man, who was going to shoot it; he had already shot its brother. It ran into Dan's house quivering, and he let it stay. Long before the grizzlies are exterminated, the last Tahltan Bear Dog will be dead. One wants to record them for the future—that they were black and pint-sized, vociferous, skinny and gutsy, that they moved on springs, lived by their wits, darted about, apprehensive as well as courageous, and that they seemed to know in these final few years that they were doomed as a race. They look up at us constantly.

The huskies are chained. Like good sleigh dogs, they exist without food or water in the summer, and don't seem to be particularly thirsty or ravenous when I offer them something. As thin as greyhounds, they suspend animation and live on the air, or an occasional pot of grease and potatoes. When they were working, Dan's pair used to be able to mush the whole distance up from the Scud in a single day, maybe stopping at the Chutine to pick up the Wriglesworths too. Last winter he loaned them to a beaver trapper, but then took them back because the fellow was overloading them, putting two beavers across each dog's withers.

The beer is stronger today, being a day older, so we've been laughing all morning, Dan slumped in his chair as if he consisted of nothing but legs and a drawn, haggy face. He raised muskmelons on his farm downriver, it was so warm, and ate a wild green called lamb's-quarter for salad. In baking he says that he didn't bother with yeast or with baking powder or sourdough "mother"; he just used an old wooden pail that he never cleaned for mixing the batter, and let the stuff stand overnight. His best friend was George Adzit, a guide with a territory about as extensive as Yellowstone Park, who ran the mail with two teams and two sleds because of the freighting he did on the side. For a price Adzit would bring anything over the trail, from a radio to an iron stove, and he worked himself dizzy at Christmas. He was a prankish hunter. He'd make his rich clients strip down to the buff in making a stalk, "like the Indians do. Follow me. Keep up close!" he would say. He would get them sniffing on their hands and knees and next to his big bare bum for the crawl, then fart. Adzit's favorite dish was to boil the nose of a moose, peel off the skin, and eat what was underneath with "bum gut," the fat off a moose's rear end, which is a delicacy and "doesn't repeat on you," according to Dan. He'd go out with nothing but salt and tea for supplies and come back a month or more later, wearing caribou shanks on his feet and carrying a caribou's stomach over his shoulder which he'd packed full with groundhog meat.

The riverboat, the *Judith Ann*, arrived this afternoon, announced by the peculiarly industrious pounding grind that the engine has. In the distance it looked like a bug; it made the river look wide. Everybody ran down for the event. The same crew, but among the passengers a jittery New York acquaintance of mine and her husband and boys. They hired a truck to drive to the relic capital of Tahltan, so I grabbed the chance to come along. It was a wonderful windy ride and I found a new metropolitan smile on my face. The couple, both likable people, live separately the whole year except for the summer, when they get together for the sake of the boys. Just as I do, they like their winter life and their summer life too. Since the wife has money of her own, the husband has no support payments to make, but he probably spends an equivalent amount on airplane fares from the West to New York.

Past Willie Campbell's farm, the canyon began to enlarge on a grand scale, with giddy cliffs and slides of rubble and volcanic chimneys and stools. Indian families were camped for the fish. From two hundred feet up we saw a huge salmon leap like a horse on a merry-go-round. A snow-headed eagle was hungrily circling close above. The Tahltan River winds back from the Stikine into its own narrow gorge, and Tahltan village is between the two rivers, but a mile off. It sits up on a strongly defendable, windblown rise, like the site of an old Berber fort, ringed with toothed ridges and crenellated slopes. We climbed up and found a doughty bell tower and church, the organ collapsed on the floor, a schoolhouse still heaped with bluebooks and maps of the world, and a smokehouse and four or five other structures that once had been homes. The smokehouse, as big as the church, contains drying racks and fire pits. It is walled with thin willow poles, spaced so that the smoke can seethe between them.

A stovepipe hung by a string in the door to one of the cabins, swinging alarmingly when the wind blew, like a phantom disturbed. The floor had caved in, exposing a storage cellar underneath, and the rooms were heaped with gold pans, garden tools, harness and rigging, bedsprings, two tables, a curtain, bits of bedding and a rocking chair with a bottle of gonorrhea medicine on it. The log walls were lined with cardboard and a layer of burlap tacked on top of that. The burlap was densely papered over with sheets of *The Illustrated London News* of 1896–97–98, and *The Tatler* of 1911–12. *After an absence from England of nearly two months, Queen Alexandra, accompanied by Queen Maud of Norway and the Crown Prince Olaf, and Princess Victoria, reached London last week on her return from Copenhagen . . . Lord and Lady Liverpool are members of a circle of which one hears comparatively little, as far as social doings are concerned. For although Lord Liverpool owns a town house in Grosvenor Gardens, he and his wife entertain only on a very quiet scale during the season.*

There are also one or two mining-camp papers, in which a doctor advertises his thirty-four years' experience in treating venereal disease. He says his practise is limited to men. A Mrs. Holborn is arraigned in court for fornication. *"Interestingly enough, the two witnesses for the prosecution are said to be Mrs. Holborn's own sons."*

Although the Tahltans accepted the presence of missionaries and never warred with the whites, they lived here into the early years of this century, negotiating with the newcomers from a position of independence and strength. The ground is footworn and littered with arrowhead chips. It's heady to wander around the site. Gaps lead through the ridges to the caribou hills beyond, and there are five salmon runs a year in the two rivers below the bowl of the town. As many as several thousand Tlingits would show up for the annual conclave in the fall, and the Tahltans, greatly outnumbered, under a lady chief then, would meet them with poise. The very last residents were Broken-jaw Dick Quash and his wife, famous snowshoe-makers, who died in the flu epidemic of the Second World War.

My friends' city youngsters had read about Tenzing, so they climbed soberly until they were dots on the ridge. We called them in and bounced home to Telegraph Creek.

"You can stay here the rest of your life, as long as I don't have to cook for you," Dan said when I got back. He had been drinking Wrangell beer on the *Judith Ann*, on top of his own "black bottom" stuff, so he was half snooted. Lazy the way I am, I went down to the boat and stood plaintively in front of the galley windows, but the cook never invited me in. "Women aren't always thinking of feeding you when they look at you, you know," Dan said.

JULY 29, FRIDAY:

THE BOMBASTIC HEALTH SERVICE nurse, the dogged Anglican minister with his slog like an overworked farm boy's, the lantern-jawed, skinny, unlikely priest—these people grow on one. I talked today to Father de Campigneulles, who was left to care for the handful of Tahltan Catholics after the Caribou Hiders moved to Eddontenajon. He's of the Oblates of Mary Immaculate, a worldwide missionary order which originated in Aix-en-Provence in 1816. He says the entire Canadian West was evangelized by them, from Winnepeg to the Alaskan border. As the southerly areas became self-supporting dioceses, they moved out and north. His bishop is in Whitehorse and his superior general in Rome is a French Canadian. As for himself, he gave up the idea of ever living in France again when he joined the order. He calls himself Father Decamp.

The church is a yellow-roofed log cabin, redone attractively indoors with tan paneling and the altar close to the congregation. The Anglicans, as the first group in town, built their church right by the stores and the riverboat landing, so the Catholics built high above on a terrace overlooking the whole. Decamp has a deep abrupt voice with a winy French accent

and a straight, powerful mouth which breaks suddenly into a
sly, boyish smile. He's thirty-seven, serious and tense unless he
turns playful. He wears a black work shirt and pants (just as
the Mountie goes around in a sport shirt most of the time), and
has big ears and a large Adam's apple. Aside from playing
chess with the schoolteachers, he drives for a chat with the
fathers at Eddontenajon or at the asbestos mine once in a while
for recreation. Otherwise, he gets a week's retreat every year,
and at the end of six years has three months off, when he goes
to his relatives in France. But that's too long a holiday, really,
he says, and before it's up, he starts touring the secondary
schools, recruiting for the order. His religion is intellectual,
"with the mind, not the feelings, because feelings are always
fooling. When people don't go to church, they don't because
they 'don't feel like it,' not because their opinions have
changed; so feelings are not to be trusted."

DeCamp speaks with forceful gestures about the pride and
honesty of the Tahltans, how they are different from the Indians he knew in the Yukon. He tutors the promising kids and
taxis the women out to their husbands in the fishing camps
along the Stikine and then back to their children again. Besides
these errands and performing the sacraments, of course, it is
his function to be a kind of a watching eye. There are three
pairs of eyes, the Mountie's and the two clergymen's, and
Decamp impresses me as probably the best. If he saw the
Indians being mulcted, he would have no direct, instant power
to interfere, but oddball that he is, he's well adapted to keeping
an eye peeled.

Later on I climbed above Dry Town to look at the river
wriggling below, quite modest in the course that it takes,
because there is scarcely room for it to get through in country
like this. Rivers seen only in passing are like other people's
children, but after two months this one in its laborious canyon
seems mine. This is my Mississippi. I love it as I have never
loved any piece of land or any other scene. I'd like to live in a
room river-gray, river-green.

Gus Adamson was in Dry Town looking for help for his

next snagging trip and not finding it. His chunky, punched face was very forlorn. We were affectionate with each other. Everybody has loosened up with me on this second visit; I'm even getting a peek at some diaries, though they seldom have anything in them but lists of work done and the weather. The Callbreaths are back. Roy appears to be dying of his ulcer,* and Eva tells me how much she hopes they go out for the winter, but I doubt that her diary hears either tale.

Wildness is a relative term. What's different here is that people write inarticulately in their diaries at night instead of watching TV. The last time I lived in British Columbia I saw two bears shot and several drunken Indians skidding their cars around Hazelton on Saturday night. But in the first week or two after I had returned to New York, I saw a man shot on the street—he sat on a stoop holding his stomach. And I was on the subway when a man jumped underneath, giving a desolate, memorable scream. And the boiler exploded in my building, setting a fire and blowing the floor out of the apartment below me.

JULY 30, SATURDAY:

TALKED TO EDDY FRANK, who is the current Tahltan chief. He's a sensible, practical, positive fellow, like Alec Jack, his colleague in Eddontenajon. Like him, he holds the post of school janitor, which is apparently reserved for these chiefs. Though there were parties going on in town, he was sanding and varnishing a door that the kids have scarred with baseballs. He wished he could take a club to them—"kill or cure." We talked about other problems he has, like the horses that crack the cement by brazenly stepping up on the porch of the school to get out of the sun. Last month when he went to Ten Mile to fight a forest fire, the kids seized the chance to break in, though they didn't do much. One of his own sons is study-

* He didn't. As of 1968, I understand that only A. J. Marion is dead in T. C.

ing instrument-flying in order to join an airline, and since his conversation is all about his job and this son, it seemed it would be condescending if I were to change the subject to my outmoded topics of pelts and trails.

I walked from the school to the Casca reserve and its bright-colored roofs. To the south the sky was a rain-mush of clouds, but I and the kids who surrounded me were standing in sunshine and shining grass. Almost every adult was away fishing. One guy had written with stove soot on his front door —"Anybody who monkeys with this cabin, you're crookeder than a dog's hind leg!" I did manage to speak with John Carlick, a vigorous, mulatto-faced man who was the chief before Eddy Frank. "Nuthin' for nuthin'," he said cheerfully. He wanted money. He's half Negro and is one of the "hard" Indians. In fact his trapline was on Hard Mountain, which is above the Sheslay, but he wouldn't give me so much as a pippin of information after saying that.

I'm installed at the Callbreaths' again, eating salmon steaks and saskatoon pie—enough of McPhee's corned-beef hash. The other customers are the fisheries helicopter crew. The pilot is a Peter Pan lad close to forty with an urbane, concentric face. Like the Kennecott pilot, the Negro, he has flown fighter planes and traveled the world. There's an air force ready room atmosphere to the place, war books strewn around. Helicopters are more difficult to fly than airplanes; you graduate to them from the air force jets, if you don't want to work for TWA. So if you're Negro or homosexual or a guy on the lam, you come out to the bush or to Malawi or to Pakistan. Bush pilots like Danny Bereza fly with their native verve and homing instinct and the seat of their pants, but these guys fly like professionals, lights winking, gear checked, engine revved up beforehand, and with a cold calm. They're the best we have here. I go out to watch them take off. Since I'm a little askew myself, the friendship comes easily. The pilot for Kennecott, like most Negroes my age nowadays, was vocal and brash in a crowd, very animated, like a pickpocket at a posh ball. He put up a bold bustly front, but he was always expecting the sheriff's hand on his shoulder and a voice to boom out, "You're Negro!" This is how I often feel when I'm not stuttering but just about to.

JULY 31, SUNDAY:

THE MOUNTIE SAW SOME real action last night. He braved a gunfight and collared his man without shooting him, unlike an American cop. An Indian in Casca was drunk and firing a shotgun out of his window at anybody who moved. The Mountie put on his dress uniform and went up and arrested him; then never mentioned it this morning, although I happened to spend a good while with him—I heard about it from somebody else. Tonight the generator is on and the lights in the jail are glaring. The Wriglesworths in their Sunday clothes are sitting up with the prisoner as paid turnkeys, spelling the Mountie off. They got the job because they are popular people and have to scrimp, not being eligible yet for old-age benefits. Tomorrow the Mountie will make the long drive to a town where there is some kind of a judge.

AUGUST 1, MONDAY:

ANOTHER WET DAY. LOTS of cloud action. In bright sunshine the rain pours down, as white as a snowfall. I'm waiting for Thursday's boat to Wrangell, which if the river rises or falls won't turn up at all, but I don't much care. I'm a person with nervous energy but not inexhaustible energy-energy, and I'm tired now—too tired emotionally to stay here any longer alone, but too tired physically to go. I've been rambling about, looking at the lofty-roofed Hudson's Bay building, architecturally noble in pattern. The kids on the steps in front, their mouths blue from berrying, are bending soda-pop cans in their hands. Mike Williams and Ah Clem's son dash out to Six Mile and back with the panel truck loaded with salmon. This is the height of the midsummer run. They give them away; every-body has a twenty-pound fish in his cooler. Gus Adamson gets plenty of fish from his wife's relatives. He fascinates me be-cause he won't answer the least of my questions, yet he's softened so much since I've come back that I bet in another week he would. He's had to postpone the snagging trip be-cause his crewmen are "cached" somewhere, hiding out, and he's depressed, a bantam man with oversized arms, like Pop-eye's, and oversized pants.

Father Decamp is in overalls, fixing a punctured muffler, showing his teeth, muttering imprecations in French. He works with the desperation of a fellow who knows that he isn't good with his hands, but hasn't got anyone else to turn to. Dan McPhee is out cutting a piece of telegraph wire from an old spool to push through his pipe from the creek. The pipe is plugged with vegetation and is itself composed of old steam-boat boiler tubing, salvaged from a wreck near the mouth of the Scud in 1949. They fished with boat hooks for the purser's cash box and for the mail sacks. Dan has a cataract in one of his eyes. He says the Indians' treatment for this would be to peel it off with a fingernail. Now that I've lived in his house he says he can tell me anything and that anyway he'll be dead when my book comes out. He claims its faults are going to be that I've talked to too few of the women. No doubt he's right. I've missed Big Mary, for one, though he says that she never speaks any more. She was six-foot-three and already supposed to be ninety when he arrived in Telegraph Creek. Now she has shrunk down to about four feet.

At dusk I went to a warehouse Dan told me about along-side the river, all iron and tin. Inside were dozens of sets of enormous antlers reaching up toward the roof like a throng of hands. Heroic, huge antlers, too big to come across now. There was something Inferno-esque about their dim groping, like souls dead and gone, but something quite jubilant too, espe-cially the outspread caribou tines. I went to Monkey Jackson's old cabin as well, where I stumbled upon an antique organ, still pumpable. I played like a gibbering ghost, hoping to scare someone. To begin with I played in the major scales so that any listener wouldn't be *frightfully* scared. Finally, getting impatient, I struck off tumultuous, grating chords, minor-key, that at least succeeded in frightening me. The creek drowned it out for the village, though, and I played for fun, remembering the Central Park carousel. I'm ready to see New York again. Am reading *Parade's End* and trying *Tristam Shandy*. Summer books.

AUGUST 2, TUESDAY:

WAS LIFTED TODAY BY my fisheries friends to the slide on the Tahltan River where the salmon are blocked. The Tahltan is the main spawning tributary of the Stikine, which is naturally why the tribe gave it their name. Lately, most of the fish are being harvested by Alaskan boats on the coast and therefore the Americans are footing part of the bill. The operation has been a fiasco so far. The first plan was to have the men on the ground scoop the fish into barrels of water that the helicopter simply lifted upriver. The fish were traumatized by this, however, and the water in the barrels became toxic to them. At present, the helicopter only ferries the men back and forth and takes the foreman on tours. His dilemma is that if he blows a passage with dynamite he will kill all the fish who are waiting and perhaps precipitate a worse slide.

The canyon is a rudimentary steep V, the walls clay and silt. The river within looks slender and white from the air, but the damaged area is like an artillery range, pitted with boulders, heaped with khaki-colored debris. Our arrival sent up legions of birds—eagles, crows, gulls from the sea. Being left to my own devices, I explored gingerly, completely alone once the pilot dropped me. It's only a little neighborhood river but it moves with violent velocity. The *water* gets through, all right; it has blasted a zigzag chute for itself with the force of a fire hose. Just to sit in the thunder and watch is awesome. There

were so many fish waiting in the slower water below the chute
that half an hour must have gone by before I was even aware
of them. I listened and looked at the gulls who had gotten the
word and had traveled so far. I thought the actual fish were
thickets of driftwood that the river had smashed together and
submerged; their fins stuck out like a welter of branches. I was
astonished instead at the carnage on shore, the bear-chewed or
beak-bitten bodies scattered about everywhere. When I did see
the living fish I gaped because there were many thousands.
The Tahltan was jammed with them, flank to flank and atop
one another, seldom moving, just holding whatever position
they'd gained, though that took continual swimming.
Hundreds of them were in water which scarcely covered their
backs. I thought of shark fins, except that there was a capitula-
tion to it, a stockade stillness, as if they were prisoners of war
waiting in huddled silence under the river's bombarding roar.
The pity I felt was so strong that I did everything I could not
to alarm the ones nearest me. They were in an eddy behind a
boulder a few feet away, and I wouldn't have dreamed of
touching one of them. Each had fought to attain that eddy, and
at any confusion or weakening of resolve he lost his hold and
was washed downstream. Like mountain climbers, the most
active fish would wiggle twenty yards further on and gain a
new cranny. It might require a number of tries, but they were
the freshest fish, unscarred, and occasionally one would get
into some partially sheltered corner of the chute itself, in one of
the zigs or zags. These dozen desperate niches were so packed
that they were like boxfuls of crated fish set into the bullet-
gray water. The salmon who were able to battle upcurrent did
so by shimmying and thrusting more than by leaping, although they did leap now and again. This was the cruelest
sight of all, because they were like paper airplanes thrown into
the hydrant blast. The water shattered and obliterated the leap
and then banged the limp, tender body down the same stretch
of rapids that it had been fighting its way up for perhaps the
past day and a half.

Most of the salmon were quite catatonic by now. They just held their own in whichever clump or eddy they'd reached, unless some pathetic impulse moved them again. They might try to better themselves, only to be dislodged and lose fifteen yards. For me, walking back and forth on the bank with absolute freedom, it was eerie to watch a spectacle of death that was measured in feet and yards. I could lift a fly out of a spider's web but I couldn't assist these salmon. The swimmer who drowns is surrounded by fish who scull at their ease, and I suppose there was something in it about spheres of existence and the difference between being on water and land. But I felt like a witness at a slow massacre. Thirty thousand fish, each as long as my arm, stymied and dying in the droning roar.

These were sockeyes. Their bodies have a carroty tint on top of the back at spawning time, often quite bright, and their heads turn a garish green. They wear a lurid, mascaraed look, a tragedian's look, as if they were dressed for an *auto-da-fé*. I could tell how long a fish had been waiting by the color he'd turned and also, especially, by the length of his nose. This was another delayed discovery. All of them were gashed from being battered on the rocks, but some, I realized in horror, had practically no nose left, as though a fishmonger had amputated it, as though he had thrown the poor fish on his chopping block and cut off the front end right by the eyes.

The Stikine is a very rough river. Permanent canyons shut off its upper tributaries to the salmon entirely. The Spatsizi, the Pitman, the Klappan have none. Tahltan Lake happens to be ideal for spawning, but this year only two individuals out of the umpteen thousands who've tried have been seen by the fisheries counters to have reached the lake. Salmon live in the ocean for four years or so before they return, by the grace of some unexplained recording device, to the fresh-water source where they were born. They lay their eggs, languish genteelly and die. Thus four generations are in the sea at a time, and when a rock slide occurs, three years can go by before the blockage *has* to be cleared. If the fourth generation is equally foiled when it tries to spawn, then the river ceases to be a salmon river because no other salmon are living with memories of how to swim there. Given that much time, the Tahltan itself, fire hose that it is, might manage to clear its bed of the debris of the slide, but in the meantime a lot of commercial fishermen will be going broke.

The seven-man ground crew, arriving on the opposite bluff, stood looking at me. I was reminded uneasily of what the Tahltans did to the early prospectors who trespassed during a salmon run: they stripped them and tossed them in. These fellows descended the bluff by means of a rope, put on rubber suits, took long-handled nets and commenced to dip salmon out of the niches and crannies along the lower sides of the chute, sixty pounds at a clip. It was a fisherman's dream until about the thirty-ninth netload, and then, as somebody said, you would never want to fish again. They'd constructed a rock-walled pool next to the chute with an exit into the river above, and in assembly-line fashion they dumped their catches in that, although it was such an onerous business one man was kept busy simply repairing the nets. They worked with care, hurrying the fish to the pool before they could smother, with the common benevolence we have nowadays, for the race but not for the individual. Yesterday they moved something like twenty-three hundred, so it seemed very promising, except I'd already been told that there is a second rockslide upriver which the fish are not able to pass and there isn't the manpower to lift them over that one yet.

The eagles were reveling in the air like bank robbers who had broken into the vault. All they could see below them was fish; the river smelled like a fish-peddler's cart. The gulls sat by the water, so fat by now that they ate only the eyes. The river raged by like a forest fire, while the living fish in it, as silent as climbers, clung to the eddies for their very lives. The level had fallen, draining several of the pools on the edge. There fish lay in the sand in spoke patterns where they'd been trapped, with gaping eyes and their gills aghast, like victims stretched in a common grave.

Walking downriver, I met grizzly tracks; also coyote and

fox tracks and tracks of black bear: then more grizzly tracks —little bears, big bears and cub bear tracks. Blood and roe were smeared over the rocks. A lynx had been licking at it. Immense fish heads stared up. But the salmon still in the Tahltan were much warier and less fatigued here. They were newcomers and were alarmed when they blundered into the shallows, instead of resting in exhausted droves. This far downstream it became like a regular salmon river, the fish dawdling along in a placid if cautious manner, keeping a decent distance from one another, though their fins filled the river and they were obviously unaccustomed to such constricted circumstances after their free-swimming years at sea. When one of them leaped, it was a superleap, a fat-bellied, splendid, classic leap, not overwhelmed. They looked startlingly large and maneuverable, as if they would not be easy to catch despite the glut and congestion and the squeezed gauntlet that they had to run. When I matched my boot with a grizzly's paws, our hind feet turned out to be the same size. His forepaws were about as broad as my boot was long. His stool consisted of nothing but berry seeds, so yesterday he was up in the meadows and this morning he was down biting salmon in half.

On my way home, I stopped at the Wood family's smoke-house above the main river to see some salmon who had come to a different end. It's an ambitious structure, like the one at Tahltan. Water from a spring flows by on a series of wooden flumes, where the fish are washed. Mr. Wood, a gentle fellow from Casca, has a couple of pickling barrels for the fish that he wants to salt. Most of them are split and hung inside, however, spitted on long poles so that they look like tobacco curing, on two levels. The smoke comes from small piles of fireweed burning under two washtubs with holes punched in them, but the red fish make the whole barn seem on fire—salmon from floor to ceiling, as thick as red leaves.

Of course there would be no salmon if every time a creek was blocked by a slide all of its spawning stock died futilely, butting the rocks. Suppressed and feeble under the instinct to return to the single site at all cost is a counterurge. After taking a terrific beating, some very few of those Tahltan salmon will let the current wash them downstream into the Stikine and down the Stikine to the Chutine or perhaps the Katete to search for another spawning ground.

AUGUST 3, WEDNESDAY:

THIS MORNING I WALKED five miles up Telegraph Creek. It could be called Toad Creek or Squirrel Creek just as properly, and except for the views of Sheep Mountain, it might be a brook in New England. I doubled back to the cliffs above Dry Town for a gaze at the river. The snorts of the Creyke family's horses below me came up like the sound of ducks flying. I watched a dog run down to the cove for his daily bath. He soaked pleasurably in the water, then ran to the garbage dump in order to move his bowels.

The rains have kept the river at a healthy height and everyone expects the boat to arrive by tomorrow night. The buzz of traffic helps make me feel ready to leave—two or three helicopters today with mining men; plus the fisheries helicopter; a survey geographer's plane which touched down to celebrate somebody's birthday; a plane from Alaska carrying hunters; and a timber company's airplane with two cruisers aboard who plan some day to log the Stikine. Even Danny Bereza was in and out, ferrying away two TB patients. Alec McPhee says ebulliently that during the flu epidemic of 1944 he was in the Indians' cabins all the time, hammering coffins and putting them in, and never caught the sickness. He just sipped a little whiskey whenever he left the room. He's been lucky in any case, all those years as a powder man snagging the river. The same way with bears: you can keep them at bay if you don't look at them. He says that he hasn't been to the city since 1911.

Alec blinks, twists his mouth, twists his head, taps his feet, like a boy sitting in the kitchen chair, not an old man. He's waiting for meat, he says. The nurse, who has gone with the TB patients to Whitehorse, has promised to bring him some. He's tired of salmon and cornmeal mush, and what good are the turnips and carrots and beets and potatoes he's raising without some fresh meat to go with them? He's had no meat the whole summer that wasn't canned—how about that? he says—a man who used to pile up his cache with enough moose and goat to feed a barracks of infantry. Can't hunt or chop his own firewood. He talks about the seven-month winters he passed on the trapline seeing not a soul, and yet they went quickly enough—and there were those long snowshoe runs to town if they didn't. He would set out his beaver traps as late as he could in the evening because the river changed level continually. Then, the next morning, it took as much as an hour to skin out one skin and fix it on the stretching board. Year by year the price fell: inflation in all the staples of life but deflation in beaverskins. There was a glacier nearby with a warm springs at the bottom, with slick clay banks, where he swam in the spring. He'd go up for a hike on the ice after visiting his traps and doing the chores, and skid down, pretending his boots were skis, and rip off his clothes and plunge in the pool. So many cutthroat trout congregated there that you could fill a fish tub in half an hour. The beaver and moose got in too, especially when there was snow around, so you'd find your whole livelihood there, the meat, the fish and the furs, and have yourself a fine swim as well.

He speaks with equal affection for all the shareholders of life —the wolves, the beaver, the moose, the marten, the Siwash, the whites and the salmon. When he prospected through to the very head of the Nahlin, the water got ankle-deep, shallow even for salamanders, but still the fantastic salmon were wiggling upstream, their dorsal fins dried to a crisp from being in the air. It was August, the stream had shrunk to a dribble, but they wiggled toward where they remembered that they ought to be. Every creek Alec came to had a miner already on it, gophering sand into a sluice which he'd whipsawed and nailed together. Maybe if the bed had gone dry he would have constructed a trestle-and-ditch arrangement bringing in water from some other creek, dug out and planked for five or six miles. It was almost beyond belief; it was Chinaman's work, Alec says, where you went out and lived for a year on rice, and yet nobody ever got tired of shoveling gold. You could work all day and the only rest that you needed was to stop for a minute and look at the dust trickling down the riffles of the sluice into the pay box.

He looks out the window at his garden. Beans and potatoes but no meat—how about that! Moose are at their best for eating right now, with the summer flesh on. Or the geese that he used to get, the size of a Christmas turkey. In September, along with the swans, they migrated through the pass just over his cabin by the thousands, fat for the jubilant journey south.

We're peering downriver, expecting the *Judith Ann* tomorrow. The Wriglesworths are puttering about in their new peacock skiff. The sun has turned the river tin-colored and written on it the swing of the current. It's a banner-blue day.

[X]

Last Talks

T HE NEXT DAY was not so happy. I waited into the night
and for most of the day after that for the boat, hearing
its counterfeit in the town's generators. I was surprised how
disappointed and even a bit panicky I felt when it became
overdue, as if I were going to be stuck in the bush for longer
than I had bargained for. The Indians were fishing and I
realized how empty the village was when they were away. My
novelty, which had animated the old-timers, had worn off, just
as their novelty was over for me. We sat reading last year's
True magazines.

The second night, after I'd almost given up watching for it,
the boat did arrive, the barge in front loaded heavily. Dan
McPhee strode down to see about a barrel of stove oil he had
ordered, and Gus Adamson to talk to Captain Callbreath about
any snags in the river which should be removed. Alec McPhee

walked down simply because he's alert and alive, and the Wriglesworths went in order to chat with the lady cook, which is a tradition with them. For years and years the quick weekly visits of her predecessors at Chutine Landing were the only feminine company Edith had. The boat brought the old men of Telegraph Creek more to life than they are at any other time, and suddenly I grew regretful.

At five on Saturday morning we weighed away. The river and sky were muddy-silver. The terraced cluster of houses slipped by, emotionally for me, and lastly the big white Hudson's Bay. Two miles below town, at Buck's Bar, where gold was discovered in 1873, we saw a black bear. He was fuddled for a moment and ran parallel to the boat with a wowsy-bowsy rocking motion. At Hudson's Bay Flats, where the first store existed on the Stikine, an Indian family was camping; a gill net was strung into the river from a long pole. Next was Shakes Creek, a tiny affair that winds back into great hunting country, where A. J. Marion built his ranch and Chief Shakes paddled up to trade with the Canadians after the Indian conclaves at Tahltan had ceased. The sandbanks were pocked with animal prints. A couple of bald-headed eagles were scouting for salmon with a slow, crowlike flap and a bomber's momentum. Low on the water, they were the first of fourteen I noticed and counted on the way down. Of course the curves and countless changing perspectives soon wiped out my possessive, personal sense of the river. Like the rest of the passengers, I was a tripper. Even the captain was that. He was a changed young man since June, however. With the extraordinary ardor of the shy, he'd discovered the thrill of public speaking. He invited guests into the wheelhouse, let them steer for a minute, and pointed out certain mountains he knew. He beamed, he swayed as if he were on the ocean, and spoke huskily.

The rising sun banded the topography with a blue haze. The delta of the Chutine was a two-mile jungle of cottonwoods and jackpine. As a clear-water river which had a pronounced,

lengthy valley of its own, it was the favorite of the homesteaders. The captain pointed out the Wriglesworth's house, right
on the bank. There were islands to squeeze around and sloping, complex overfalls of water off the sandbars. One very
bumpy swathe was called the Grand Rapids. A truck was
riding on the front of the barge, jouncing up and down, and a
dog was tied under it, howling in fear.

In a pretty fireweed meadow we picked up two prospectors
who had just dropped a thousand dollars, mostly in transporta-
tion costs, and not found an ounce of gold. They were blow-
cheeked, side-of-beef heavies in the good old dumbbell tradition. They said that marble was a form of granite, and they
had brought a goofy "pump" from Juneau with the idea of
somehow "pumping" the gold out like oil, except that the
Chutine had too many boulders even to test the contraption—
you "would need money." Having been raised in Telegraph
Creek, Captain Callbreath had seen too many eightball prospectors to hide his scorn. They were a wet, chilled, crestfallen
pair. They had borrowed the money, they dreaded facing the
folks at home, and were thoroughly sick of each other by now;
one guy was a prodigious pig of an eater and his partner had
hated him for every mouthful all the way along. In fact, if the
boat had come any later they would have starved, because he'd
eaten the last supplies. Now they were out to recoup a little of
their loss in bragging to us. They'd encountered a grizzly, but
it had been a draw. He didn't cross the river to beard them and
they didn't fire, remembering the reputation wounded bears
have. One guy, as it turned out, had distinguished himself in
Wrangell twenty years ago by ripping down the old Russian
mission in order to get some second-hand lumber for a shack
that he wanted to build. The other, the eater, had been supported by his wife throughout his married life; she worked in a
dry-goods store. He had been such an oaf he had driven his son
to become a bishop, indeed.

On every side of the boat small rutted glaciers hung down
the mountain slopes—green ice the color of copper oxide. At

Oksa Creek, eighty miles in from the sea, a seal was basking on a mud bank. In the distance a grizzly mother ducked away with two light-colored cubs, one bicycling frantically to cross over a slippery log. The mountains mounted into major land-forms but the Stikine minced into a ticklish, short canyon that simmered around us, widening out into shallows which the boat had to creep and grope through. The water remained the same uninstructive silt color whatever its depth was. We passed the tents and caches of fuel which the snagging crew used —a rich, rain-forest, wild, pathless shore. Too many glaciers above us to count, but alongside the boat a thick tropic smell. Four geese were tucked into the mouth of the Scud, and a seal was nearby. They flew up; he dived. Above the Anuk, we caught sight of a bull moose swimming the river. His rack was in velvet still, and he swam so hard, wagging his ears, that he raised himself in the water as if he were hurdling windfalls. As we pressed just behind him, he seemed to be pulling the boat. On the bank, he ran along opposite us and finally paused, in his innocence, and simply faced us. Parting the willow forest like a curtain with one shoulder, he disappeared.

Scooting by with the current's push as we were, the tumultuous vegetation and this lavish potpourri of the animal kingdom beat on our eyes like a replica of the week of Creation. The mountains went up as if they weren't going to stop. They built into elephant backs and cat backs and shard peaks. Close to the Porcupine River there were seven more geese and another seal. The Stikine became such a maze of islands and sloughs that I couldn't have managed to guess even which direction we ought to take. The beaches were heaped six feet high with drift logs. Sweepers lay over the water—newly fallen trees with the leaves still on. I expected monkeys to chatter at us. Suddenly the channel appeared when we were on top of it, a sucking, boiling slot of water in the lake of mud. There were blue-water sloughs and gray-water sloughs and broad cottonwood stands like Louisiana's. The sun was too bright and strong and the banks too far off for me to see anything on the shore. The river had gotten too big for me to feel even in memory that it was mine. I was already lonely with the slight parcel of knowledge I had.

This was the section of the Stikine which was mythic for the Tlingits, with their Raven Father. The Iskut River came in at last, a magnificent valley in its own right, proportioned symmetrically, *andante con brio*, and with real alps just visible up at the curve where it turned for the hundred-mile straightaway sweep towards Eddontenajon. The vegetation was of machete density—sea air, moist clouds, a year-round spelunker's temperature. Alaskans call this southeastern panhandle of theirs the Banana Belt. Smack on the International Boundary was Alec McPhee's trapping cabin, looking as sprightly as he and surrounded by beaver sloughs, with the mouth of the fecund Katete directly across the way.

We steamed past diminishing mountains, past the naval graveyard of great trees in the estuary of the Stikine, where the water was like silty glass. Being ahead of the tide, we sounded and wiggled ourselves across the flats. We were all Americans on the boat—forceful, flat-toned, matter-of-fact. Once there was no shore to watch it was like being already home.

The traffic in Wrangell was like a percussion section. Signs for a salmon derby and for a plexiglass boat regatta were up. The tourists were swaggering widows who stood about getting acquainted, like men of the same regiment who have recognized each other's collar tabs. I looked up the news in the paper and tried to find a stock that I'd bought in May—except I'd completely forgotten what the stock was. The country still disliked itself. President Johnson was telling the press which of his daughters was his favorite; Negroes were rioting in Cleveland and Lansing; and a couple of bad-tempered nationwide strikes were on. I supped on shrimp, peas and fresh milk, and then placed a long-distance phone call, fumbling with the dialing, and planned an important letter, or postponed planning it.

Though my face pursed sourly at my countrymen, actually I was relieved to be with them again, where the boredoms and dangers were familiar ones and my small store of savvy counted for something. When I dropped in on Joel Wing, the magistrate, it seemed excruciating to listen to how his brother and he had whipsawed their cabin together and divided a moose. I was between two worlds, since I didn't want to discuss Vietnam either. I was impatient with everybody. More than that, I felt claustrophobic. The rhythm, the rat-tat activity, seemed rigidly ceaseless, a sense I'd first had at Hyland Post when I looked at the goats on the mountainside and the horses flirting and the moose cow and calf, and compared them to Morgan and me, both of us stitching away like sewing machines at our work, or sitting tapping our feet at mealtimes with the same incessant attentiveness. Here in Wrangell radios were playing, boats leaving, stores opening and closing at five o'clock, planes buzzing off, people phoning for appointments —and yet of course as compared to New York it was like Hyland Post! I was in it again, clued in to clocks and timetables and when the mail left and who was the person to see about getting rid of my sleeping bag. I was already beginning to jump, as if electrodes had been attached to my skin. I was hoping to see the Surveyor General in Victoria, if he hadn't gone off for his holidays. I booked space on the plane. Should I book a room ahead?

Gerry Andrews, in the Parliament Building, was as interested in picking my brain as I was in picking his. First, however, he brought out a voter's list for Atlin and set it in front of me to determine if I was a fake. It was a closely spaced sheet of names with code numerals for each man's occupation. I did well with Charlie Gairns and Norman Fisher, so we relaxed and exchanged impressions. Andrews is short, humane, martial—a quite glamorous man—compact, sense-talking and low key, like an engineer or an Englishman in his manner. As Surveyor General he presides over a real confraternity of surveyors, many old and retired now, who have helped to explore this incredible province. He has a large "battle map" on the wall which shows the gaps that remain unexplored. He's obviously a first-rate leader but lately the quality has been exercised in arranging funerals for his friends; they seem to be wearing out before the supply of raw country does.

Andrews himself is talked about everywhere—he and Skook Davidson, that fellow Steele Hyland told me about who is still holding out alone, arthritis and all, far up the Kechika Valley, with a hundred wild horses and two dozen wolves. Skook packed for several of the surveyors originally, so Andrews knew him—a drummer boy in the First World War, a wild man in town, a biter and kicker, but good on the trail once you had gotten him out of jail. He laughs and confesses that the thrust of his job is to help speed the obliteration of the very wilderness in which he's involved himself his whole life. Mapping from the air, his men go along so fast they can't think up names for the features they find. He says, though, that barring a tremendous mineral discovery, the Stikine should remain just about as it is into the 1970s. For one thing, the highway contractors keep going broke trying to build south down the Iskut valley, and most of the province's development money is tied up between now and then in damming the Peace and Columbia rivers.

During the twentieth century, exploring became the bailiwick of the specialist and wasn't left to mere trappers and packers like Carson and Boone to carry forward in their spare hours. A man with the itch apprenticed himself to a surveyor and began to explore professionally. Andrews directed me to his own mentor of forty years ago, a hard-edged figure named Frank Swannell, whom I'd both read and heard about. He lives here in an old people's residence home.

Victoria is a sunny city of manicured sidewalks dotted with lawns. Besides the capital buildings and a stately variety of tourism, the main industry must be these homes. Swannell's is respectable-looking, like the others close by. It has a small garden and porch, a TV room with deep, inexpensive stuffed chairs, a cramped dining room whose door is kept closed, a pleasant staircase, a pleasant young girl to answer the phone and to sweep the floors, and a few euphemistic notices tacked up on three-by-five cards, which announce in effect that any guest unable to make it downstairs for meals had better go into the hospital on his own or the management will have to see that he moves.

Swannell was out walking the first time I came. It was assumed I must be his grandson. The message that I would be back was written down with the sort of expression that suits good news. One of the delights of the summer has been to search out extraordinary neglected old men whose achievements nobody else seems to know about, and when we met later on in the TV room the other guests asked if I wasn't his grandson. He said no, that I was an interviewer. They asked what he'd done, in that case, and he answered that he had been a surveyor. He smiled because that was a proud profession; I smiled because, for our era, I was sitting next to the equivalent of De Soto.

We could smile at each other more easily than we could talk. Like many live wires, he found my stutter disturbing, and he would have been brusque anyway. At first I wondered if he wanted me to go, but he only wanted to get on with the important business of putting into my mind what had been in his. He was very much interested in knowledge and in passing it on, but every answer was a single sentence, maybe two, after which he would whistle tensely under his breath, tight-lipped. Frequently he broke off in the middle of a phrase, if he thought the gist of it had been conveyed, his eyes glinting a little, waiting for the next question. Yet I didn't feel I was doing badly. I was no harder to understand than he, and I was the last stranger of thirty or so who would ever be asking him anything. (In other words, I felt a bit brutal.) He paid due heed to my own professionalism, nevertheless. To him, that was precisely the point: to cross the barrier between specialties. He had an abrasive voice, a terse mind, and he was well fed and for-

mally dressed in a dark suit, unlike the wiry ragamuffins I had
been meeting. Snowshoes and rifles hung on his wall, oiled until they resembled exhibits. The tiny room was crammed with
bookcases and a big polished desk which held his files. Although he said he'd had no adventures—it was the greenhorns
who suffered adventures—he wasn't a self-effacing man. He
was a technician, a narrow man, whose memories were never
of people, only of terrain. He described the many assistants
he'd worked with only in terms of how good they were, or how
much trouble, and whether they were half-breeds or quarter-
breeds. He was a geographer and a traverser, and so it was
rather like talking to a ship captain about the sea—the conception of distance, of smooth going and rough going. He never
stopped anywhere to homestead or farm, and didn't speak of the
country he saw for either its beauty or bounty, only its wild
obstacles and its distances. It seemed, as I pressed him on this,
that he simply couldn't; he was an explorer, never a settler.
Now that he no longer leads the old life, he cruises around the
world on freighters in the winter. He likes the Norwegian
freighters the best.

Swannell's diaries are straightforward, brief, unflowery,
though humorous too, and invariably include what the Indian
girls looked like in the hutments he passed, both their figures
and clothes. An apprentice surveyor's work was usually a
matter of dividing newly homesteaded land into sections—cre-
ating property, as it were. Arriving in British Columbia in
1899, he did considerable amounts of this, or else worked for
the mining companies free-lance, clinching their claims. By
1908 his competence had been recognized and he was surveying the Nechako River for the government; later the Omineca,
north of Fort St. James. In 1914 he went up the formidable
Finlay River by canoe, from its mouth almost to its source.
This put him in the history books because the feat has not been
duplicated by anybody except the original discoverer, Samuel
Black, in 1824. Then after the First World War he was active
in the Bella Coola country and from Ootsa Lake to the coast,

where Jim Morgan, as a boy of fifteen, meat-hunted and wrangled for him. Morgan, wide-eyed, took him as a hero and model, but Swannell speaks slightingly of Morgan as "just a kid."

In those same best years, when he was forty, he was exploring the Ingenika, which drains into the Finlay (a mountain range and a tributary river are named after him); and was in the Groundhog country of the Skeena; and in the country above and about Bear Lake; and on the Peace River; and was helping to survey the Rocky Mountain Trench. His diaries are stitched with mathematics because he did temperature and barometric readings three times a day. He was constantly calculating triangulations with his transit for the heights of the mountains around. At noon he shot the sun to determine his latitude. At night he shot the stars for an azimuth of his direction, the compass being just a rough check, and for the exact time, which, compared to Greenwich mean time, gave him his longitude. Whether he was canoeing or walking, he would stop and climb the mountains alongside his route to fix cairns and sketch the configurations of the country in his book and to estimate "traverses"—distances, such as from where he was on the river to the next bend. These added laboriously into the mileages between valley and valley. Winters he spent in Victoria with his wife, working up his reports. He was certainly no freewheeler, but he was the ace of them all and his trips were the boldest and most resplendent. As Morgan described, he would go out alone ahead of his party for a week with rice and tea and a bit of fishline in order to climb a distant range.

For two seasons during the 1920s Swannell traced as exactly as possible the last leg of Alexander MacKenzie's expedition to the Pacific in 1793. This dash antedated Lewis and Clark's by twelve years and was the first crossing of the American continent. MacKenzie was a driving, impersonal, zealous man, much like Swannell. Always traveling at top speed, he made the twelve hundred miles from Fort Forks on the Peace River to saltwater near Bella Coola in seventy-four days. There he wrote in vermilion on a rock the flamboyant words, "Alexander MacKenzie, from Canada, by land." Then he started back with his party, subsisting on dried fish roe boiled with flour and oolakan grease, the oolakan being the candlefish (smelt). Since he knew the route now, he went even faster, averaging thirty miles a day. Swannell's group found the ruins of the "Friendly Village" where MacKenzie was helped along, and of the trade trail he used, showing at first as only an indentation in deep moss, but underneath as packed earth. It was called a "grease trail" because the chief article of commerce with the interior Indians was this oolakan grease, and they found several of the old cedar boxes the stuff was put in, as well as fish weirs.

Individual years are blurring for Swannell now, so he gave me some published material to read about his most notable and grueling trip, up the Finlay. I had read about it in New York before I imagined the man who had made it might still be alive, so that to see *Swannell* on the page again brought back an image of a person laughably wan—a dead man, in other words—as compared to this ruddy, well-groomed personage across from me with the gnarled voice and harsh blue eyes— gay, pagan, Pan eyes.

He had three companions on the Finlay, including George Copley, a boyhood friend, and Jimmy Alexander, a strong Scotch half-breed. Alexander became a famous walker, has a mountain named after him on the Nation River, and ended his days as a ferryman at Fort St. James. The cook, Jim Nep Ah Yuen, was a Cantonese who had come to work on the Canadian Pacific Railroad in 1885 and finally went home fifty years later to run guns to Mao and Chiang.* They would breakfast on

---

* A picture of Swannell in 1911 shows him wearing a bandoleer and a pencil mustache. Jim Nep Ah Yuen is there, with unsteady eyes and a round henchman's look. Also Jimmy Alexander, a tall central figure with raffish hair and a curved pipe. He has long arms, husky legs, and a flat-brimmed hat, and he looks rough and ready—ready to go to work in an instant. In a much later picture Swannell appears in the midst of a circle of shawled Indian ladies like a plumped-out roué, a crude P. T. Barnum.

"Hudson's Bay honey," a mixture of molasses and bacon grease which was spread on camp bread, and spend the days chipping and charring the butt log of a cottonwood tree, until they'd constructed a dugout canoe. When they had the hull, they filled it with water and dropped in stones heated red hot, till the water boiled and the sides of the craft became pliable. They shaped and spread them, fastening in thwarts and nailing extra boards to the gunwales which flared out and lessened the chances of swamping. The intention was not to imitate primitive man but only to build a boat that wouldn't smash up. The trouble was that they'd made it so sturdy and heavy they couldn't portage with it.

At last, when they were ready, they headed north sixty miles to Fort Grahame, the one-man post where Jack Lee and Gunanoot and various of the Caribou Hiders hung about at different periods. However, the peg-legged trader was away. A band of twelve Indians had shown up recently in a starving state and were camped in the yard, too honest and shy to break the padlock on the door, although they could look through the window and see the foodstuffs on the shelves. Indeed, five of them had already died and the rest were down and ill from living on nothing but flour boiled as a gruel. As Swannell says, they were "hunters pure and simple." If they starved, they really starved. He and Copley picked the lock, passed out supplies and collected a basket of strawberry leaves to stew for them as a restorative.

The valley north narrowed and grew ruggeder. At Deserter's Canyon, where two of Samuel Black's party had decamped in the night, the river became so dangerous with whirlpools that large spruce trees floating down were sucked underwater, not to reappear for hundreds of yards. Then for a while, as they continued poling upcurrent, it was wide and reasonably free of rapids, though very swift. An old Klondike trail ran alongside, with a few rotting cabins where people had wintered miserably, without vegetables, without stoves. Occasionally they noticed the skeleton of a horse, still rigged in its pack, which had given out in the snow and been shot. Fires dating from the Gold Rush had devastated this part of the valley, so that no game was evident.

Falling on discouraging times, Swannell's group used up their sugar, flour, oatmeal, molasses, and one night they bivouacked in a chute of a canyon where the river, normally 250 yards wide, stormed through a 50-foot opening. They had to forget their tent and their supper and sleep in the drenching spatter, each curled round a tree on a skinny ledge under the cliff, stunned by the roar. A succession of cascading canyons started in earnest now, with walls too sheer to portage over, even if they had had a bark canoe. They battled their way, usually standing in water up to their hips, though it was September by now and the water was achingly cold. Struggling for every two dozen feet, slipping on the ledges that were submerged, they lifted and "frogged" the heavy dugout for many miles. They were living on trout and grayling, muskrats, rabbits, partridge and grouse—whatever came to hand that particular day, a skimpy, dreary diet. Once when they had a good chance at a moose, the rifle wasn't handy and it seemed to be getting away. Jimmy Alexander plunged into the river, caught up with it and cut its throat, riding as it died and then steering it like a boat in the torrent until it floated aground on a sandbar a quarter-mile down.

After the Finlay turned westward at the junction of the Fox, still worse canyons confronted them, which Black had carried his canoe around. But they had to stick to the river, pulling themselves along with lines to the shore, or frogging up to their chests in the water. Whole days were occupied in schemes which failed, in unloading what they had with them in order to pass the dugout over a single smoldering rock. These worst canyons merged into a sort of tube, a unity of violence which they fought through yard by yard, until their bodies ceased to shiver and their eardrums to hear. Eventually they reached the valley of the Toodoggone, where the Finlay slithered by a bunch of sloughs and reed-choked lakes, the Fishing Lakes, with flocks of herons and ducks and muddy beaches that the caribou had trampled like a barnyard. Knowing from Black's journal that they had overcome all of the river's obstacles, they turned back, in a snowstorm, sick of their all-meat diet. Later on, Swannell did reach the three deep lovely lakes which are the Finlay's final source by going up the Ingenika to its head and hiking across.

Sweeping down, of course, they hit hair-raising speeds, nearly smothering in the rapids numerous times and tilting at the passing cliffs with their poles and paddles as the walls rushed at them. The water's force was bent now on smashing them, drowning them, instead of stymying them. A trapper had tied a red rag to a tree, which had a two-month-old newspaper attached, notifying them of the First World War.

This had been too furious, youthful a feat for much map-making, and so Swannell and a sizable company of men came back on foot in 1941 to survey the Finlay in detail, or at least the section between its mouth and the debouchment of the Fox. They were scouting an alternative route for the Alaska Highway, and they walked up the Fox through Sifton Pass to the head of the Kechika and down the Kechika to where it empties into the Liard. This was four hundred and fifty miles, all in the curious fault formation which is known as the Rocky Mountain Trench. It goes so straight that when they drew their completed map they found that the information fit on a strip of paper fifty-six feet long and three feet wide. The same year, Jack Lee was making his walk of six hundred miles from Hazelton on the Telegraph Trail, measuring the snow on the ground. These walks were just about the last go-round—the last exploration of the continent by foot that we'll ever have.

Swannell's formality toward me broke at lunchtime. Boyish and embarrassed, he said that he couldn't ask me to lunch because the home didn't allow it. "They don't give you anything but soup anyway. Maybe that's the explanation." He'd added a good deal to what I was reading, flattered that I was with him, and it seemed as though part of his earlier hard-guy tautness had been a harkening back to when he was in the bush, driving himself.

After he came upstairs, I tried to retain the mood of intimacy. "Everybody's dying," he said, almost angry about it. But he was no better at describing his colleagues than he was at telling me about the settlers he met in those raw vivid valleys. And I couldn't persuade him to admit to a twinge of regret that he'd never picked up a lush farm somewhere for back taxes. He was a traveling man. Once, behind Smithers on a mountainside, he noticed a grizzly below him, peaceably grazing. Though he was unarmed and above treeline he yelled to the bear convivially, "Hey, bear!" Instead of bolting, the bear right away climbed toward him quickly, as if he had called. When it was within a few yards it reared up to see over the brush, and Swannell, reckless but shaking, could just take its picture. The old-fashioned camera exposed so slowly that when he got home he discovered 44 bears on the plate. Meanwhile his surveying assistant, racing up the other slope of the basin with a gun to beat the bear to him, had won.

I prompted him with names from the Finlay that I'd heard from other people and got no particular response until I mentioned that remarkable fellow Shorty whom Jack Lee told me about, whose trapping partners invariably disappeared just before the fur sales. Then, like every man with a registered trapline, he got a new partner the next season from among the drifters who wandered in. He was phenomenally quarrelsome and is said to have bushwhacked his neighbors in their own cabins. One day he paddled into Finlay Forks after several months' isolation, and as the trader was helping him tie up his boat, Shorty said, "Well, how's the old bitch?"

"What old bitch?"

"Your old bitch. Your wife. You know, Lucille."

Swannell's acquaintance with Shorty was brief. He was in a skiff going upriver to survey a Crown grant, when he noticed a cabin on the bank and stopped to ask directions. There was no answer when he knocked and he was about to try the door and wait inside, except that the latch looked tampered with. Shrewd Swannell took a stick and touched the latch with caution. Instantly a crosscut saw rigged with heavy stones dropped like a guillotine and cut off the end of the stick.

Swannell's assistant began gathering shavings from the wood-pile to burn the house down, but Swannell, being a government man, prevented him.

I idled in Victoria for several days. It's a city of greenery and channel views. I was savoring my tiredness, proud of myself, and already fizzing with thoughts of New York—the wistful phone calls I make to my ex-wife every couple of weeks, the overfull sex life. Other men commute to their jobs, but I work at home and commute uptown to stay overnight. You arrive for a date and watch the girl get dressed from the buff for you. And the parties. I'm usually quite happy at parties, though I do put my back up against a wall when I can. There's the sense of being young and, all of a sudden, the opposite feeling, of *not* still being young, and of having used up the series of people who have loved me. One person makes a declaration of love and the other remains relaxed and gently affectionate about it, and at first it seems that the person who made the declaration has lost somehow, but of course, on the contrary, they've won. They go on and marry somebody else while the one who was so relaxed remains in his passivity. I'm tired of being a man on the loose and of being childless.

Crossing by ferry to Vancouver, I found myself in a metropolis, the skids really under me now. My head was full of anticipatory scenes, phone calls I'd try from the very airport when I got home. I had the address of E. C. Lamarque, my last explorer, and I bussed out from the hotel to see whether or not he interested me. I was still elated, because although I knew nowhere else in the city to go, there was nowhere else I wanted to go, and apparently no one but me in the city even knew he existed.

Immediately I was very taken with Mr. Lamarque. I saw him for two afternoons, only short visits, and each night I looked out my window at the wide spread of lights to pick out the neighborhood where he lived. He's a year older than Mr. Swannell, living with a wife ninety-two who is dying. From time to time as we talked she would start sobbing and gibbering in the bedroom, like a bumblebee humming, and would try to come out. Old Lamarque stood up and went to her patiently. "Yes, hello. Hello there. Yes, hello. Yes, hello." With no one else in the household, he cooks for them both, though he isn't up to such an exacting schedule, living as he is with his own death too. He seems to be looking around at the details of its approach, the way many old people do who are given enough forewarning. They notice the change in the tops of their feet; they watch their thighs shrink and their steps grow bumpy. It's so personal that it's not terrifying; it simply settles slowly around them in the form of new habits.

Lamarque is a slender, frail, alert man, still wearing the baggy wool pants of a woodsman, though misbelted, and with a firm swing to his hands as he walks. He has a large, individual nose, a floppy mustache, sloping, observant eyes, a grumbly stomach and a good-humored mouth. Walking a few feet, he moves with the lilting aplomb of a grandfather entering a maternity ward. He lives in a green, rundown clapboard home hidden away among overgrown shrubs in an otherwise brand-new suburb very conscious of price. The lawn is uncut and the house looks as if it must have been the first one built on the whole hill. You duck through a sleeve of vines to get on the porch. Inside is a clutter of old wicker chairs and crowded daybeds and cushions and clocks and memorabilia; a caribou skin blocks off the front of the fireplace. Light cords run out from the chandelier to awkward lamps across the room. On the walls are a couple of dozen sketches which Lamarque drew of passes and rapids that only a pathbreaker would have reached. The walls which aren't decorated with these are peppered with snapshots—Lamarque in a parka in front of an Indian hut with thirteen kids; Lamarque with a wild-headed pioneer; Lamarque with a dog team of brindled bears. By now I'd seen lots of old photographs, but the startling thing about these was that there was no contrast—this was the same man, thin and humane, with that fluffy, sub-zero mustache.

He's an Englishman who already by 1897 had charge of a

trading post in the Northwest Territories forty miles from another settlement. He worked until the First War as a factor for Hudson's Bay, moving to a post on the MacKenzie River, then to one on the Athabasca at Fort McKay, and finally to Hudson Hope on the upper Peace, where the only interpreter he could find was afflicted with a tubercular hip and limped about on a crutch on their trips. They traveled by sled or canoe, buying furs, and at night he would play his banjo for the people, dancing the Prairie Chicken Dance. The communities were "nondescript," as he calls them, of no more than ten families or so, and no other whites, but the tribes were expert boatmen, especially the Crees. A missionary only came through at Christmas and Easter; yet the Indians kneeled down with their backs to the fire every evening and prayed.

Later he left the fur trade and became a surveyor. Compared with Swannell, Lamarque's style was soft-nosed, as competent but much milder, and just as Swannell's reports to the Province were chockablock full of mathematics, his were interspersed with pen-and-ink sketches which he had done from his horse or while he ate lunch: views that a traveler would recognize, down a lake or of a skyline. In 1930, his apprenticeship over, he led a scout group to the headwaters of the Columbia, looking for possible routes for a road. The next summer he spent at the sources of the North Thompson River on the same sort of errand, and another season he went to Bella Coola, inspecting pack routes into the interior. Then, again in the north, he went to the confluence of the Liard and the Kechika to try to improve on the system of trails that reached Lower Post.

Lamarque's favorite trip—that larky brisk trip I've heard about from so many men, wherever it happened to take them —was in 1934. He was a cool fifty-five by that time, and along with an Indian named Jack Stone, he mapped the Finlay-Fox-Turnagain country, en route from the head of the Muskwa River to Dease Lake by a way which had not been previously explored. They constituted the advance party of the Bedaux expedition. This was a *bouffe* private expedition equipped with tractors, whose aim was to mow a path six feet wide through one of the wildest regions on earth. Bedaux, a millionaire adventurer, an efficiency expert by profession and a naturalized American, was interested in the tractors because he'd invented them. He'd taken them through the Sahara and the African jungles. He was also attempting to film a movie, so it was a mad assemblage, complete with late-sleeping French ladies and maids, a Swiss ski instructor and several Hollywood camera technicians. One pack horse carried nothing but novels, another nothing but ladies' shoes. The hundred-plus horses had to be shot, as they starved in the bush or their feet went lame, but the people came out of it pretty well. They complained that they got diarrhea from the tractor fumes, and when the tractors broke down Bedaux turned back. He wasn't as prudent a few years later; he killed himself while under indictment for treason, an alleged sympathizer with Vichy.

Swannell was right in the thick of that expedition, noting down humidity readings and triangulations and the look of the French and Indian girls, while Lamarque, out ahead on his own, was having a very different experience. He was scouting in earnest, behaving as though there was no buffoonery going on in the company behind him. Jack Stone and the other Sikannis hadn't any knowledge of the territory which they had entered because on the rare occasions when one of them wished to cross to Dease Lake from the Finlay he went roundabout by Caribou Hide, and no white man had ever crossed directly either. But they moved along as smoothly as two swimmers, both professional woodsmen, and they didn't stint on their comforts. They brought a fly to sleep under and horses to ride and to carry the dunnage, the dried milk and fruits, rice, bacon, porridge and flour and butter and Lamarque's portfolios and instruments. Fort Ware was their last stopping point. Ware was a pleasant, decent little man, but the thirty or forty Indians living nearby were not in good shape, being starve-or-feast types. The valley was chilled and menaced by the river.*

Afterwards, for two ringing weeks they saw nobody. It was that airy, aerial moment in time when a man is in country which nobody has ever set eyes on before, feeling blithe and surrounded by the sublime, yet constantly moving, as though to stop would be to founder and fall like a trapeze artist. They discovered a passage between key watersheds, now called Lamarque Pass, and a creek that led down from it, Jackstone Creek. On the slopes of the pass they counted forty goats, and later on seventeen moose at a lake. Lamarque named the lake Hattah Lake because of its palindromic shape. This was misunderstood in Victoria, where the spelling was changed to Hottah, it being assumed that he must have heard and adapted some Indian name. Succinct set pieces stood about everywhere. A grizzly and three cubs were digging ground-hogs out of a patch of snow, encircled by a caribou herd who ignored them. The mama lay on her side, reaching into a hole like a cat feeling after a chipmunk. Lamarque calculated direction and pitch more by his eye than by the gadgets that he had with him, and distances just by his traveling time. He sketched and wrote notes as he rode, all of which were incorporated in the map that he drew during the winter, marking his line of travel. It's on a ten-foot sheet of paper. Along the borders fifty-one of the significant views that he saw are inked—brush ridges, voluptuous peaks and massifs and sober fir forests, along with written advisories, such as "Great spring gushes from side of hill," "Mountains of bald, castellated outline," "Undulating treeless region," "Green-coloured hill," "High massive range with pinnacles," and "Gravel benches and fire-swept pasture." He's especially specific about pasturage.

On my second day at Lamarque's a garrulous neighbor

---

* Fort Ware is now a placid community of 120 surviving Sikannis. It's said to be the happiest Indian town in all of British Columbia, as well as the most isolated. To fly there costs upwards of $300 from the nearest point.

dropped in, in a string tie. (I have yet to like anyone who wears a string tie.) He wanted to tell us about his trailer trip through Banff National Park. Poor Lamarque stirred his gentle old bones to be hostly, but he was exhausted and shaking. His wife was still gibbering through the wall and I was stuttering excitedly at him; the two sounds seemed very similar. He was listening with patience to the three of us, catching what each of us had to say. I finally got rid of the neighbor and then decided I ought to get rid of myself as well. When I said so, he quickly agreed. His wife, like a doleful hallucination, was wandering into the hall. He needed to fix their suppers and he needed to rest. The ten-foot map was unrolled on the floor—we were standing on it in stocking feet—and to my astonishment, as we rolled it up, he gave it to me. I didn't know what response to make except that I can't ever remember being any more pleased. He smiled; he knew that. He said that he had no use for it now, nodding good-bye politely, the weight of his present exigencies pulling his eyebrows down. His pants were falling down too, and I was touched and sorry for him.

"I love thee. Love to thee. I love thee," I mumbled over and over, preparing to go to the airport, already trying to explain where I'd been to the people I would be seeing again soon. The trouble was that even in my mind's eye I really had nobody to say I love thee to. And I was still disoriented by the relentless, metronome scurry around. Instead of being only one rhythm of many, it was the whole. People never *do* stop, and I'd come from a world where the people were few. Birds and insects are as active as man, but they don't take up room and they don't live as long. I was worn out just watching the tempo. It wasn't like coming home from one of the ancient cities of Europe or a month's isolation in one of the second-growth forests of Maine. This was a return to man himself from the previous existence, about to be sealed off and stoppered. I was alarmed by the crush.

Of course the future takes care of itself. All we know is

what is lost, not what will be invented. If people haven't the room we have known, presumably they will punch out a new kind of room. In the meantime we become more selective, as to season and latitude when we travel, as to friends when we don't. We can either enjoy the Halloween sixties or turn into hobbyists, down on our hands and knees, watching how the deer mice get along, and we brush past more and more hordes of people in our hurry to save ourselves time.

In the lounge of the air terminal the count-down announcements proceeded, between tinkle-bells. Then the big, big try of the jet getting off the ground. The patterns of lights below were ethereal and the night was placid and calm. The plane coasted sleekly across the face of the continent. We had snacks at midnight and dawn. Sunrise on the Atlantic was one of those great space sights of the new century which we usually see only in *Life*, and which seem at the time to mean more than they do. Laid lushly as wool, the orange and yellow colors intensified and intensified, as gorgeous as organ music and spreading the width of the world.

About the Author

EDWARD HOAGLAND has published *Cat Man*, a novel about circus life (1956), and *The Circle Home*, a fictional study of boxing (1960). His third book, *The Peacock's Tail* (1965), was about a modern Pied Piper. He alternates traveling with teaching as avocations, and is married, with one child. He is thirty-six.

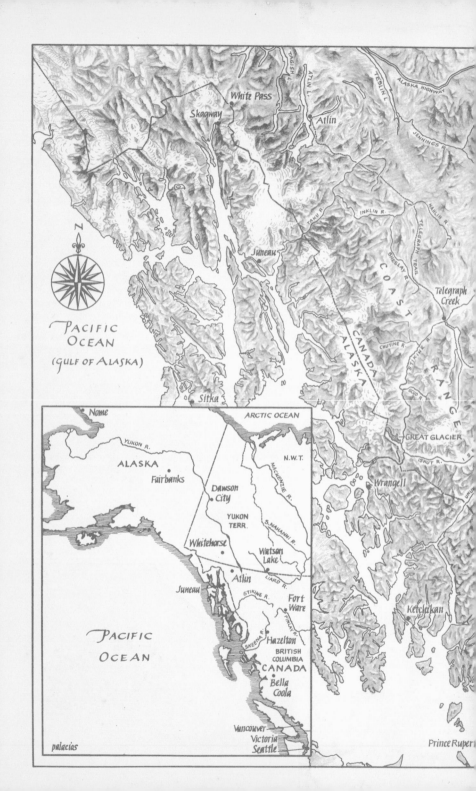